D1349239

The Beatles

The Beatles

igloo

igloo

Published in 2010

by Igloo Books Ltd

Cottage Farm

Sywell

NN6 0BJ

www.igloo-books.com

Copyright © 2010 Igloo Books Ltd

All rights reserved. No part of this publication may be reproduced, stored in a retrieval system, or transmitted in any way or by any means, electronic, mechanical, photocopying, recording, or otherwise, without the prior written permission of the publisher.

10 9 8 7 6 5 4 3 2 1

ISBN: 978-0-85734-260-7

Produced by BlueRed Press Ltd

Written by Mike Evans

Printed and manufactured in China

Every effort has been made to obtain permission to reproduce copyright material, but there may be cases where we have been unable to trace a copyright holder. The publisher will be happy to correct any omissions in future printings.

Page 1: *The Beatles (top to bottom, Paul McCartney, John Lennon, George Harrison, and Ringo Starr) backstage at the London Palladium in October 1963.*

Page 2: *(Left to right) Paul McCartney, George Harrison, John Lennon, and Ringo Starr take a dip in the swimming pool of their hotel during The Beatles' US tour in 1964.*

This Spread: *(Clockwise from top left) John Lennon, George Harrison, Paul McCartney, and Ringo Starr in stills from The Beatles' movie "Help!".*

Contents

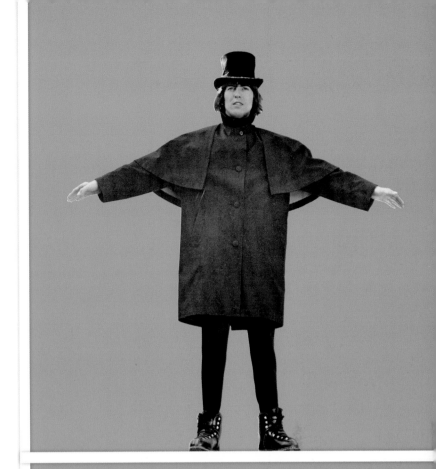

Introduction

Over 40 years after their final records were made, The Beatles are still the most popular band in pop music history. Their name is known by countless millions around the world, and their music is timeless.

From "I Want To Hold Your Hand", the first Beatles song to conquer the American charts in 1964, through ballads such as "Yesterday" and "Something", to the rock 'n' roll excitement of "Twist and Shout", their records formed the soundtrack to the Swinging Sixties, and featured songs that are now seen as modern-day classics. Throughout the decades since, their work has topped the charts again and again, showing The Beatles' universal appeal

The Beatles' story, starting in the cellar clubs of Liverpool and Hamburg and taking them to giant stadia, is one of success, of tragedy and triumph; of four young men named John, Paul, George, and Ringo, who became famous musicians, icons for a generation.

Right: *(Left to right)*
John Lennon, George Harrison,
Ringo Starr, and Paul McCartney,
in a publicity shot from 1963.

Chapter 1: The Early Years- 1940s–1959

Decades after the band broke up in 1970, The Beatles remain the most important rock group of all time. Their impact was not just on the world of music, though they changed the face of rock and pop forever; they also provided a soundtrack to the Sixties that still sounds as fresh and familiar today, even to generations born long after the band stopped playing together.

Theirs is a story of an amazing rise to fame—just six months after their record debut, they were the biggest name in British entertainment and, less than a year after that, they had become the most famous faces on the planet. But fame did not arrive overnight; all four Beatles served a tough apprenticeship in the sweaty cellar clubs of Liverpool and all-night haunts of Hamburg before finally releasing a record. It was a hard road to success. And a road that can be traced back to the very earliest days of rock'n'roll.

The Beatles—Ringo Starr, the eldest, was born in 1940; George Harrison, the youngest, in 1943—were part of the first generation to be called "teenagers." In the post-war years of the mid-1950s, young people had begun to enjoy an amazing independence, which came with a whole new youth culture in fashion, movies, and—most importantly—music. Like the rest of the world, the English seaport of Liverpool in north-west England echoed to the birth of rock'n'roll.

Right: *The Silver Beatles: (left to right) Stuart Sutcliffe, John Lennon, Paul McCartney, Johnny Hutch, and George Harrison, on stage in 1960. Drummer Johnny Hutch was sitting in, as the band did not have a regular drummer at that time.*

The new cult of youth was heralded by movies like *Rebel Without A Cause* with James Dean, *The Wild One* with Marlon Brando, and *Blackboard Jungle*—which had Bill Haley's "Rock Around the Clock" as the soundtrack to its opening scene. Haley hit the charts in 1955, followed by Elvis Presley, whose first UK hit charted early in '56. For some youngsters, the music and the new attitude was to be life-changing. Among them was a young John Lennon who would later remark, "Before Elvis, there was nothing."

John Winston Lennon was born on October 9, 1940, to Julia and Alfred Lennon. His parents separated when he was just three years old, after which he was brought up by his mother's sister, "Mimi" Smith, and her husband George, in the leafy Liverpool suburb of Woolton. He still saw his mother almost every day and, in contrast to the more serious Mimi, she was a happy-go-lucky woman who would joke and fool around constantly. But it was Mimi and George, with no children of their own, who cared for John as if he were their son. Mimi encouraged a love of books, and enrolled him in school—Dovedale Primary, near Penny Lane—when he was only four years old; the young Lennon was learning to read before he was five. As a boy, John loved reading, writing, and drawing. Throughout his years at Dovedale he wrote stories, and even made little books, which he illustrated.

John was also beginning to enjoy the music that was an everyday part of his life. His uncle George bought him a harmonica, and Julia sang and played the banjo. It was John's mother who taught her son his first chords—on the banjo—and the first song he learned as a teenager was an early rock'n'roll hit, Fats Domino's "Ain't That A Shame". Julia also bought him

his first guitar in 1957, the year before she was killed in a car accident. Aunt Mimi didn't wholly approve of the gift, remarking, "The guitar's all very well, John, but you'll never make a living out of it." John, always something of a dreamer, thought it was wonderful, and in March 1957 formed The Quarry Men skiffle group.

The craze for "skiffle" music, which had been imported from America, saw bands playing swing music or traditional jazz and blues on improvised instruments such as cigar box fiddles and drums made from tins and jugs. Alongside these, skiffle bands usually had one or two guitar or banjo players. Skiffle swept teenage Britain in the mid-1950s, triggered by Lonnie Donegan's hit "Rock Island Line".

Above: *A young John Lennon with his mother, Julia. John's cousin, Stanley Parkes, took the photograph.*

DID YOU KNOW?
The Quarry Men played an early gig at the Cavern club, which Paul McCartney missed because he had to be at a Boy Scout camp in North Wales.

Top: *John's father, Freddie Lennon, relaxing on a park bench.*

Above Left: *A portrait of John Lennon in school uniform, taken in the late 1940s.*

Above Right: *John Lennon at home in Liverpool during his schooldays.*

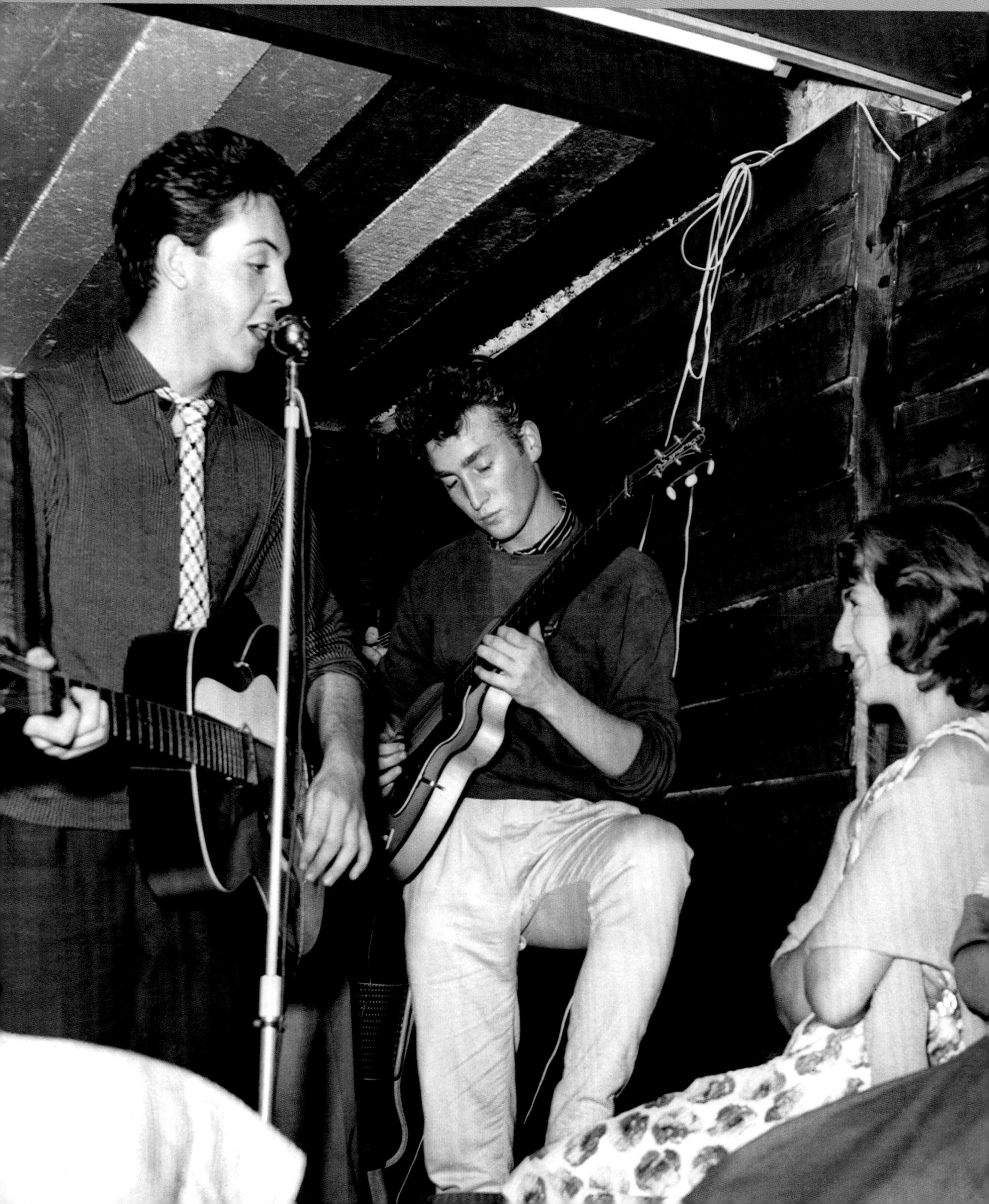

Formerly a jazz banjo player, Donegan and his Skiffle Group had no less than 10 singles in the UK charts through 1956 and '57, and hundreds of do-it-yourself groups sprung up across the country as a result. Like most of them, The Quarry Men consisted of a couple of guitars backed by home-made instruments—a packing crate bass and washboard. But while most skifflers, including Donegan, performed souped-up versions of old American folk tunes, The Quarry Men also played current rock'n'roll numbers by musicians such as Little Richard, Jerry Lee Lewis, and—of course—Elvis Presley.

The band was formed with classmates from Quarry Bank High School, which John had attended since 1952. Despite his earlier promise, John was never an achiever at Quarry Bank. He fooled his way through school, always acting the class clown—when he wasn't playing hookey from lessons with his friend and ally Pete Shotton—and his school reports grew steadily worse. His only talent seemed to be in art and the young Lennon would spend hours drawing caricatures of teachers in a self-produced classroom "magazine" *The Daily Howl*. Other than that, his consuming passion was rock'n'roll. Lennon lost his mother, Julia, in a car accident in 1958, when he was still in his teens.

The Quarry Men started off playing casual dates such as school dances and such and, on July 6, 1957, performed one of the most important gigs in the history of The Beatles. Held at a garden party in the grounds of St. Peter's Church in Woolton, it was here that John Lennon was introduced to Paul McCartney by a mutual friend, Ivan Vaughan, himself a member of The Quarry Men. Backstage, McCartney chatted to Lennon and showed him the guitar chords for Eddie Cochran's "Twenty Flight Rock". John was impressed, and soon invited 15-year-old McCartney to join the group.

Born on June 18, 1942, James Paul McCartney grew up in a musical household. His father, Jim, had been a professional trumpet player and pianist—leading Jim Mac's Jazz Band during the 1920s—and encouraged both Paul and his brother Michael to learn instruments.

Left: *The Quarry Men (Paul McCartney, left, John Lennon, right) perform their first gig at the Casbah Coffee House.*

Unlike John, Paul was a good pupil. At 11, he won a place to the Liverpool Institute for Boys, the city's oldest grammar school, and seemed destined for success, doing well academically and never causing trouble. But his driving passion was always music. Apart from the short-lived piano lessons, Paul's first instrument was a trumpet, given to him by his father, but when the skiffle craze took off Paul decided to trade it in for a guitar, after realizing he couldn't sing and play trumpet at the same time. The trumpet was soon exchanged for a Zenith acoustic guitar and, being left-handed, Paul had to learn to play it strung the "wrong" way around. He soon began writing songs on it; the first was called "I Lost My Little Girl" when he was just 14. By the time he met John Lennon and The Quarry Men, Paul had become a fairly confident guitarist and immediately accepted their offer of a place in the group.

Soon after joining, he suggested bringing in another

There was an upright piano in the family home but, when Paul asked his father to teach him, Jim insisted he went for "proper" lessons. For a seven-year-old, the lessons were too much like school, especially when he was given homework, and the formal tuition lasted about a month. This was to be the only professional musical training Paul McCartney ever received.

Paul's mother, Mary, who worked as a domestic midwife, died of cancer when Paul was 14. He would later recall how it was the first time he ever heard his father cry, saying, "You grow up real quick, because you never expect to hear your parents crying."

teenage guitar player: George Harrison. Paul had known George since 1954, after meeting him on a bus while returning home from the Liverpool Institute, which Harrison also attended.

Like all his band mates in The Beatles, George Harrison came from a family of modest means. He was born on February 25, 1943, and his father Harold was a bus conductor while his mother, Louise, worked as a shop assistant. The home where he spent his first six years was a small terrace house with an outside toilet. Nevertheless, it was full of music. Harold Harrison loved to play records he'd bought when he was a merchant seaman, some of them discs he'd brought back from the US. From these American recordings, George would always remember Jimmie Rodgers, the legendary "Singing Brakeman", who was the first country singer he ever heard. George's eldest brother Harry also had a record player, a modern portable model that George would "borrow" when Harry was out. As in every home in those pre-television days (TV didn't catch on as a mass medium in the UK until the mid-1950s) the radio was where George heard the hits of the day.

George's first school was Dovedale Primary, which John Lennon had attended two years ahead of him. George moved up to the Liverpool Institute in 1954, by which time he'd decided he wanted a guitar. His first instrument was bought from a boy George had known at Dovedale and cost him just under $10 (£3 and 10 shillings in the old British currency). He applied himself to learning it enthusiastically and was given some lessons by a friend of his father, who taught him the chords to various old standards like "Dinah" and "Sweet Sue"—songs that would influence George greatly later in his career. When he met Paul McCartney on the bus from school, the two boys found they had a love of music in common, and it wasn't long before George, too, joined The Quarry Men. He had already been in a short-lived skiffle group with his brother Peter, called the Rebels (who had played just one official gig) so, when he auditioned for The Quarry Men playing a version of the Bill Justis hit "Raunchy", he looked—and sounded—more competent than his youth might have suggested. It was February 1958, and three members of The Beatles were playing together for the first time. Around the same time, a couple of miles from the leafy suburbs of Allerton where The Quarry Men were based, in the dockside district of the Dingle, another of Liverpool's many skiffle outfits was playing the rounds. Formed in 1957, the Eddie Clayton Skiffle Group consisted of Eddie Miles and Frank Walsh on guitars, Roy Trafford on tea-chest bass, John Dougherty on washboard, and Richie

Far Left, **Top:** *Paul McCartney with his father, James "Jim" McCartney, and brother, Mike.*

Far Left, Below: *Beatle-to-be Paul McCartney at the age of six, with his eight-year-old brother, Mike.*

Left: *George Harrison plays acoustic guitar for a childhood portrait.*

Starkey on drums. Richie, who would later begin calling himself Ringo Starr, had formed the group with Eddie Miles (there was no Eddie Clayton; they just thought it sounded better).

Richard Starkey was born in the working class Dingle area on July 7, 1940, to Richard and Elsie Starkey. His parents split up when he was just three and, after a bout of appendicitis at the age of six, his childhood was often troubled with illness. At 13 he developed chronic pleurisy, which hospitalized him for the next two years, after which he never went back to school. Also when Ritchie was 13, his mother Elsie married Harry Graves, a keen music fan who would encourage his stepson's interest to the extent that, in 1957, he bought Richie his first full drum kit.

Ritchie had already tried playing on a single drum. He had become a fan of rock'n'roll after seeing Bill Haley's *Rock Around the Clock* at the local cinema, during which the teenage audience ripped up the seats. Being a sickly child, Richie didn't join in but, like millions of others in 1956, he'd caught the rock bug—and this was to be one infection he didn't want to shake off.

Recovered from illness, Richie worked for a short time as a railway messenger boy, then took a job as a barman on a Liverpool-to-North Wales ferry out of the River Mersey. After that he became an apprentice at the engineering firm H. Hunt & Sons. It was when his stepfather bought him a drum kit for $28/£10 in London (bringing it back by train) that Richie formed the Eddie Clayton Skiffle Group with Eddie Miles, all five of the band's members being employees at H. Hunt & Sons. The group was soon playing regularly around the Liverpool rock and skiffle circuit, and even performed a number of dates at the soon-to-be-famous Cavern club in city center Matthew Street. In 1959, Richie joined another group, called the Raving Texans. It was then that he adopted the cowboy-sounding name Ringo Starr. When George Harrison joined them in February 1958, The Quarry Men line-up was Colin Hanton on drums, Len Garry on bass, Eric Griffiths on guitar (he left soon after George's arrival) plus Lennon, McCartney, and

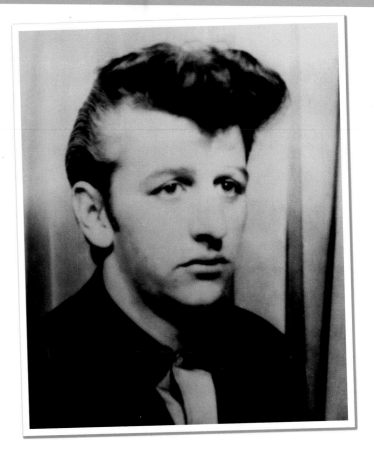

Above: *A late 1950s photo of Ringo, before he joined The Beatles.*

Right: *A crowd dances on the sidewalk outside a cinema showing the groundbreaking "Rock Around the Clock". Starring American rock 'n' roll band Bill Haley and His Comets, the movie helped raise the popularity of rock 'n' roll around the world, and inspired four young boys in Liverpool to start making their own music.*

Harrison. Garry, too, would soon depart, after contracting meningitis and, by mid-1958, the band had become a quintet with the addition of pianist John Lowe, though he only played at venues where there was a piano. The group mainly played rock 'n' roll hits, but Lennon and

DID YOU KNOW?
Although he missed much of his education at Dingle Vale Secondary Modern school through illness, Ringo showed great potential talent for art, drama, and practical subjects including mechanics.

McCartney had also started to write their own songs. One of these early compositions—"One After 909"—would eventually appear on The Beatles' final album release, *Let It Be*.

After failing his final exams miserably, John managed to get a place at Liverpool College of Art in September 1957 and, with the other members similarly occupied, The Quarry Men continued as a part-time band, performing a few gigs at local clubs and private wedding functions. When John's mother Julia was killed in a road accident, on July 15, 1958, the band didn't play at all for almost six months after.

The loss of his mother traumatized John, who had had more than his fair share of emotional turmoil to deal with. He'd seen his father leave when he was just three, and in 1955 his uncle George—who'd brought him up, taught him to draw, and even bought him his first harmonica—had died.

Nevertheless, The Quarry Men started playing again at the end of the year and were hired to play gigs every other Friday at the art college dance, where they were billed as "The College Band." Other dates were few and far between and, though John and Paul carried on developing their song writing, it was obvious that The Quarry Men were finished. George even left for a short period, joining The Les Stewart Quartet, which included guitarist Ken Browne. Then, in August 1959, a woman named Mona Best, whose son Pete played drums, opened the Casbah Coffee Club, and offered the Stewart group a regular gig. Stewart turned it down, so Harrison and Brown brought in Lennon and McCartney to make up a quartet, using the name The Quarry Men. They played every Saturday night for seven weeks, until they walked out after an argument with Mona over cash.

Eight days after they quit the Casbah, The Quarry Men—as a trio without Ken Browne—became Johnny and the Moondogs in order to audition for a popular TV talent show, *Carrol Levis's Discoveries*. They made it to the second heat in nearby Manchester the following month, but missed the final judging because, having no extra money to pay for a room overnight, they had to catch the last train home.

Although the Johnny and the Moondogs period is a short one in The Beatles' history, it marked an important development: the recruitment of Stuart Sutcliffe on bass guitar. Sutcliffe, born in June 1940, had been at the art college a year longer than John, and the two became firm friends after being introduced early in 1959. John was intrigued by Sutcliffe, who had a James Dean look about him but, in many ways, it was an attraction of opposites: Stuart the serious artist, John the couldn't-care-less cynic who once declared in the art students' pub Ye Cracke, "avant garde's just French for bullshit!"

By now, John, perhaps surprisingly, had settled into the art school scene. He had started dating Cynthia Powell, a prim-looking, quiet, and neatly dressed girl who later became his wife and, in early 1960, moved into the bohemian flat that Stuart shared with fellow art student Rod Murray. It was a typically squalid student "pad" which, in July 1960, featured in a Sunday newspaper article exposing "The Beatnik Horror"; the first time, but certainly not the last, that John Lennon's picture would appear in a national newspaper.

Unlike Lennon, whose talent in visual art seemed to be restricted to satirical caricatures and nonsense cartoons, Stuart Sutcliffe was considered one of the bright sparks of the college, a student with great potential in abstract painting. But, while he was dedicated to his art, Stuart also loved rock'n'roll and had already been taught a few guitar chords by his father. When he sold a painting for $180/£65 (a huge sum for a student) he was easily persuaded by Lennon and McCartney to spend it on a Hofner President bass guitar. With "Stu" on bass, all Johnny and the Moondogs needed was a drummer.

Through the first half of 1960, the group performed with a succession of drummers, including Tommy Moore and Norman Chapman. None of them lasted very long. They also acquired yet another name, thought up by Stuart and John. The Silver Beetles was a name inspired by Buddy Holly's Crickets, and the Beetles motorcycle gang in the Marlon Brando film The Wild One. It later evolved into the double-meaning Silver Beatles and, finally, The Beatles in August 1960.

Above: *A photograph of Stuart Sutcliffe, taken before The Beatles' rise to fame.*
Left: *(Left to right) George Harrison, John Lennon, and Paul McCartney standing outside Paul's Liverpool home.*
Right: *The Silver Beatles on stage in 1960. The drummer Johnny Hutch was sitting in.*

It was as the Silver Beetles that the band's next break came, via local promoter Allan Williams. Williams ran the Jacaranda, a coffee bar/basement club used by art students, and gave the group an occasional gig. Welsh-born Allan Williams was something of a bohemian hustler. As well as running the Jacaranda coffee bar, the ex-plumber and door-to-door salesman was involved in various money-making schemes, including the small-time promotion of rock'n'roll groups on the growing Liverpool music scene. In May 1960, he announced that the famous London pop agent Larry Parnes was coming to Liverpool to hold auditions. This was big news for the band: Parnes handled many big names of the day, the most famous being Billy Fury, himself from Liverpool.

Williams arranged for Parnes to hear some local beat groups in the Wyvern Social Club, which he'd just bought. And, despite stiff competition—several of the best bands in the area were there—The Silver Beetles got the gig. Parnes

contacted Williams, who was now acting as their unofficial manager, and offered the group a tour of Scotland, backing one of his singers, Johnny Gentle.

The tour wasn't a great success. The venues—local clubs and church halls—were half-empty and the band had little money. They slept in the group van most of the time while Gentle stayed in local hotels. But, in their eyes, it made them "professional" for the first time. Paul, much to his parents' dismay, left for Scotland when he should have been working toward exams; John missed a crucial art school exam; George, working by this time as a trainee electrician, gave up his job; and drummer Tommy Moore took two weeks off from his job at a bottle factory.

Allan Williams' role in the band's history would be far more important than just the trip to Scotland, though. Through a series of bizarre events, he would launch the next stage in The Beatles' career, in the German port of Hamburg.

Chapter 2: Hamburg and Liverpool- 1960–1962

In the summer of 1960, The Silver Beatles were once again without a regular drummer. After the short Johnny Gentle tour of Scotland, drummer Tommy Moore had walked away from a rock'n'roll career and the remaining four group members found it difficult to get proper gigs without him. In fact, they became so desperate for work that they said "yes", immediately, when Allan Williams offered them a regular afternoon job in a seedy venue. The gig was in a strip club around Liverpool's Upper Parliament Street, just a walk from the Jacaranda and the bustling city center. Grandly named the New Cabaret Artistes Club, the venue was part-owned by Williams and managed for him by a West Indian man known as Lord Woodbine or, more usually, "Woody".

The Silver Beatles, with Paul on drums, were to play backing music for a stripper named Janice, in front of a small male audience. As they prepared to go on, Janice handed out sheet music for them to follow which, of course, none of them could read. Janice was expecting to shed her clothes to "The Gypsy Fire Dance", but the boys decided to play the Duane Eddy instrumental "Ramrod" instead, and then struggled on with standards such as "Moonglow". For later appearances behind the hard-working Janice, they decided to put Paul back on guitar and play without drums.

Right: *(Left to right) Paul McCartney, Pete Best, Stuart Sutcliffe, George Harrison, and John Lennon, performing onstage in Hamburg.*

Above: *Ringo Starr, behind the drums, performing with Rory Storm and the Hurricanes.*

Meanwhile, Williams was learning that there was money to be made in the nightclubs of Hamburg. Through his connections in the local West Indian community, which was far more firmly established in the seaport of Liverpool than in other parts of England, Woody had employed a group of steel drum musicians, the Royal Caribbean Steel Band, to play Williams' Jacaranda. They had become a regular fixture in the dark basement club until, to Williams' dismay, they left suddenly without warning, having been tempted away by a German promoter to play a club in Hamburg.

Williams was furious at first, but calmed down when letters began arriving from the Royal Caribbean musicians. They told him there was a lively club scene in the German port and suggested he send some of his Liverpool beat groups over. Williams decided to go to Hamburg in person and, in order to show the German promoters what Liverpool rock'n'roll had to offer, he intended to take The Silver Beatles with him. However, it was too expensive for the band to make the trip so Williams settled for a quickly assembled tape recording.

Arriving in the German port with Lord Woodbine as his travelling companion, Allan Williams headed for the Reeperbahn area, which he had heard was the center of the night scene, and found himself in a busy side street called Grosse Freiheit Strasse. It was lined with neon-fronted clubs, bars, and strip joints. There, he met a stocky, tough-looking man named Bruno Koschmider, who owned the Kaiserkeller, a typical dance venue. Disaster struck, however, when Williams offered to play his "audition tape" on Koschmider's tape recorder. The recording hadn't been made correctly and all that came out of the machine's speakers was static.

Returning to Liverpool, Williams renewed contact with the big-time London promoter Larry Parnes. At that time, Derry Wilkie and the Seniors was the most musically able of Williams' groups, and Parnes promised the band a summer show spot in the nearby seaside resort of Blackpool. The group's members all gave up their regular jobs to take up the offer, only to be let down at the last minute when Parnes informed Williams the gigs had been canceled. The Seniors were furious, and threatened to go to London to complain to Larry Parnes. Williams convinced the angry band members to go to find alternative gigs instead, and agreed to drive them and their instruments in his Jaguar. Once in London, Williams and the Seniors headed straight for the 2 I's coffee bar, which, since the mid-1950s, had become famous as a place to hear new rock'n'roll talent.

As Derry Wilkie and the Seniors set up on the tiny stage (singers and groups were allowed to just "get up" and play at the 2 I's) Allan Williams spotted a familiar face in the coffee bar. It was Bruno Koschmider of the Kaiserkeller, who was there by amazing coincidence. The German promoter had been intrigued by Williams' claims for British rock'n'roll, and traveled from Hamburg in order to see and hear it for himself. Arriving in England, Koschmider had come to the only place he knew of where he would be sure to find rock'n'roll: the legendary 2 I's.

Koschmider had already booked a solo singer, Tony Sheridan, and was now planning to hire an English band. After they played a short, but sensational, set at the 2 I's, Derry Wilkie and his group were immediately offered the job. Williams was delighted, and even more so a few weeks later when, the Seniors and Sheridan both doing well at the Kaiserkeller, Koschmider indicated that he wanted a third group to play at another of his clubs, the Indra.

Before offering the gig at the Indra to The Silver Beatles, Williams tried to hire at least two other bands. The first was Rory Storm and the Hurricanes, who had changed their name from the Raving Texans and whose drummer was Ringo Starr. With none available to make the two month trip to Hamburg, however, Williams finally suggested that the less-experienced The Silver Beatles should go.

John, Paul, George, and Stuart accepted immediately, though there were several problems to be settled first. In Paul's case, his father's permission was required, but Jim McCartney eventually said "yes" because his son had just completed his final school exams and would be ready to continue in college after the trip. John, on the other hand, had failed his art school exams and it looked unlikely that he would be asked back. Stuart's position was more difficult because he had promised to start a teaching course at the end of his art college studies. At first he said "no" to Hamburg, but the others talked him into it and the college agreed that he could postpone the course. At 17, George was the youngest member of the band, but he had finished school and his parents said they would let him go as long as he promised to keep out of trouble and write regularly. The biggest problem, however, was the fact that The Silver

Beatles still had no drummer. Allan Williams warned the band that if they didn't find one quickly, he would have to give the Hamburg opportunity to another group.

It was August 1960, and the group had started playing at Mona Best's Casbah club again. Since their previous gigs there as The Quarry Men, the club had become very popular and one of the Casbah's best groups was The Black Jacks, which included Mona's son Pete, on drums. Luckily for The Silver Beatles, The Black Jacks were about to disband because their leader, ex-Quarry Man Ken Browne,

was moving away from Liverpool. Pete Best, who had just left Liverpool Collegiate School, had nothing to do. Living upstairs from the club, he was familiar with all the groups that appeared there so, when Paul McCartney phoned him to ask if he'd like to join The Silver Beatles and go to play in Hamburg, he said "yes" without hesitation.

On August 16, 1960, the group—having now dropped the "Silver" from their name on John's insistence, in favor of simply The Beatles—left for Hamburg. They travelled in an old cream and green "minibus" belonging to, and driven

Above: *Photographed at the Arnhem War Memorial are (left to right) Allan Williams, his wife Beryl, Lord Woodbine, Stuart Sutcliffe, Paul McCartney, George Harrison, and Pete Best.*

Left: *A publicity shot of The Beatles (left to right, Pete Best, George Harrison, Paul McCartney, and John Lennon) taken not long after Pete Best joined the group.*

by, Allan Williams. As well as the band, Williams had brought along his Chinese wife Beryl, her brother Barry Chang, and Lord Woodbine. A famous photograph was later taken by Barry Chang in front of the Arnhem war memorial in Holland,

with Allan, Beryl, Woody, George, Paul, Stu, and Pete in front of an inscription that reads: "Their Names Liveth For Ever More"; John had decided to stay in the minibus.

Before The Beatles left Liverpool, John had boasted around the College of Art that they were going to make $280/£100 a week, but whatever dreams the five musicians might have had about living the high life as pop stars in Hamburg were soon shattered when they arrived in Grosse Freiheit Strasse. They were to be paid $42/£15 a week each by Koschmider, which seemed a reasonable sum at the time considering George's bus conductor father earned about half that amount, but they had not imagined the working conditions. The Indra was a small basement club at the shabby end of the street, away from the bright neon lights of the Kaiserkeller. The band was expected to play a total of four and a half hours every week night, and six hours on Saturdays and Sundays. Across the road from the club was a small movie theater, the Bambi Kino, run by Koschmider. The Beatles' living quarters were at the back. Here, in a filthy room and two small ante-rooms, right behind the cinema screen and its booming soundtrack, they were meant to sleep, or try to sleep.

The first week at the Indra saw a change in The Beatles' performances. On their first night, they were greeted by a sparse audience that consisted mainly of prostitutes and their clients. Depressed by the atmosphere, the five boys shrugged their way through the set with a couldn't-care-less attitude, which just added to the desperate gloom of the place. Bruno Koschmider, and the Allan Williams party, who stayed in Hamburg for a week, were all there and on the second night Williams urged them on, shouting from the bar for them to "Make a show of it!" Koschmider took up the chant, shouting "Mak show, mak show" and, this time, the boys responded, leaping about the stage and stamping their feet in a rock'n'roll frenzy that would become their trademark over the next few months.

Word spread around the local scene and the Indra soon began to fill up each night with customers eager to see the five Liverpudlians and their manic stage act. The challenge of long hours of performing made The Beatles tighten their act and polish their stage skills, so much so that when Derry Wilkie and his group came down from the Kaiserkeller to hear The Beatles they were amazed at the improvement.

The Indra club had long been the target of complaints about noise, especially from the old lady who lived directly

Above: *The Beatles on stage in Hamburg. (Left to right) George Harrison, Stuart Sutcliffe (seated), and John Lennon.*

above the club. Now, with The Beatles and their growing following at full throttle every night, the club was closed down by local authorities in October. It was good news for The Beatles, however; Bruno Koschmider moved them to the far bigger and more popular Kaiserkeller.

It was while they were playing the Kaiserkeller that the boys first came into contact with a group of Hamburg

Left: *(Left to right) George Harrison and John Lennon on stage with Tony Sheridan.*

Below: *(Left to right) Photographs of Jürgen Vollmer, Astrid Kirchherr, and Klaus Voorman taken around the time when they first went to see The Beatles performing in Hamburg.*

art students who would have a huge influence on them in the coming months. The group included photographer Jürgen Vollmer, artist and musician Klaus Voorman and his girlfriend, photography student, Astrid Kirchherr. It was Voorman who first saw The Beatles at the Kaiserkeller, and he became an immediate fan. Voorman raved about them to Astrid, who was unwilling to venture to the notorious Reeperbahn district to see the band. She was from a respectable, middle class family, and more interested in philosophy than rock'n'roll.

Left: (Left to right) George Harrison, Stuart Sutcliffe, and John Lennon, photographed on a truck by Astrid Kirchherr.

Above: (Left to right) Pete Best, George Harrison, John Lennon, Paul McCartney and Stuart Sutcliffe, photographed by Astrid Kirchherr at Hamburg Funfair.

Below: Astrid Kirchherr with Stuart Sutcliffe, after she changed his hairstyle.

Voorman visited the club several more times before his girlfriend eventually joined him, by which time he had started chatting to the band between sets and had formed a particular friendship with Stuart Sutcliffe. When Astrid came to see The Beatles for the first time, she was fascinated by them, but was immediately attracted to Stuart. Over the next few weeks, Astrid Kirchherr would change the way The Beatles looked forever. She offered to take photographs of the group and posed them in a local fairground and on industrial sites around Hamburg. The resulting photos were certainly not ordinary pop group portraits and the boys were delighted; the pictures gave them a unique image.

From the first, Stu and Astrid had been drawn to each other and it wasn't long before she and Klaus Voorman were no longer a couple, though her former boyfriend remained a keen fan of The Beatles. Astrid was besotted with Stu's delicate good looks and suggested he change his hairstyle from the swept back "Teddy Boy" look inspired by Elvis Presley and James Dean.

She cut his hair so that it was long at the side but flat on top, a little like Marlon Brando's, not like a rock'n'roller's. Although the other Beatles laughed at Stu's haircut, they soon cut theirs, too. Only Pete Best kept his slick quiff.

Like all the art student crowd, Astrid made much use of black, often wearing black sweaters and black stockings with white make-up. She sewed a black leather jacket and skin-tight leather trousers, just like her own, for her new boyfriend. Once more, the rest of the band followed Stu's lead, adopting a new uniform of black leather jackets, pointed "winklepicker" shoes and black t-shirts. This was a completely new look that marked The Beatles out from the other flashily-dressed groups on the rock 'n' roll scene.

It was while they were at the Kaiserkeller that the classic line-up of The Beatles, with Ringo Starr on drums, recorded together for the first time. When Derry Wilkie's season at the club ended, his band's place had been taken by Rory Storm and The Hurricanes. Rory's bass player, Lu "Wally" Walters, also sang, and wanted to make a disc in a record-your-voice booth. These machines, for a small sum, allowed customers to cut a primitive disc and pay for a few copies to be pressed. Lu invited John, Paul, and George to back him, along with The Hurricanes' drummer Ringo, and two tracks were recorded: Peggy Lee's hit "Fever" and the Gershwin classic "Summertime". The disc 45-rpm disc was credited as *The Beatles mit Wally*.

But the days at the Kaiserkeller were coming to an end. In November 1960, a new club opened in a huge underground space not far from Grosse Freiheit Strasse. Called the Top Ten, its owner, Peter Eckhorn, offered a better rate of pay than the Kaiserkeller, and accommodation above the club that was far better than anything Koschmider provided. Tony Sheridan was the first to leave the Kaiserkeller and was soon followed by The Beatles, putting them in breach of their contract with Koschmider, which banned them from playing anywhere else in the city. On December 5, the police raided the Top Ten and demanded to see George Harrison's passport. At only 17, he was too young to be in a club, let alone play in one after midnight. As The Beatles were preparing to play their debut date at the Top Ten, George was ordered to leave Germany. The remaining four played a few nights at the club, before Paul and Pete were arrested and then deported after setting fire to a condom when they returned to pick up some clothes they'd left at the Bambi Kino.

Above: *George Harrison (left) and John Lennon (right) pictured onstage in Hamburg wearing their new uniform of black leather jackets and black t-shirts.*

Left: *A concert poster promoting The Beatles' stint at the Kaiserkeller as support act to Rory Storm and the Hurricanes.*

The Beatles first stint in Hamburg, which had lasted nearly four months, had ended in disarray, though the experience on stage certainly helped the group in the long run. A few days later, Stuart flew home on a ticket paid for by Astrid's parents, and John went home by train and ferry.

The band kept a low profile for a couple of weeks after their return but, just before Christmas 1960, The Beatles got together again. First for "welcome home" gigs at Mona Best's Casbah Club, and then a memorable date at Litherland Town Hall, just north of Liverpool. The Litherland date was presented by a part-time disc jockey, Bob Wooler, who had run recently into The Beatles for the first time in the Jacaranda, where the boys were hustling Allan Williams for some new gigs. Although he had never heard them play, Wooler took a chance and booked them for the gig, billing them on the posters as "Direct from Hamburg".

The Beatles' performance at Litherland was sensational. The band played with all the manic charisma of their best nights in Hamburg and scores of girls rushed the stage. Many of the audience, taken by surprise and having not heard of the group before, assumed that they were German. Wooler, meanwhile, realized that these leather-clad rock'n'rollers were special.

Left: *John Lennon (left) and Stuart Sutcliffe (right) photographed by Astrid Kirscherr on a rare day off at a beach on the Baltic coast.*

Below: *The Beatles (left to right): Pete Best, Paul McCartney (at piano), George Harrison, John Lennon, and Stuart Sutcliffe, performing onstage at the Top Ten club.*

DID YOU KNOW?
As well as originating the Beatles "mop top" haircut, Stuart Sutcliffe was also the first to wear a collarless jacket, later to become a Beatles' trademark.

Just three days after that Cavern evening debut, the Beatles returned to Hamburg, this time playing at the Top Ten for an impressive $112/£40 a week each. Over the next few weeks they performed alternating sets with Tony Sheridan between seven at night and three in the morning. Stu, however, was becoming less and less enthusiastic about The Beatles. His relationship with Paul had broken down to the point that, on one occasion, the pair nearly fought on stage, and he had also thrown himself back into his painting. Although Stu's promised return to Liverpool College of Art had never happened, he was urged by Astrid and her friends to try for a place at Hamburg's State Art College. Funded by a grant from the Hamburg City Council, he enrolled under the tutorship of Eduardo Paolozzi, one of his artistic heroes and, for just over a month, led a dual life of playing at the Top Ten at night and attending art school during the day. Then, he quit The Beatles, leaving Paul to take over on bass guitar.

The Cavern Club in Liverpool's Matthew Street had opened as a jazz club in January 1957. The Beatles played their first date there a little over four years later, on February 9, 1961. It was at lunchtime, the first of many daily lunchtime sessions The Beatles would play over the next couple of years. Bob Wooler, whom owner Ray McFall had engaged as DJ, had recommended them, promising they would bring in a lot of fans. He was right. The band had played several Wooler presentations around the Merseyside area since the Litherland gig and the boys were beginning to attract a following. Following several more successful lunchtime gigs, they played their first evening gig there on March 21.

It was during this Hamburg trip that The Beatles made their first commercial recording. Bert Kaempfart, well known in Germany as a bandleader, was also a producer for Polydor,

Above: *The Beatles playing at the Cavern following their return from Hamburg. (Left to right, George Harrison, Paul McCartney, Pete Best, and John Lennon.)*

Left: *Resident DJ Bob Wooler and owner Ray McFall, pictured outside the Cavern Club.*

Above: *The Beatles perform at the Top Ten club, Hamburg, in April 1961. (Left to right, John Lennon, Paul McCartney, and George Harrison.)*

Left: *A leather-clad Paul McCartney on stage at the Cavern Club.*

and had just signed Tony Sheridan to the German record label. For a backing group, Sheridan chose The Beatles and, billed as Tony Sheridan and the Beat Brothers, they recorded eight tracks, two of which "My Bonnie" and "The Saints", Polydor released in August 1961 as a single. Although the disc was a big hit in Germany, The Beatles were only paid a flat fee of about $72/£26 each.

When the rest of his former band mates returned to Liverpool in early July 1961, soon after the Sheridan recordings, Stuart Sutcliffe, no longer a Beatle but still a close friend of the group, decided to stay in Hamburg with Astrid and continue his art school studies. Back in Liverpool, the group was soon back onto the Merseyside gig circuit, though their fan base was steadily increasing. The local beat group scene was growing and there was even a local music paper devoted to it, *Mersey Beat*, launched on July 6, by John and Stu's old art school colleague Bill Harry. The Beatles quickly resumed their regular lunchtime and evening dates at the Cavern, and played all the local village halls and ballrooms. There was, however, nothing new until the end of October, when a local record shop manager noticed customers asking for "My Bonnie" by The Beatles, and wondered what was happening.

Chapter 3: Enter Brian Epstein-1962

Brian Epstein was the manager two record shops, both called NEMS, which was short for North End Music Stores. It was his family's business, and the city-center stores he supervised were among the major music outlets in the northwest of England. In August 1961, Epstein had started writing a record review column in Bill Harry's new *Mersey Beat* newspaper, which often reported on the group, and their name appeared regularly on gig posters around town. Unknown to him at the time, the four Beatles were also regular customers in his store. However, when customers started asking for the Sheridan single, on which The Beatles were billed as the Beat Brothers, he could find no mention of the band in the UK record catalogs. Intrigued, Epstein asked Bill Harry who the group was and where they played, so that he could contact them to find out which record label they were on.

Right: *Brian Epstein, manager of the North End Music Stores, before he became The Beatles' manager.*

Far Right: *John Lennon (left), Paul McCartney (middle, seated), and Pete Best (right), performing at the Cavern Club.*

Above: *An expectant line of teenagers await entry to the Cavern Club in the early 1960s.*

He'd never heard of the Cavern club until Harry told him it was just a short walk from his store in Whitechapel, and that The Beatles played there most lunchtimes. Epstein decided to see them.

Bill Harry arranged for Brian and his assistant, Alistair Taylor, to visit the Cavern on November 9, 1961. As they were ushered in by the bouncer, Paddy Delaney, without having to pay the 15 cent/1 shilling (5p) membership, the smartly dressed shop men wondered if the visit was such a good idea. Descending the narrow steps into the cellar of the Cavern, they were met with the ear-splitting sound of pop records played at top volume, and the smell of sweating bodies. Standing in the dimly lit basement, with its dungeon-like walls and archways, surrounded by trendy teenagers, they felt completely out of place.

Epstein, as manager of the biggest record shop in the area, was well-known to the Cavern management as well as to most of the customers, and his visit was marked with a certain sense of occasion. The DJ, Bob Wooler, even announced a greeting over the club's PA system. Then, to cheers from the crowd, Wooler introduced The Beatles, who launched into an almost non-stop set of frantic rock, and rhythm and blues.

The group's set consisted almost entirely of covers of American rock'n'roll songs, some well known, by musicians such as Chuck Berry, Little Richard, and Carl Perkins, and others less familiar. The crowd, three quarters female, went wild before and after each song, while The Beatles goofed around on stage, calling out to members of the audience by name and showing a warm familiarity with the fans.

Brian Epstein was fascinated, not so much by the music—he preferred classical music—but by the directness of its delivery, the visual image of the four young men in tight-fitting leather, and the effect they had on the crowd. "I was immediately struck by their music, their beat, their sense of humour on stage," he would later recall. "Even afterwards, when I met them, I was struck again by their personal charm. And it was there that, really, it all started."

After The Beatles had finished their first set, Brian went into the tiny Cavern band room to meet them. "And what brings Mr Epstein here?" George joked. Mr Epstein stayed for the second set and, afterward, over lunch with Alistair Taylor, said he thought they were "tremendous." He even hinted to his assistant that he might consider managing them. Taylor, however, thought the group was "absolutely awful."

Epstein watched The Beatles at the Cavern several more times over the coming weeks, getting to know them and politely asking where they played, as well as how much they usually got paid. At the same time, he began investigating, via the record representatives who serviced his stores, the ins and outs of pop management and recording deals, a business that was firmly based in London. By December 3, he felt that he had learned enough to arrange a meeting with The Beatles, at which he proposed managing them. A very punctual man, Epstein was less than impressed when Lennon, Harrison, and Best arrived without Paul, but with Bob Wooler as their "adviser," long after the agreed time, having been drinking in The Grapes pub after their lunchtime gig in the Cavern. The Beatles were yet to be convinced they needed Epstein as a manager, but Brian was not going to give up easily.

He met with their one-time informal manager Allan Williams, who was still resentful that the group had not paid him his commission for their last series of Hamburg dates, having arranged the gigs with the Top Ten club themselves.

Top: *John Lennon on stage at the Cavern Club.*

Above: *Paul McCartney (left) and John Lennon (2nd left) goof around with members of the audience at the Cavern Club.*

Williams assured Epstein that he was no longer connected with The Beatles, and warned him, "not to touch them with a barge pole." There were several more meetings, including some with The Beatles' parents, and John's Aunt Mimi, who were not fully convinced that the boys should enter a management contract with Epstein, but who had to give their consent in the case of Paul, George, and Pete, all of whom were under 21 years of age. Eventually, on January 24, 1962, Brian Epstein signed a five-year management contract with The Beatles that would be the key to their future progress.

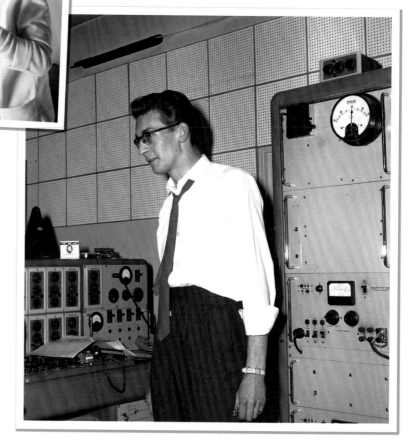

At that time, any progress was far from certain. Over a month earlier, Epstein had caught the attention of Dick Rowe, head of the A&R (Artiste and Repertoire) division at the powerful Decca record company. On December 13, Rowe sent a young assistant in the A&R team, Mike Smith, to Liverpool to audition the hopeful band on their home ground, live on stage at the Cavern. Smith was impressed with what he heard, but decided the band needed to prove their worth in a recording studio before they could be offered a deal. A further audition was fixed for New Year's Day, 1962, and, on a freezing New Year's Eve, The Beatles set off to London with all their equipment in a van driven by Neil Aspinall, a friend of Pete Best and a genial character who had been acting as the band's road manager.

The Beatles, partly on the advice of their manager-to-be, ran though a low-key selection of standards, novelty songs, and three Lennon and McCartney numbers, with only "Money" and Chuck Berry's "Memphis Tennessee"

hinting at the rock'n'roll that was at the core of their live act. The group was not happy with the audition, though Mike Smith assured them that it had gone well, and told them he would let them know Decca's decision in a few weeks.

When it came, however, the decision was negative. Decca had turned The Beatles down, saying they thought the band sounded too much like British pop sensation Cliff Richard's backing group, the Shadows, who were big stars with rival company EMI at the time. He also told them that guitar groups were "on the way out." The group, and Brian Epstein, were devastated.

On their home turf, though, The Beatles could do no wrong. Their brush with the London record scene went almost unnoticed as their popularity in the Cavern and around Merseyside grew with

Top Left: *John Lennon's Aunt Mimi, pictured in 1971, standing in front of a photograph of her famous nephew.*

Above: *Mike Smith of Decca Records in the recording studio.*

each gig. Early in January 1962, the group topped the readers' poll in *Mersey Beat*, ahead of local rivals Gerry and the Pacemakers. Meanwhile, Brian played the Decca tapes to other record companies. The answer from each of them was "no," so The Beatles new manager turned his attention to how he could improve the group's chances of getting attention.

First, he decided, they should change their image. Although he liked their "leather look," he wasn't sure it was right for a wider audience. It was too similar to the way "biker boys" dressed, and the motorcycle "rockers" were already behind the times in terms of fashion. Brian decided the boys should, instead, start wearing smart suits; not the flashy mohair or lamé uniforms that many of their rivals wore, but neat Italian-style box jacket suits with narrow lapels, worn with shirts, ties, and cord waistcoats.

Initially, John resisted, but reluctantly went along with the majority; Paul had seen it as a positive move from the start, and George and Pete thought it was a good idea if it helped them make "the big time." The change of style certainly didn't seem to matter to their growing number of fans around Merseyside.

Above: *The Beatles performing at a Liverpool club in a club in early 1962. (Left to right, George Harrison, John Lennon, Paul McCartney, and Pete Best.)*

Above and Below: *The Beatles on stage at the Cavern in their new "smart" outfits, 1962.*

By the time they first appeared on stage in their new outfits, late in March 1962, the Beatles were undisputed kings of the local beat scene, and their home following was often fanatical. Girls would follow them from gig to gig around England's northwest, never missing a show, and some fans would even begin lining up in the early hours of the morning before their Cavern shows, just to make sure they had a seat in the front row. There was still a one-to-one familiarity between The Beatles and their fans, especially in the confines of the Cavern where, during breaks, "the boys" would mingle with the audience and knew most of the regulars by name. On stage, they would read out hand-written requests that had been passed into the band room before the set, joking with the crowd before launching into the next number.

Each Beatle had his own fans; girls who preferred baby-faced Paul, hard-edged and confident John, shy-looking George, or handsome Pete. If there had been a poll among the fans to identify the most popular Beatle at that time, Pete Best would very possibly have won, with his clean-cut good looks and quiet charm.

But acclaim for The Beatles was still limited to Merseyside and nearby areas; a gig in North Wales, over 20 miles away by road, was about as far as their one night stands took them. Brian knew that the London recording scene was the only way forward, but continuous rejections from all the big companies, including Phillips, Pye, and EMI, made the prospect of fame and fortune in the capital city seem increasingly distant. They still had a fan base in Hamburg though, and the group was delighted when Brian told them they would be returning to Grosse Freiheit Strasse to open an important new venue, the Star-Club, on April 13. The six weeks residency would give them a chance to renew their German links and, most importantly, allow them to visit their old bass player, and now aspiring painter, Stuart Sutcliffe.

Attending Eduardo Paolozzi's Master Class at the Hamburg art school, Stuart's painting was developing every day and had a raw intensity that impressed both his fellow students and his tutor. But since settling in Hamburg the previous year, Stu had complained of increasingly frequent headaches. On a Christmas visit to Liverpool with Astrid, he told his mother, Millie Sutcliffe, about them. Millie spoke to a specialist who told her that Stu's condition could be serious, but she hoped that overwork and the late nights of his new life in Hamburg were to blame. Astrid, too, was becoming concerned. Stu complained ever more regularly and, as his headaches became more painful, he locked himself in his attic studio for long periods. He also started to suffer from blackouts. More than once, he fainted during an art class and the Kirchherr family doctor, suspecting a brain tumour, sent him for an X-Ray, though no tumor was detected.

Above: *Stuart Sutcliffe, photographed in Germany by his girlfriend Astrid Kirchherr.*

Then, on April 10, just three days before he and Astrid had planned to see The Beatles opening at the Star Club, Stuart had an attack far worse than any before. He was rushed to hospital, but died in the ambulance, in Astrid's arms. The cause of death was given as a rare condition that led to an expansion of the brain, though later post mortem X-Rays revealed, as earlier suspected, a small tumor.

The four Beatles were devestated by the news. Flying to Hamburg that same day, they were met by Astrid at the airport, and Paul, George and Pete couldn't hold back the tears. John showed little emotion; his was a private grief, hidden behind a dry-eyed, stony face.

While his "boys" were once again on the stage of a Hamburg beat club, at the end of April, Brian Epstein decided to make a final attempt with the London record companies. This time he made an acetate "demo disc" of The Beatles' Decca tape, and managed to get it to the head of A&R at Parlophone Records, George Martin.

Above: *The Beatles performing, in May 1962, at the Star Club in Hamburg, with guest pianist Roy Young (far left).*

Unlike the major label Columbia, which had already rejected The Beatles, Parlophone was a less important part of the EMI group. Martin's track record included hits by the Vipers Skiffle Group and novelty jazz outfit the Temperance Seven, not exactly cutting-edge rock'n'roll. However, Martin liked what he heard enough to suggest a recording test for The Beatles in June, after they had finished their stint in Hamburg. Although only the test was scheduled, it was enough for *Mersey Beat* to announce that The Beatles had actually signed with Parlophone, adding that the band would be releasing a single in July. When they turned up at the Abbey Road studios on June 6, 1962, the group themselves believed this, because Brian never told them more than that they had a recording session at EMI.

Martin took an instant liking to the four Beatles, and they to him. John was particularly impressed by the fact that the producer had worked with Peter Sellers and Spike Milligan, British comedians who had been his heroes since school days when they were part of the surreal radio comedy series *The Goon Show*. But while Martin got on well with the group, he didn't instantly like the music.

He liked their raw approach, and that they had good voices, capable of singing harmony. What he wasn't so sure about was their material. As well as rock'n'roll classics from the 1950s, which weren't considered to have chart potential in 1962, they played a collection of standards; oldies such as "Red Sails In the Sunset", which Martin didn't think had any commercial appeal. The band also failed to impress him with the handful of songs they'd written. In fact, Martin wasn't fully convinced that The Beatles had a recording future. The one thing he was sure of, and it was a point he voiced to Brian Epstein during the audition, was that if The Beatles did make a record for Parlophone, it would be without Pete Best. Martin assured The Beatles' manager that it would make no difference to the group "because no one will know who's on the record anyway," but he didn't think Pete was a good enough drummer. Martin insisted he would use a studio session musician for any records they might make.

It was nearing the end of July before Epstein heard from George Martin. The Beatles were offered a two-single deal over a year, with four further one-year options should Martin decide to take them up. This was a minimal singles-only offer, common practice in the early 1960s when no pop band was ever offered an album deal unless one of their singles topped the charts in a big way.

After the Abbey Road recording test, rumors began to circulate that the other members of the band wanted to change Pete Best for a different drummer. None of this gossip reached Pete, apart from one whisper at a gig, which he laughed off. However, he wasn't made aware of the Parlophone offer. Then, on Thursday, August 16, Pete Best was summoned to Brian Epstein's office at 11.30 am. There was nothing unusual in this; Brian often spoke to the group individually about small matters, but when Pete came face to face with the manager this time, he could tell instantly that he had serious news. Brian came straight out with it, though he'd obviously been dreading having to utter the words: "The boys want you out of the group."

Pete was, not surprisingly, devastated, and his mother Mona, who'd played her part in nurturing the group (her Casbah club was where The Beatles usually met before traveling to gigs) was furious. Since he'd joined them in August 1960, Pete Best had been with The Beatles two years, on the road to a success that now seemed just around the corner.

Nobody outside the inner circle of The Beatles was ever really sure why Pete was fired, but a big factor was undoubtedly George Martin's views about Pete's drumming.

The Beatles had become friendly with Ringo Starr, the drummer with Rory Storm and the Hurricanes, while both bands were playing in Hamburg in 1960. John, Paul, and George liked Ringo, and when the decision to replace Pete Best was taking shape, his name came up. In August 1962, the Hurricanes were playing the summer season at the Butlin's holiday camp in Skegness, 150 miles east of Liverpool on the North Sea coast. John Lennon contacted the drummer at Butlin's and offered him the job. Ringo accepted immediately.

News of Best's departure and Starr's recruitment was broken officially in the August 23 edition of *Mersey Beat*, which stated that it was an amicable agreement among all concerned. It also announced that The Beatles were going to

London to record their debut single for Parlophone on September 4.

That same day, almost in secret and certainly not broadcast to the fans in the pages of *Mersey Beat*, John Lennon married his long-standing art college girlfriend, Cynthia Powell. She was expecting a baby, and John did what was then considered "the right thing." The couple's simple wedding took place in the Mount Pleasant Registry Office, and was attended by Cynthia's brother Tony, Brian Epstein, George, and Paul. A road drill outside made it impossible for anyone there to hear most of the brief ceremony.

The real truth about Pete's dismissal soon became common knowledge around Liverpool. In response, hundreds of fans signed petitions, demanding that the rest of the band bring him back, and sent them into the *Mersey Beat* office. At their next Cavern gig, The Beatles were greeted by chants of "Pete for ever, Ringo never" from some of the crowd, and George Harrison appeared on stage with a black eye, received in a fight with angry Best supporters as he entered the club. The outcry, however, soon died down and, over the next few weeks, Ringo's place in the group was accepted by all but the most stubborn Pete Best fans.

Meanwhile, the first record to be released under The Beatles own name was due to hit stores on October 5. On both sides of the single were songs written by John Lennon and Paul McCartney and the A-side was a song George Martin had originally passed over during their recording test, "Love Me Do".

> **DID YOU KNOW?**
> During the summer of 1962, John and Paul made a secret trip to the holiday resort of Skegness, where Rory Storm and The Hurricanes were playing a summer season, to ask the band's drummer, Ringo, to join The Beatles. When Rory asked Ringo why John and Paul had come, he refused to answer.

Chapter 4: Please Please Me-1963

It was the moment The Beatles had been waiting for, and Brian Epstein was sparing no expense—after months of work on Brian's part, and years of hard gigging by John, Paul, George, and, in his separate career, Ringo, the four Beatles boarded a plane and flew down to London to make their first record.

When they arrived at EMI's Abbey Road studios on September 4, producer George Martin had no idea the band had changed drummers since the June recording test. Not that it concerned him; he just hoped Ringo would impress him more than Pete Best had. Martin had brought along a song he wanted the group to record as the A-side of their first single, "How Do You Do It", written by the professional songwriter Mitch Murray. After a rough run through of one of their own songs, "Please Please Me", the group settled down to record the Murray number, though with little enthusiasm. They were eager to release one of their own Lennon–McCartney songs on their first disc, but recorded "How Do You Do It" anyway, if only to please Martin.

After a break, they returned to the studio for an evening session, during which they made a number of versions of their own song "Love Me Do", none of which pleased either the band or Martin. Paul wasn't happy with Ringo's drumming, the vocals weren't going well and, after 20 or more "takes" (versions recorded or part-recorded) they decided to stop.

Right: *The Beatles perform at the Empire Theatre, Sunderland, on February 7, 1963. (Left to right, Paul McCartney, Ringo Starr, George Harrison, and John Lennon.)*

Above: *The Beatles and their producer, George Martin, at an early recording session. (Left to right, Paul McCartney, George Martin, George Harrison, Ringo Starr, and John Lennon.)*

"Love Me Do" Facts

B-side: *"P.S. I Love You"*
Recorded: September 4 and 11, 1962
Released: October 4, 1962
Label: Parlophone (UK)
Writers: Lennon/McCartney
Producer: George Martin
Chart Success: UK No. 17,
US No. 1 (1964)

Returning to Abbey Road on September 11, they once again tried to get "Love Me Do" to sound right. This time, George Martin was taking no chances with the drummer, and brought in a session player, Andy White, to sit in for Ringo. The new Beatle didn't seem to mind being replaced and, instead, played tambourine on the rhythm track. On the single's B-side, "P.S. I Love You", another number written by John and Paul, Ringo played only the maraca. The A-side now included a catchy harmonica part played by John Lennon, which was apparently influenced by the hit "Hey Baby" by Bruce Channel, whom The Beatles had supported for a gig earlier in the year; it was a sound that would feature on several of their early recordings.

After the second session, Martin, and the group, were satisfied. They had a single to release. Excitement over the release of "Love Me Do" on October 5 was largely limited to Merseyside. Apart from a few basic adverts that EMI placed in the national music papers, such as *NME* (*New Musical Express*), the record company put no promotion behind the single. Neither Parlophone nor George Martin were part of the company's pop royalty and the small label couldn't expect EMI to spend much advertising an unknown group. Nevertheless, for a first disc by an unheard of band from the north of England, it sold well, if only around Liverpool.

Brian Epstein, with his local record shops, made sure of that. He ordered 10,000 copies of the disc, a massive number that would prove difficult to sell, even though The Beatles had hundreds of fans in, and around, Liverpool. Brian had been told that this was the minimum number of copies that had to be sold to get a record into the national Top Twenty. The record was an instant hit in shops (not just Epstein's NEMS) around the northwest of England, and shot to Number One in *Mersey Beat*'s Top Twenty chart. And, mainly on the strength of those regional sales, it also crept onto the national listings, making the Number 17 spot in the *NME*.

Oddly, not all The Beatles' Liverpool fans bought the single. A hard core of Cavern regulars decided to boycott it, believing that once the band had a hit, The Beatles would leave town and not be "their" group anymore. A few months later, after the release of the second single, they would be proved right.

As copies of "Love Me Do" continued to sell, The Beatles made their first appearance on television, on October 17. It was not a national broadcast, but a local news/review program called *People and Places* that was put out by Manchester-based Granada TV. Pre-filmed in the Cavern on August 22, just after Ringo had replaced Pete Best, the footage showed them singing one of their many covers of US rhythm and blues numbers, Richie Barrett's "Some Other Guy".

Producer Johnny Hamp had battled with his bosses at Granada to get the film shown, but would go on to put The Beatles on the show several more times over the coming months. He later recalled, "I first saw The Beatles in a club in Hamburg. They were very scruffy characters, but they had a beat in their music which I liked...I got into a lot of trouble over it. Everyone said they were too rough, too untidy. But I liked them. I put them on again and again." On October 29, Hamp even brought the group into the Granada studio, where they were filmed performing "Love Me Do" and "A Taste of Honey". The new footage was transmitted on *People and Places* on November 2.

Above: *A poster advertising a Beatles performance, now top of the bill, at the Tower Ballroom in Brighton, England, on September 14, 1962.*

Left: *John Lennon on stage at the Cavern Club in 1962.*

Above: *A 1962 group portrait of the band (left to right, John Lennon, George Harrison, Ringo Starr, and Paul McCartney) taken by Astrid Kirchherr.*

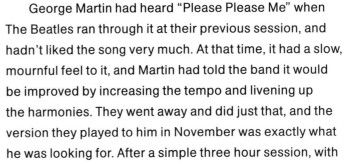

The end of 1962 was a busy period for The Beatles. Their next single was due to be released by Parlophone early in the New Year, and they had been booked to play another season at Hamburg's Star Club through the last two weeks of December. With the German trip looming, they went into Abbey Road on November 26, to record the single before they left.

George Martin had heard "Please Please Me" when The Beatles ran through it at their previous session, and hadn't liked the song very much. At that time, it had a slow, mournful feel to it, and Martin had told the band it would be improved by increasing the tempo and livening up the harmonies. They went away and did just that, and the version they played to him in November was exactly what he was looking for. After a simple three hour session, with Ringo now behind the drums, and during which they also taped the B-side "Ask Me Why", The Beatles had a sensational track on their hands. When he heard the final take of "Please Please Me", George Martin commented from the control room, "You've just made your first Number One," and his instinct would be proved correct.

The Beatles were not looking forward to the Star Club engagement, especially as it meant they would miss both Christmas and New Year's Eve at home. The engagement had been booked in the summer, before they had signed with Parlophone and, with all the excitement at home, the last thing they wanted was to play long sets to a noisy crowd in Germany. To add to their gloom, The Beatles weren't even top of the bill, and the boys would have preferred to stay in Britain promoting "Love Me Do", instead of banging out old cover songs.

Above Left: *John Lennon (left) and Paul McCartney (right), in December 1962, during their final residency at the Star Club in Hamburg.*

Left: *The Beatles performing at the Star Club in December 1962. (Left to right, John Lennon, Ringo Starr, Paul McCartney, and George Harrison.)*

Above: *Paul McCartney (left) and Ringo Starr (right) performing during a Beatles' appearance on the British TV show "Thank Your Lucky Stars" in February 1963.*

As soon as the German dates were finished, the band returned to England as soon as possible, arriving back immediately after New Year. By now, they didn't have time to worry about promoting "Love Me Do"; the new single was due to be released on January 11, and this, they hoped, would be the big one. Key to its success would be exposure and, the day after its release, the band appeared on the prime time Saturday night TV pop show *Thank Your Lucky Stars*. This was the first time most people outside the Merseyside area had seen or heard The Beatles, and it was their first national television appearance. However, the teenage audience at the show, which was broadcast from Birmingham, seemed to know

exactly who they were: as The Beatles mimed along to "Please Please Me", the sound was almost drowned out by the screams of fans.

The following week, all the British music papers carried excellent reviews of the new release, and the single started its climb to the Number One spot in the *NME* and *Melody Maker* charts, making Number Two in the trade magazine *Record Retailer,* on which many other charts were based. George Martin's prediction about The Beatles' second single had come true.

Now well known pop names, at the beginning of February The Beatles starred on a countrywide "package" tour on which they shared the bill with other acts. Headlining was the popular 16-year-old singer Helen Shapiro. This was the first time that new fans across the UK had a chance to see the band live and, though they were only fourth on the bill, The Beatles' short set was always greeted by the deafening screams that would become commonplace at their concerts over the next three years. Driven by a frantic press campaign, "Please Please Me" topped the charts on February 16, by which time The Beatles had, unofficially, become the main attraction on the tour.

"Please Please Me" Facts

B-side: *"Ask Me Why"*
Recorded: November 26, 1962
Released: January 11, 1963
Label: Parlophone (UK)
Writers: Lennon/McCartney
Producer: George Martin
Chart Success: UK No. 1, US No. 3 (1964)

Above: *The Beatles (left to right, Paul McCartney, George Harrison, John Lennon, and Ringo Starr) read a letter in their dressing room while on tour in 1963.*

Above: *Paul McCartney, George Harrison, John Lennon, and Ringo Starr goofing around in an elevator at the Empire Theatre, Sunderland, in February 1963.*

For George Martin, a hit single meant a new challenge: to cash in on the band's success with an album as soon as possible. What he didn't want was an album that fit the usual record industry formula of hit singles mixed in with a selection of lightweight "filler" tracks, because he was convinced The Beatles could do better. At first, Martin thought a live album recorded at the Cavern might be the answer but, for technical reasons, recording at the Cavern was ruled out. Instead, he decided to record The Beatles "live" in the studio, with as few "takes" as possible. The resulting album, *Please Please Me*, was recorded in a one-day session on February 11, 1963, and it was a sensation.

The two singles and their B-sides were included, of course, and the rest of the songs were a cross section of The Beatles' act at the time. There was a selection of cover versions from their stage show, ranging from the ballad "A Taste Of Honey" to the wild show-stopper "Twist And Shout", alongside four original Lennon–McCartney songs. From the opening track, "I Saw Her Standing There", the *Please Please Me* album confirmed The Beatles as more than one-hit wonders. Released on March 22, 1963, it catapulted the group to the top of the UK album charts, where it would remain for the next six months.

DID YOU KNOW?
Please Please Me is the only Beatles album on which the original songs are credited to "McCartney/Lennon"; after that they would be always be credited as the more familiar "Lennon/McCartney".

Top: *The Beatles (left to right, Paul McCartney, George Harrison, Ringo Starr, and John Lennon) perform in a London record shop, in March 1963, to promote the release of the album "Please Please Me".*

Above: *The Beatles (left to right, George Harrison, Paul McCartney, John Lennon, and Ringo Starr) posing in front of a display of "Please Please Me" album covers.*

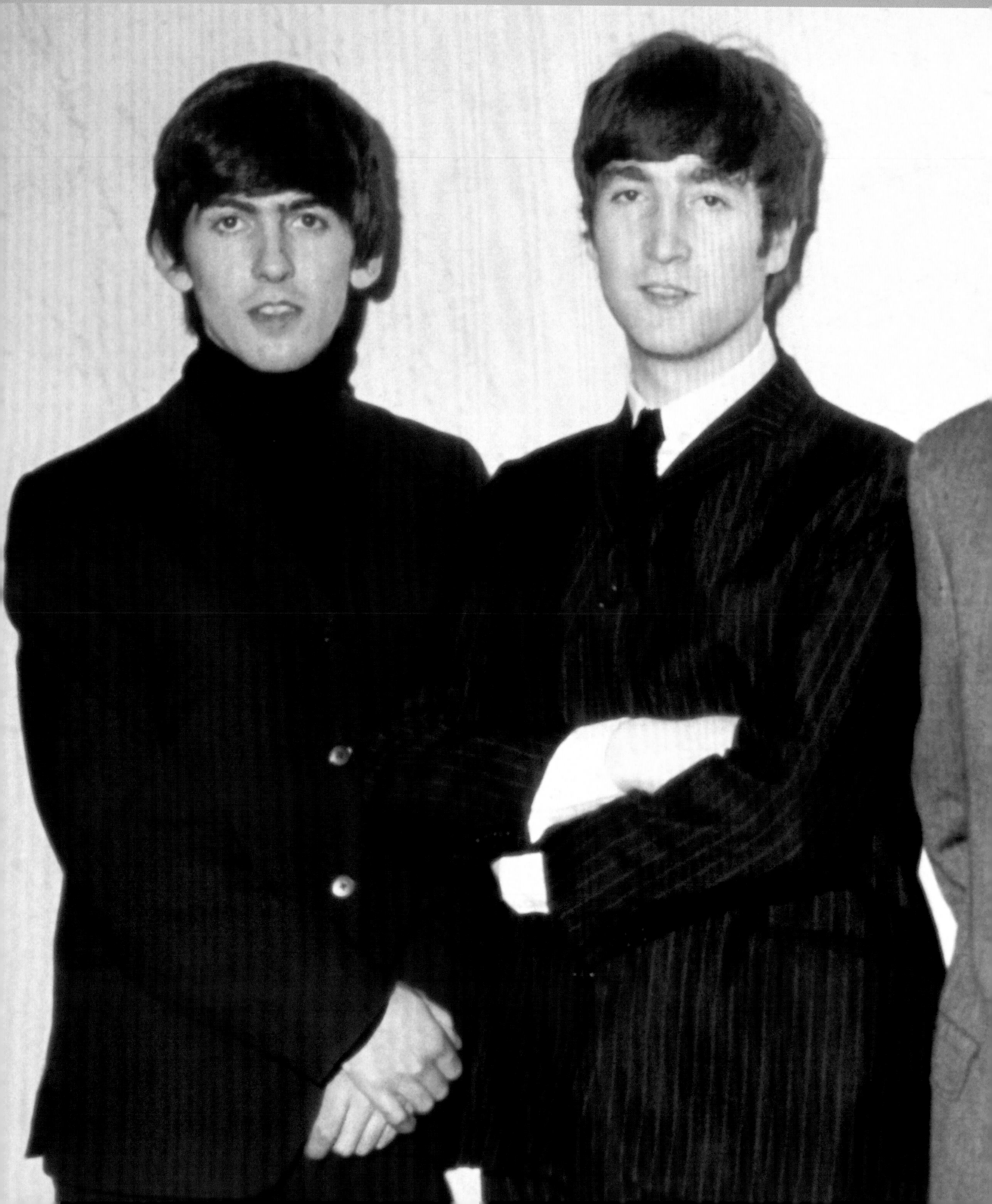

This spread: *(Left to right) George Harrison, John Lennon, Paul McCartney, and Ringo Starr pictured in a 1963 publicity shot.*

Please Please Me Facts

Recorded: February 11, 1963
Released: March 22, 1963
Label: Parlophone (UK)
Writers: Lennon/McCartney
(except songwriters as noted below)
Producer: George Martin
Chart Success: UK No. 1

Please Please Me Track-By-Track

Side 1

I Saw Her Standing There (2min 52sec)
A crowd-pleaser at the Cavern, this track proved that John and Paul could write solid rock'n'roll when they wanted.

Misery (1.47)
John and Paul shared vocals on a song they originally wrote for Helen Shapiro, but which she never recorded.

Anna (Go To Him) (2.54) (Arthur Alexander)
Typical of the slightly obscure American material The Beatles sometimes picked, Arthur Alexander had hit the US R&B charts with this song the previous year.

Chains (2.23) (Gerry Goffin/Carole King)
Originally recorded by the US girl vocal group The Cookies, and composed by the legendary Goffin and King songwriting team.

Boys (2.24) (Luther Dixon/Wes Farrell)
Ringo's chance at a vocal came on this cover of a Shirelles B-side from 1960.

Ask Me Why (2.24)
B-side to The Beatles' first Number One, "Please Please Me".

Please Please Me (2.00)
The chart-topping title track, without which there would have been no album.

Side 2

Love Me Do (2.19)
The first recording of their debut single, with session man Andy White on drums. A second, with Ringo playing, was released as the single.

P.S. I Love You (2.02)
B-side to "***Love Me Do***".

Baby It's You (2.35) (Hal David/Burt Bacharach/Barney Williams)
Another cover of a Shirelles hit, the original charted in the US Top Ten in June 1962.

Do You Want To Know A Secret (1.56)
George's only stab at lead vocals on the album.

A Taste Of Honey (2.01) (Ric Marlow/Bobby Scott)
One of Paul's ballad moments that always went down well with his fans at live shows, it was the instrumental theme tune of the 1961 film of the same name.

There's A Place (1.49)
A very good example of John Lennon's early ballad writing skill.

Twist And Shout (2.33) (Bert Russell/Phil Medley)
A 1962 US hit for the Isley Brothers, this was The Beatles' roaring version, which regularly climaxed their stage shows in 1963.

Above: (Left to right) Paul McCartney, Ringo Starr, George Harrison, John Lennon, performing at the Majestic Ballroom, Finsbury Park, London on April 24, 1963.

Left: The Beatles hold a silver disc, awarded for UK sales in excess of 250,000 of their single "Please Please Me". (Left to right, Paul McCartney, George Harrison, Ringo Starr, George Martin of EMI, and John Lennon.)

Chapter 5: Beatlemania-1963

Two weeks before the *Please Please Me* album was released, The Beatles began a UK tour, for which they had, again, been booked in a support spot. Promoter Arthur Howes, who had staged the earlier tour with Helen Shapiro, had engaged the band for a string of dates with US stars Chris Montez and Tommy Roe, both of whom had recently hit the British charts. However, by the start of the tour, The Beatles, with a Number One single on their hands, were a far bigger attraction than the two Americans and Howes changed the billing at the last minute, so it was The Beatles who closed the show, to ear-splitting screams every night.

Above: *The Beatles fool around for the cameras. (Left to right, Ringo Starr, George Harrison, Paul McCartney, and John Lennon.)*

Right: *The Beatles perform on the British TV program "The Ken Dodd Show" in 1963. (Left to right, Ringo Starr, George Harrison, Paul McCartney, and John Lennon.)*

"From Me To You" Facts

B-side: "Thank You Girl"
Recorded: March 5, 1963
Released: April 11, 1963
Label: Parlophone (UK)
Writers: Lennon/McCartney
Producer: George Martin
Chart Success: UK No. 1

While the band played to adoring new fans, the media frenzy surrounding them grew through March and April. They appeared on the top BBC radio shows *Saturday Club* and *Easy Beat*, while *Thank Your Lucky Stars* proved just the first of TV appearances on all the major shows on the national networks. By now, the popular press, not just the music papers, was also taking notice. When The Beatles' third single, "From Me To You", which was recorded on March 5, shot to Number One soon after it was released on April 11, a press campaign bigger than anything seen in British pop began. This was the beginning of what, throughout 1963, would become a national obsession, as The Beatles captured the public imagination.

Below: *The Beatles (left to right, Paul McCartney, George Harrison, Ringo Starr, and John Lennon) rehearse for a British TV appearance in 1963.*

Left: *The band pictured in the studio on the day that they recorded "From Me To You". (Left to right, George Harrison, Paul McCartney, Ringo Starr, and John Lennon.)*

Below: *Brian Epstein (far right) pictured in June 1963 with three of his most successful bands of the time. From left to right, The Beatles (John Lennon, Ringo Starr, George Harrison, and Paul McCartney), Gerry and the Pacemakers, and Billy J Kramer and the Dakotas.*

The same week that "From Me To You" went to the top of the charts, Cynthia Lennon gave birth to a son in Sefton General Hospital, Liverpool, on April 23, 1963. John wasn't present for the birth, because The Beatles were still on tour with Chris Montez and Tommy Roe and, when he did visit the hospital a few days later, he had to be smuggled in, to avoid the fans outside. John named his son Julian, in remembrance of his mother, Julia.

Meanwhile, Brian Epstein had signed another Liverpool group, The Beatles' friendly rivals, Gerry and the Pacemakers.

Also with George Martin on Parlophone, Gerry and his band recorded the song that Martin had wanted The Beatles to debut with, "How Do You Do It?" and, on March 22, it also hit Number One. Over the next three months Brian signed Billy J.Kramer, the Big Three, the Fourmost, and Tommy Quickly, all Liverpool acts. With Kramer and the Fourmost both having hits with songs written by Lennon and McCartney, and another chart-topper arriving for Gerry and the Pacemakers, by June 1963, Brian's artists were dominating the British charts.

Above: *The Beatles pictured with their instruments in a small backyard in London, 1963. (Left to right, George Harrison, Ringo Starr, Paul McCartney, and John Lennon.)*

It wasn't just Brian Epstein who had discovered that that there was money to be made from Liverpool's talent, though. London record companies had quickly signed up other Merseyside groups, including The Searchers and Swinging Blue Jeans, and both of those bands had hits in June. The press even invented a label for the new music phenomenon. It was now known as the "Mersey Sound".

But it was The Beatles that led this northern invasion of the charts. They had by far the biggest fan following and grabbed most of the headlines. By the summer of 1963, everyone in Great Britain could name John, Paul, George, and Ringo. Their pictures appeared in hundreds of magazines and every national newspaper, they were on TV pop shows and featured in cinema newsreels, and their image seemed to be everywhere. In fact, their faces were just as familiar to

They even saw their first EP (a four-track Extended Play 7-inch disc) enter the singles chart. Titled *Twist and Shout*, it featured four tracks from the *Please Please Me* album, topped the UK EP chart for a record-breaking 21 weeks, and reached Number Two in the singles chart. It sold over 800,000 copies, a remarkable amount considering all the tracks were on the LP that had already been at the top of the album charts for ten weeks. With its iconic cover picture by Dezo Hoffman of The Beatles leaping in the air, *Twist and Shout* is still the biggest-selling EP in British pop history.

All four Beatles had been growing their hair longer since the beginning of 1963 and, by the summer, their "mop tops" had become an essential part of the group's look, as they shook their heads on stage to whoops of delight from frantic audiences. At the same time, their style was also becoming more "cuddly", as Brian strived to make them acceptable to all

Above: *The famous image of the band (left to right, Ringo Starr, George Harrison, Paul McCartney, and John Lennon) that was used for the cover of the "Twist and Shout" EP.*

"Twist and Shout" EP Facts

Recorded: February 11, 1963
Released: July 12, 1963
Label: Parlophone (UK)
Writers: Lennnon/McCartney
(except songwriters as noted below)
Producer: George Martin
Chart Success: UK No. 1 (EP chart),
UK No. 2 (singles chart)

Track-By-Track
Side 1
Twist and Shout (2.33) (Bert Russell/
Phil Medley)
A Taste Of Honey (2.01)
(Ric Marlow/Bobby Scott)
Side 2
Do You Want To Know A Secret (1.56)
There's A Place (1.49)

During a studio session in the early summer, photographer Dezo Hoffman snapped the most familiar image of The Beatles of the time. They wore neat, gray, collarless suits designed by Pierre Cardin. It was an image that would appear on countless fan magazines and pin-up photographs, and was also used for a boom of merchandising. The Beatles' faces appeared on cosmetics, toys, bubble gum, bed clothes, wallpaper, and in an avalanche of souvenir books and pictures. Only Elvis Presley in the late 1950s had had his picture marketed as widely; for a British pop act to exploit their image in this way was unheard of. Smiling down from a million bedroom walls, in their button-down shirts and high-fastened jackets, this was The Beatles of the summer of '63, the summer of "She Loves You", which would be their biggest hit yet.

Recorded at the beginning of July and released on August 23, with advance orders of half a million copies, "She Loves You" went straight to Number One and stayed there for six weeks. The single remained in the British charts for eight months and is one of the biggest selling British singles of all time. The catchy "Yeah, Yeah, Yeah" at the end of each chorus became a line used by all the newspaper headline writers, who now covered The Beatles' every move. And, as summer turned to fall, the press invented a word to describe the madness that was gripping the nation: "Beatlemania".

The word was invented after The Beatles appeared on the country's top TV variety show, *Sunday Night at the London Palladium* on October 13. This, in itself, was a measure of how popular the band had become. Broadcast

Below: *(Left to right) Paul McCartney, George Harrison, Ringo Starr, and John Lennon wearing matching gray, collarless suits designed by Pierre Cardin.*

"She Loves You" Facts

B-side: "I'll Get You"
Recorded: July 7, 1963
Released: August 23, 1963
Label: Parlophone (UK)
Writers: Lennon/McCartney
Producer: George Martin
Chart Success: UK No. 1,
US No. 1 (1964)

"live" every Sunday from the famous old theater in London's theater district, the show featured a mixture of comedians, novelty acts, and even had a game show in the middle, before ending with an international star as headliner. As The Beatles themselves well remembered, the American rock'n'roll legend Buddy Holly had appeared on the show in 1958, and pop fans across the nation had clustered around black-and-white TV screens to see his short set.

The Beatles' appeared, like Holly, in the star spot at the end, and attracted a bigger viewing audience than even the great rock'n'roller. In fact, it was the highest rating edition of the show ever broadcast. Fifteen million people across Britain tuned into the program that night but, next day in the newspapers, it was events outside the theater that attracted the most attention.

The usual collection of fans, mostly female, had gathered to see their idols arriving at, and leaving, the Palladium and, though later accounts suggested there was nothing unusual in their conduct that night, the morning papers were full of reports of a "riot", involving thousands of hysterical fans, that had to be stopped by police. "Beatlemania" more than one headline screamed, and the word stuck.

Below Left: *John Lennon dances with Helen Shapiro during rehearsals for an appearance on the British TV show "Ready Steady Go" in 1963.*

Below: *The Beatles (left to right, Paul McCartney, George Harrison, Ringo Starr, and John Lenon) on stage during their performance on "Sunday Night at the London Palladium".*

thousands of Beatles fans, each hoping to catch a glimpse of John, Paul, George, or Ringo.

The Beatles performed a short, four-song set, climaxing, as their stage act always did throughout 1963, with "Twist and Shout". The royals seemed to genuinely enjoy it, and the papers next day called it a "triumph" for the four mop-tops. John Lennon gave the press their best quote when he asked the audience, "Will people in

Riots or not, the staggeringly successful Palladium appearance confirmed The Beatles' place in the traditional show-business establishment, something the band members would have never imagined, or even wanted, a year earlier. Even the formerly rebellious John accepted that joining the establishment was the price of fame. So, when it was announced that the group would appear on that year's Royal Command Performance on November 4, it was no surprise to anyone.

The annual Royal Command event showcased the best of "light entertainment", including pop music, excerpts from hit musicals, and comedy acts, for the entertainment of Britain's Royal Family. The Beatles were being awarded the ultimate honor of the UK entertainment industry. The Queen herself, soon to have a baby, was unable to attend that year, so The Beatles were to perform in front of her sister, Princess Margaret, and Elizabeth, the Queen Mother. The show was held at the Prince of Wales Theatre in London and, by the time the royal party arrived, the venue was almost surrounded by

the cheaper seats clap your hands? All the rest of you, if you'll just rattle your jewellery..." Beneath a heading that simply ran "Yeah! Yeah! Yeah!" the popular *Daily Mirror* newspaper began its main editorial, "You have to be a real sour square not to love the nutty, noisy, happy, handsome Beatles. If they don't sweep your blues away—brother, you're a lost cause."

During 1963, The Beatles had risen from playing local Liverpool gigs to the most popular band in Great Britain. At the end of November, they released their second album, With The Beatles, and their fifth single, "I Want To Hold Your Hand". These would be the keys to their becoming the most popular band in the world.

Far Left: *Police outside the London Palladium hold back teenage Beatles fans. The girls were hoping to catch a glimpse of the group after their performance on "Sunday Night at the London Palladium."*

Left: *The Beatles (left to right, John Lennon, Paul McCartney, George Harrison, and Ringo Starr) relax backstage at London's Prince of Wales Theatre, before the Royal Command Performance of November 4, 1963.*

Above Right: *(Left to right) Paul McCartney, Ringo Starr, John Lennon, and George Harrison during rehearsals for the Royal Command Performance at the Prince of Wales Theatre, London, on November 4, 1963.*

Right: *(Left to right) Paul McCartney, John Lennon, Ringo Starr, and George Harrison take a break during the recording of their radio show, "Pop Go The Beatles", in August 1963.*

Did You Know?
The Beatles had their own BBC radio series in the UK, called *Pop Go the Beatles*, that ran from June until September 1963.

Chapter 6: With The Beatles-1963

The Beatles had been working on their second album since July, 1963, scheduled for release at the end of November. A month before, on October 24, the band took off for a six-day "European tour" that was actually just a series of concerts in Sweden. It was clear as soon as the group landed in Stockholm that The Beatles fame wasn't limited to the UK; hordes of hysterical teenagers greeted them, and the band had to be escorted by police back to their hotel after every gig. Even their mop-top hairstyle was being imitated by Swedish boys; the local papers called it the "Hamlet".

Above: *George Harrison (left) and John Lennon (right) rehearse in a Stockholm, Sweden, hotel room in October, 1963.*

Right: *The Beatles (left to right, Ringo Starr, John Lennon, Paul McCartney, and George Harrison) pose for the cameras in 1964.*

Arriving back in London, the group was greeted with more mayhem. As The Beatles descended the steps of their plane at Heathrow Airport, hundreds of girls, who had crowded on to the observation roof of the terminal, screamed and waved "Welcome Home" banners, even though the band had been away for less than a week. An army of press photographers swarmed around the aircraft.

Late in October, Brian Epstein moved his NEMS music operation south to London. The Liverpool offices had become too small, and Brian knew it would be better to move the business to the capital, which was, of course, also the country's show-business and commercial capital. He also found places to live in London for himself and three of The Beatles. Brian took a luxury apartment in the fashionable Knightsbridge area; George and Ringo shared a place in the

same mansion building. John, Cynthia, and baby Julian moved to Emperor's Gate in Kensington. Paul took a spare room in the family home of his actress girlfriend Jane Asher, whom he'd started dating four months earlier. Although they visited family and friends on Merseyside regularly, The Beatles were now officially London residents. The group had played their final gig at the Cavern on August 3, and, apart from brief visits, had now left Liverpool forever.

EMI records had intended to delay the release of The Beatles' next album until the sales of *Please Please Me* and its spin-off EPs (four-track "extended play" discs) had run their course. However, mounting coverage of "Beatlemania" in the press, and the impact of the Palladium and Royal Command shows, persuaded the company to bring the release forward, though *Please Please Me* was still at Number One. The album

Above: *The Beatles (left to right, John Lennon, George Harrison, Paul McCartney, and Ringo Starr) riding donkeys on a beach in Weston-Super-Mare, England, before a concert in July 1963. The man on the right is the donkey owner.*

was released on November 22, and, before anyone had even listened to it, *With The Beatles* caused a stir with its choice of cover photograph. Taken a few months earlier by Robert Freeman, the stark black-and-white picture of the four unsmiling Beatles was a very different image to that of the happy-go-lucky mop-tops of their regular publicity shots; it was clear the band wanted to be taken seriously. The photo would also appear on their first American album release, in January 1964, which was called *Meet The Beatles!* and featured a different track selection to the UK album.

Unlike *Please Please Me*, which the group recorded in one day, the group had spent eight days in the studio, between July and October 1963, making *With The Beatles*. Again, American R&B classics appeared alongside Lennon–McCartney numbers, plus a song written by George. This time, however, there were no "repeats" of already-released singles; every track was new, and none would be released as singles in the UK.

With UK advance orders alone topping 300,000, sales of the album quickly passed the half million mark, and it replaced *Please Please Me* at Number One the week after its release. Unusually, *With The Beatles* even appeared in the singles chart, which at that time was calculated on the sales of any record, whatever its size. A week after the album had hit the stores, The Beatles released the single "I Want To Hold Your Hand". With advance sales of over a million copies, it became an instant Number One, replacing "She Loves You", which had returned to the top spot. The "fab four" ruled the UK charts, and the whole British music scene. The band was, by now, praised at every level of society; even a classical music critic, William Mann, wrote in *The Times* newspaper that Lennon and McCartney were the "outstanding English composers of 1963."

Below: *The Beatles recording with producer George Martin in 1964. (Left to right, George Harrison, Paul McCartney, George Martin, John Lennon.)*

"I Want To Hold Your Hand" Facts

B-Side: "This Boy"
Recorded: October 17, 1963
Released: November 29, 1963
Label: Parlophone (UK)
Writers: Lennnon/McCartney
Producer: George Martin
Chart Success: UK No. 1, US No. 1

Above: *(Left to right) John Lennon, Paul McCartney, Ringo Starr, and George Harrison on the British TV show "Juke Box Jury" in December 1963.*

Their genius for songwriting set The Beatles apart from the other "Merseybeat" groups and, indeed, any of the British pop stars who had gone before them. Songs on *With The Beatles,* such as "All My Loving", were easily good enough to be singles; the rich Lennon–McCartney output meant that the band's albums included strong, self-written tracks where other rock'n'roll groups would have used the usual, and expected, lightweight "fillers." In fact, most pop artists relied on professional songwriters to provide their material, or played cover versions of American hits, but by now The Beatles were even writing hits for rival groups, from other NEMS artists such as Billy J.Kramer and the Fourmost, to London's Rolling Stones.

As the new album and single crashed into the charts, The Beatles began a frantic UK tour that saw them playing to packed crowds at local theaters and cinemas across the country. It finished with a three-week Christmas Show at the Finsbury Park Astoria theater in London; a show The Beatles also took back to their home town for a date at the Liverpool Empire on December 22.

For The Beatles, 1964 began with a three week trip to Paris in January, where they performed at the city's Olympia theater, one of the most important venues in the French capital. Although the money they were being paid was hardly enough to cover expenses, especially as Brian Epstein had booked the party into the exclusive George Cinq hotel, Brian saw it as a necessary publicity exercise in a country where

British pop had never made a big impact. The French press were alerted to stories of the riots and mayhem that followed the group's appearances in England, and the British press were sent over in force to cover "our boys" conquering the French pop scene.

Nevertheless, Beatlemania failed to erupt on the streets of Paris. The audience at the Olympia was mostly male, which puzzled the band, and were obviously more interested in the local star Sylvie Vartan and American singer Trini Lopez, who shared the bill. Apart from some chants of "Ring-o, Ring-o" and a flurry of applause for rock'n'roll numbers like "Twist And Shout", the band played to lukewarm crowds, though, at least, they could hear themselves playing on stage for the first time in months.

The reviews of the Olympia concerts were no better; any plans Brian and the band had of taking France by storm were over, for the moment at least. However, far more important news had come through while The Beatles were in Paris; news that stunned the band into shocked silence when Brian told them. "I Want To Hold Your Hand" had hit Number One in the American charts.

DID YOU KNOW?
Two of The Beatles were left-handed: Paul (a more well-known fact because he plays bass guitar that way) and Ringo.

Left: *(Left to right) John Lennon, Paul McCartney, Ringo Starr (top), and George Harrison in costume for a segment of their 1963 Christmas Show at the Finsbury Park Astoria theater in London.*

Below: *John Lennon (far left) plays his guitar while (left to right) George Harrison, manager Brian Epstein, Ringo Starr, and Paul McCartney relax in a hotel room in Paris in January 1964.*

DID YOU KNOW?
For three weeks in December 1963, The Beatles were Number One and Two in the UK singles chart, Number One and Two in the album chart, and Number One and Two in the EP (extended play) chart.

This spread: *George Harrison, Ringo Starr and John Lennon with British comedian Eric Morecambe, during rehearsals for a 1963 appearance on Morecambe's British TV show.*

With The Beatles Facts

Recorded: July 18 and 30, September 11–12
and 30, October 3, 17, and 23, 1963
Released: November 22, 1963
Label: Parlophone (UK)
Writers: Lennnon/McCartney
(except songwriters as noted below)
Producer: George Martin
Chart Success: UK No. 1

Track-By-Track
Side 1

It Won't Be Long (2min.11sec.)
John's lead vocal was double tracked on this powerful opening number.

All I've Got To Do (2.01)
Unlike most tracks on the album, this was fully recorded during the same session.

All My Loving (2.06)
One of the Beatles' most popular album tracks.

Don't Bother Me (2.26) (George Harrison)
George Harrison's record debut as a songwriter.

Little Child (1.45)
As well as bass, Paul also played piano on this rhythm and blues-style song.

Till There Was You (2.14) (Meredith Willson)
Paul's version of this song, from the 1957 Broadway musical *The Music Man*, had long been treasured by fans at the Cavern.

Please Mister Postman (2.34) (Georgia Dobbins/
William Garrett/Brian Holland/Robert Bateman/
Freddie Gorman)
Another cover, the original was a 1961 US chart-topper for all-girl vocal group the Marvelettes.

Side 2

Roll Over Beethoven (2.44) (Chuck Berry)
Another crowd-pleaser from the days of playing Liverpool and Hamburg, George played brilliantly on the Chuck Berry classic.

Hold Me Tight (2.29)
Like many Beatle tracks of this period, hand-clapping forced the beat along on this solid rocker.

You Really Got A Hold On Me (3.00) (Smokey Robinson)
Another US vocal group classic, this had been a hit for Smokey Robinson and the Miracles early in 1963.

I Wanna Be Your Man (1.56)
A song that was also recorded by The Rolling Stones as their second single.

Devil In Her Heart (2.25) (Richard Drapkin)
Originally by the American all-girl group the Donays, the lyric was changed slightly for George's lead vocal.

Not A Second Time (2.05)
Only two Beatles, John and Ringo, played on this track, which also features George Martin on piano.

Money (2.47) (Janie Bradford/Berry Gordy)
Recorded by Barrett Strong in 1959, like "Twist And Shout" this track had become a Lennon-led show-stopper. It was recorded with George Martin on piano.

Top: *Paul McCartney (left) and John Lennon (right) pictured backstage at the Finsbury Park Astoria during the Beatles' 1963 Christmas Show.*

Above Left: *Ringo Starr relaxes backstage at the Finsbury Park Astoria during the Beatles' 1963 Christmas Show.*

Above Right: *George Harrison takes a break backstage at the Finsbury Park Astoria during the Beatles' 1963 Christmas Show.*

Chapter 7: Conquering America-1964

The Beatles' breakthrough in the USA took everyone by surprise, not least The Beatles themselves. Although their records had been on sale in North America since February 1963, when Capitol Records, owned by EMI, released "Love Me Do" in Canada, the United States branch of the company had not been interested in the band. George Martin had tried to get Capitol US to release "Please Please Me" after it topped the UK chart, but had been told by an executive, "We don't think The Beatles will do anything in this market."

Instead, "Please Please Me" had been released in the US by Vee-Jay, a small independent label, and didn't even make the *Billboard* Hot 100 chart. Similarly, "From Me To You" reached no further than Number 116 on *Billboard*. It was left to another independent label, Swan, to release "She Loves You" in July 1963. That single, too, failed to chart.

On November 4, 1963, Brian Epstein took matters into his own hands, and flew to New York to persuade the executives at Capitol Records in person. He took with him an advance copy of "I Want To Hold Your Hand", which was due to be

Did You Know?

New York disc jockey Murray "The K" Kaufman accompanied the group around the city during their first visit, interviewing them live from their hotel room and dubbing himself "the fifth Beatle."

Right: *(Left to right) Paul McCartney, John Lennon, Ringo Starr, and George Harrison wave to the crowd as they arrive at JFK airport, New York, in February 1964.*

Above: *Ed Sullivan (left) talking to George Harrison (center) and Ringo Starr (right) during a photo-call to promote The Beatles' appearance on "The Ed Sullivan Show" in February 1964.*

released in Britain at the end of the month. It was a successful trip for Brian; though they weren't wild about the single, staff at Capitol agreed to release it and set a date for January 13, 1964.

While in New York, Brian also had a successful meeting with Ed Sullivan, host of the biggest prime time variety show on US television. Sullivan was aware of The Beatles' popularity in Britain, having met them in London in October, at which time he had suggested that they might appear on his show early in 1964. Brian closed the deal; the band were to be given top billing on the *Ed Sullivan Show* on February 9, and were also booked for another broadcast, one week after that. All that was needed to secure the band's success in the US was for "I Want To Hold Your Hand" to sell well in January, though, with Capitol still unexcited about the single, that seemed far from certain.

On December 10, 1963, CBS News anchorman Walter Cronkite presented a film about the Beatle craze sweeping Britain, which included footage of the group playing "She Loves You" to a screaming live audience. It was watched by 15-year-old Marsha Albert in Silver Spring, Maryland. She became a fan instantly, and wrote to a radio disc jockey in nearby Washington, D.C., telling him he should be playing The Beatles' records.

The DJ, Carrol James, was intrigued by the letter and tried to buy the band's latest single. When he found he couldn't get a copy of "I Want To Hold Your Hand" in the US, he had someone working for the British airline BOAC bring in a copy from London, and invited Marsha into the studio to introduce his first broadcast of the disc. She announced it with the words, "Ladies and gentlemen, for the first time on the air in the United States, here are The Beatles singing 'I Want to Hold Your Hand'."

James found that the record was a hit with listeners and played it again and again.

Staff at Capitol Records were dismayed by the news that a radio station in Washington, D.C. was playing the record ahead of its January release date, and more upset when

Above: The label of the US seven-inch single "I Want to Hold Your Hand", released by Capitol Records.

Above: (Left to right) Paul McCartney, Ringo Starr, George Harrison, and John Lennon hold a press conference at JFK airport in February 1964.

others began following suit. A station in Chicago, followed by one in St Louis, soon began airing "I Want To Hold Your Hand", from tapes passed from DJ to DJ. With teenagers beginning to clamor for the disc, the company decided to make the best of the situation and rush-release it, with "I Saw Her Standing There" as the B-side. "I Want To Hold Your Hand" hit the stores on December 26, 1963, and quickly became America's fastest-selling British single ever. Capitol ordered a million copies to be pressed by New Year and it entered the *Billboard* chart at Number 45 on January 18. By the time it had hit the Number One spot on February 1, the single had already sold all of those, plus an extra 500,000.

Knowing they had a Beatles' bonanza on their hands, Capitol were quick to react and, on January 20, 1964, released the first "official" American Beatles album. Using the same sleeve photograph as *With The Beatles,* but choosing different tracks for the actual record, *Meet The Beatles!* shot to the top of the US album charts, where it stayed for nearly three months.

By the time The Beatles landed at Kennedy Airport on February 7, they had three records in the US singles chart, and two records competing for the Number One album spot: *Meet The Beatles!* and Vee-Jay's *Introducing... The Beatles,* which made it to Number Two.

Introducing... *The Beatles* **Facts**	**Track listing** Side 1	**Side 2**
Released: January 1, 1964 (version #1) and February 10, 1964 (version #2)	I Saw Her Standing There Misery Anna Chains Boys	P.S. I Love You (replaced by "Please Please Me" on version #2) Baby It's You Do You Want To Know A Secret
Label: Vee-Jay (US) **Chart Success:** US No. 2	Love Me Do (replaced by "Ask Me Why" on version #2)	A Taste of Honey There's A Place Twist and Shout

Beatlemania had arrived in the US, and 3,000 screaming fans were at the airport to prove it.

The Beatles had never seen anything like it, and they'd seen a lot in the past year. Girls threw themselves against the thick glass windows that kept fans out of the press area where The Beatles were interviewed, and hundreds of photographers struggled to get close to the English lads. A line of police was almost overwhelmed by the crush. This was Beatle-mayhem.

Before they arrived, Capitol had circulated promotional records and biographies of the group to almost every radio station in the nation. New York stations were playing Beatle records almost non-stop, and shops and souvenir stands across Manhattan sold everything from Beatle dolls to Beatle wigs.

Below: *The Beatles talk to Ed Sullivan during rehearsals for their appearance on "The Ed Sullivan Show" on February 9, 1964. (Left to right) Ed Sullivan, Paul McCartney, George Harrison, John Lennon, Ringo Starr (top).*

Above: *(left to right) Paul McCartney and George Harrison share a microphone, Ringo Starr (top), and John Lennon, performing during their 1964 US tour.*

Below: *(Left to right) Ringo Starr, Paul McCartney, John Lennon, and George Harrison play in the snow outside the Coliseum in Washington, D.C. on February 13, 1964.*

The Ed Sullivan Show had received 50,000 applications for its 700 available seats and, on the night of the broadcast, an estimated 73 million viewers, in 23 million households across the country, tuned in to watch. Police reports stated that crime rates across the USA fell sharply that night, especially among juvenile offenders.

The Beatles performed five numbers over two spots, ending with "I Want To Hold Your Hand". Sullivan presented them in his usual casual fashion, much has he had Elvis Presley on another historic TV moment back in 1956, and announced that Elvis himself had sent them a good luck telegram via the show. At that moment, The Beatles must have felt that they had truly arrived in America.

Two days after their debut on the Sullivan show, The Beatles made their first concert appearance in the USA, at the Coliseum in Washington, D.C. Thousands of fans greeted them when they arrived in the nation's capital, and 10,000 more flocked to the gig itself.

A sign of things to come, the stadium concert was on a scale The Beatles had never experienced before. After two more gigs, this time at New York's "home of classical music", Carnegie Hall, and another Ed Sullivan appearance (aired from Florida, it drew another 70 million viewers), The Beatles flew home to England on February 22.

Did You Know?

"My Bonnie", recorded by Tony Sheridan and the Beat Boys in Hamburg, made the US Top 30 in July 1964, billed as "The Beatles with Tony Sheridan".

This spread: *Ringo Starr, George Harrison, Paul McCartney, and John Lennon splash about in the surf at a Miami beach in February, 1964.*

Left: *(Left to right) Paul McCartney, George Harrison, John Lennon, and Ringo Starr on stage during a concert at Carnegie Hall, New York City, during the band's 1964 US tour.*

Below Left: *(Left to right) Ringo Starr, Paul McCartney, and John Lennon enjoy the swimming pool of the Deauville Hotel, Miami, in February 1964.*

Despite the hysteria surrounding the band's first visit to the United States, their domination of the American charts had not yet peaked. On March 13, *Cashbox* magazine placed Beatles singles in the top four places, also reporting that Meet The Beatles! had sold 3,600,000 copies to date, an unheard of number for an album. Their next single, "Can't Buy Me Love", had nearly two million advance

***Meet The Beatles!* Facts**
Released: January 20, 1964
Label: Capitol (US)
Chart Success: US No. 1

Track Listing
Side 1
I Want To Hold Your Hand
I Saw Her Standing There
This Boy
It Won't Be Long
All I've Got To Do
All My Loving

Side 2
Don't Bother Me
Little Child
Till There Was You
Hold Me Tight
I Wanna Be Your Man
Not A Second Time

orders. In April, *Billboard* put Beatles singles in all top five places, just as the group's second Capitol album, *The Beatles Second Album*, was released.

In England, meanwhile, the boys began working on their first movie, *A Hard Day's Night,* at the beginning of March.

***The Beatles Second Album* Facts**
Released: April 10, 1964
Label: Capitol (US)
Chart Success: US No. 1

Track Listing

Side 1
Roll Over Beethoven
Thank You Girl
You Really Got A Hold On Me
Devil In Her Heart
Money
You Can't Do That

Side 2
Long Tall Sally
I Call Your Name
Please Mr. Postman
I'll Get You
She Loves You

Below: *Police struggle to hold back the crowd at London airport as The Beatles return from their US tour.*

Chapter 8:
A Hard Day's
Night-1964

Just before they left for America, The Beatles had spent a day in EMI's Paris studio, where they recorded two of their most successful songs, "I Want To Hold Your Hand" and "She Loves You", in German. More importantly, at the end of the same session they also recorded what would become their next international hit, "Can't Buy Me Love". The new single was a worldwide smash, topping the charts in almost every country where it was available, and earning a US gold disc within a week of its March 16, release.

Right (main picture): *Prince Philip, Duke of Edinburgh (left), shares a joke with The Beatles (left to right, Ringo Starr, George Harrison, John Lennon, and Paul McCartney) at an awards ceremony held at the Empire Ballroom in Leicester Square, London, in March 1964.*

Right: *George Harrison (left) and Ringo Starr (right), relax with cigars after an awards ceremony at the Empire Ballroom in Leicester Square, London, in March 1964.*

"Can't Buy Me Love" Facts
B-Side: "You Can't Do That"
Recorded: January 29, 1964
Released: March 16, 1964
Label: Parlophone (UK), Capitol (US)
Writers: Lennnon/McCartney
Producer: George Martin
Chart Success: UK No. 1, US No. 1

With America, and most of the rest of the world, now at their feet, The Beatles had become national heroes in their home country by the time they arrived back from their first American trip. They were honored by Oxford colleges, discussed in the "serious" press, and givenawards by the armload.

One ceremony took place on March 19, when a show-business charity, the Variety Club of Great Britain, made John, Paul, George, and Ringo (jointly) Show Business Personality of the Year. After the award the four Beatles were guests of honor at a lunch attended by various celebrities and politicians, but left after John Lennon announced, "We've got to go now, 'cause the fella on the film wants us, and he says it's costing him a fortune."

The "fella" was movie director Richard Lester, and the film was The Beatles yet-to-be-named cinema debut, *A Hard Day's Night*.

The movie was a comedy in which The Beatles played themselves. Opening with the band being chased by fans as they board a train in Liverpool, the plot follows 24 hours in their lives. The Beatles are mobbed by the press, pestered by Paul's grandfather, and Ringo goes missing before a TV gig in London.

Above: *British Prime Minister Harold Wilson (center), pictured with The Beatles (left to right, John Lennon, Ringo Starr, Paul McCartney, and George Harrison) after presenting the band with their Variety Club of Great Britain award in March 1964.*

Right: *A 1964 film lobby card advertising The Beatles' first movie, "A Hard Day's Night".*

Right: *(Clockwise from top left) Ringo Starr, Paul McCartney, George Harrison, and John Lennon pictured in stills from "A Hard Day's Night".*

The four Beatles were portrayed as the fans pictured them: John the witty one, Paul the cute one, George the shy one, and Ringo the quiet one. In fact, Ringo earned special praise from the critics for his performance, some comparing him to the Hollywood silent-movie legend Charlie Chaplin.

It took just seven weeks to make, and shooting was well underway before a title was decided. The producers had wanted to call the movie *Beatlemania* at first, but this title was soon dropped because the band disliked it. *Moving On* was suggested next, followed by *Travelling On*, and *Let's Go*. It was only after a particularly long day in front of the cameras, when Ringo was heard to say that it had been "a hard day's night," that the perfect title was found.

Between finishing the movie and its July release, The Beatles began a 26 day tour, on June 4, that took them to the other side of the world. After playing in Denmark and Holland they flew to Hong Kong for two dates, then made a string of appearances in Australia and New Zealand.

For the first half of the tour, however, there were only three Beatles on stage; Ringo was taken to hospital with tonsillitis, and rejoined the group in Melbourne, Australia, on June 15. For the earlier dates, an unknown musician named Jimmy Nichol took his place behind the drum kit, and found worldwide fame for 11 days.

Proof that the Beatlemania wasn't just a British and American phenomenon came when the group (without Ringo) landed in Adelaide for the first of their Australian dates. As they were driven into the city, they were met by the biggest crowd ever to turn out for The Beatles, before or after.

An estimated 300,000 people took to the streets to welcome the band, and about 250,000 crowded into the middle of Melbourne three days later, when all four Beatles waved from the balcony of the Town Hall.

Back in Britain, *A Hard Day's Night* had its world premiere at the Pavilion Theatre in London on July 6,

Did You Know?
When Ringo's tonsils were removed, a BBC newsreader read his script wrong, saying the Beatle had had his toenails removed!

Left: *The Beatles before their June 1964 tour of Denmark and Holland, with drummer Jimmy Nicol who replaced Ringo Starr due to illness. (Left to right) Paul McCartney, John Lennon, Jimmy Nicol (seated on drums), and George Harrison.*

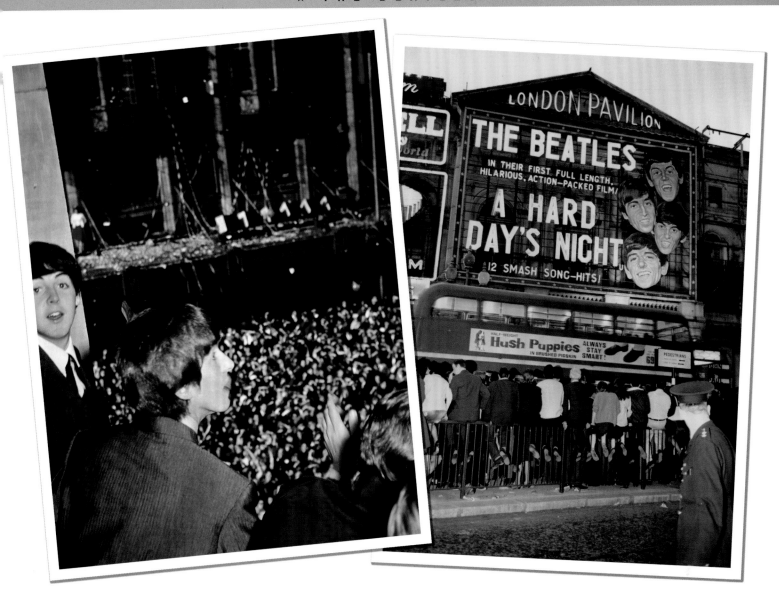

Above Left: *Paul McCartney (left) and George Harrison (right) above the huge crowd that met The Beatles at Melbourne Town Hall, Australia, in June 1964.*

Above Right: *Fans crowd the street outside the London Pavilion cinema before a screening of The Beatles' first movie, "A Hard Day's Night".*

with the Queen's sister, Princess Margaret, heading the guest list. The Beatles flew to their home city from London the next day, Ringo's 24th birthday, and were greeted at Speke Airport by 3,000 fans. They were driven the seven miles to the Town Hall in a police cavalcade, with an estimated 200,000 people, or roughly a quarter of the city's population, lining the route. The group would later recall how strange it felt, driving past tens of thousands of waving fans through the same suburbs where they

Did You Know?
It was on the set of "A Hard Day's Night" that George Harrison met his future wife, Patti Boyd. A model at the time, she was playing one of a group of schoolgirls on the train out of Liverpool.

Above: *(Left to right) Paul McCartney, George Harrison, Ringo Starr, and John Lennon in a still from "A Hard Day's Night".*

had grown up, and even seeing people on the sidewalk that they remembered from their teenage days when they were still in schoolboy skiffle groups. Arriving at the Town Hall, they were greeted as guests of honor at a civic reception with the city Mayor before appearing at a special "northern premiere" of the movie.

Reviews of *A Hard Day's Night* were full of praise, on both sides of the Atlantic, with New York's *Village Voice* calling it "The *Citizen Kane* of jukebox musicals." Leading film critic Leslie Haliwell awarded it four stars; it was the only UK film to receive his top score in 1964. The movie was also nominated for two Oscars: for Best Screenplay (by Alun Owen) and Best Score Adaptation (George Martin). Artistically, as well as at the box office, the movie was an immediate hit, and had a direct influence on the Monkees' TV series, future pop videos, and even 1960s spy movies. *A Hard Day's Night* also set a record in the movie industry, with 15,000 prints made for worldwide distribution.

> **"A Hard Day's Night" Facts**
> **B-Side:** "Things We Said Today"
> (US: "I Should Have Known Better")
> **Recorded:** April 16, 1964
> **Released:** July 10, 1964
> (US: July 13, 1964)
> **Label:** Parlophone (UK), Capitol (US)
> **Writers:** Lennnon/McCartney
> **Producer:** George Martin
> **Chart Success:** UK No. 1, US No. 1

Four days after the film's premiere, the album and single of *A Hard Day's Night* were released in Great Britain.

The single, with its stunning opening guitar chord, was the first time Lennon and McCartney had written a song "to order," having composed it around the ready-made title.

The album featured new songs from the film, plus "Can't Buy Me Love" and its B-side, as well as "I'll Cry Instead", which was written for the movie but not included. Another version of the soundtrack album had already appeared in the US. Released on June 26, by United Artists (the film company that produced *A Hard Day's Night*), it had a different track listing. United Artists was only allowed to use music recorded for the film, so it used all the movie songs, plus some George Martin orchestral pieces from the soundtrack.

With their popularity hitting ever greater heights, The Beatles flew to the United States for the second time in August. On August 19, at the huge Cow Palace arena in San Francisco, the band were due to start their first North American tour. Playing 24 cities across the United States and Canada in just a single month, they would be shuttled from hotel room to stadium, to airport lounge, to the next hotel room with hardly a break, and feel the full impact of Beatlemania, US-style, for the first time.

Did You Know?

An alternate version of "Can't Buy Me Love" included the sound of a studio toilet flushing at the end; The Beatles wanted that version released, but George Martin said "no".

Above: *(Left to right) Ringo Starr, John Lennon, George Harrison, and Paul McCartney leave London airport for their August 1964 US tour.*

A Hard Day's Night Facts

Recorded: January 29 – June 3, 1964
Released: July 10, 1964
Label: Parlophone (UK)
Writers: Lennnon/McCartney
Producer: George Martin
Chart Success: UK No. 1

A Hard Day's Night Track-By-Track
Side 1
A Hard Day's Night (2.32)
A perfect track to be played over the movie's opening titles.
I Should Have Known Better (2.42)
In the film, this song featured in an early scene where The Beatles were playing cards on the train.
If I Fell (2.16)
A ballad in which John leads solo on the first verse, with Paul coming in to duet with him for the rest of the song.
I'm Happy Just To Dance With You (1.59)
George sings lead here, with Ringo playing Arabian bongo drums.
And I Love Her (2.27)
A McCartney ballad that went on to be an international standard, covered by many artists over the years.
Tell Me Why (2.04)
One writer described John and Paul's harmonizing as sounding like a crowd of children.
Can't Buy Me Love (2.15)
The hit single from three months earlier, included here because it featured in the film.

Side 2
Any Time At All (2.10)
Like all of the album's second side, this track was not featured in the *Hard Day's Night* movie.
I'll Cry Instead (1.44)
This rockabilly-influenced song was intended for the film, but didn't make it to the soundtrack.
Things We Said Today (2.35)
The guitar in this track has a sound reminiscent of the Shadows, the biggest guitar group in Britain before The Beatles.
When I Get Home (2.14)
A track that was apparently influenced by John's love of the Motown sound and American soul music.
You Can't Do That (2.33)
Ringo was listed as playing drums, bongos, and cowbell on this, the B-side to the "Can't Buy Me Love" single.
I'll Be Back (2.22)
A good title to end the album on.

A Hard Day's Night Facts (US version)
Released: June 26, 1964
Label: United Artists (US)
Chart Success: US No. 1

Track Listing
Side 1
A Hard Day's Night
Tell Me Why
I'll Cry Instead
I Should Have Known Better (George Martin Orchestra)
I'm Happy Just To Dance With You
And I Love Her (George Martin Orchestra)

Side 2
I Should Have Known Better
If I Fell
And I Love Her
Ringo's Theme: This Boy (George Martin Orchestra)
Can't Buy Me Love
A Hard Day's Night (George Martin Orchestra)

Above: *(Left to right) Ringo Starr, Paul McCartney, John Lennon, and George Harrison attend the premiere of "A Hard Day's Night".*

Left: *(Left to right) George Harrison, Ringo Starr, Paul McCartney, and John Lennon in stills from "A Hard Day's Night".*

This spread: *Ringo Starr uses a long cable release to take his own picture during a break in the shooting of "A Hard Day's Night" in London.*

A Hard Day's Night Movie Fact File

Directed: Richard Lester
Produced: Walter Shenson
Written: Alun Owen
Music: The Beatles/George Martin
Cinematography: Gilbert Taylor
Edited: John Jympson
Distributed: United Artists
Released: July 6, 1964 (UK), August 11, 1964 (US)
Running Time: 87 minutes
Budget: £200,000 ($500,000)
Gross Revenue: £2,500,000 ($6,165,000)

Principal Cast List

John – John Lennon
Paul – Paul McCartney
George – George Harrison
Ringo – Ringo Starr
Paul's Grandfather – Wilfrid Brambell
Norm – Norman Rossington
Shake – John Junkin
TV Director – Victor Spinetti
Millie – Anna Quayle
Police Inspector – Derek Guyler
Man on Train – Richard Vernon
Hotel Waiter – Edward Malin
TV Floor Manager – Robin Ray
TV Choreographer – Lionel Blair
Dolly – Alison Seebohm

Above Left: *The Beatles (top to bottom, Paul McCartney, John Lennon, George Harrison, and Ringo Starr), walk down a stairway in a scene from "A Hard Day's Night".*

Above Middle: *(Left to right) George Harrison, John Lennon, Ringo Starr, and Paul McCartney pictured during the filming of the cinema trailer for "A Hard Day's Night".*

Above Right: *Ringo Starr (left), George Harrison (jumping), and John Lennon (right) on the set of "A Hard Day's Night".*

►18   ►19

Left: *(Left to right) Ringo Starr, Paul McCartney, John Lennon, and George Harrison in a still from "A Hard Day's Night".*

Plot

After being chased by fans, The Beatles board a train from Liverpool to London; Paul has to look after his troublesome grandfather on the journey. They get to their hotel, where they feel trapped, so they go to a casino, where the old man causes more problems. The next day The Beatles are at the theater where they are to be filmed for TV, but Ringo gets bored and goes off for a walk by himself.

The drummer tries to have a quiet drink in a pub, and walks alongside a canal while the rest of the group are trying to find him. After a series of funny events that lead to Ringo being arrested by the police (along with Paul's grandfather), he returns to the theater where the concert goes ahead as planned.

►18   ►19

Chapter 9: Beatles For Sale-1964

From the moment The Beatles got off their flight at San Francisco airport, it seemed that madness had gripped the American nation. The group was driven from their plane into a huge metal cage, intended to protected from the gathered mob of fans as they were moved to the airport terminal. The cage, however, began to collapse as hysterical teenage girls pressed in from all sides, and The Beatles had to be rescued by police.

For the next four weeks, similar scenes greeted them in city after city, and the group was in fear for their lives on numerous occasions. Their private plane, a Lockheed Electra (an aircraft that didn't have a perfect safety record) got into trouble more than once, including a frightening incident when a landing in Jacksonville, Florida, had to be aborted because of a hurricane.

Right (main picture): *The Beatles (left to right, Ringo Starr, George Harrison, Paul McCartney, and John Lennon) performing at the Convention Center in Las Vegas, Nevada, on August 20, 1964.*

Right: *(Clockwise from top left) Ringo Starr, John Lennon, Paul McCartney, and George Harrison arrive in the US for their second tour.*

Above: *A line of police officers prevent fans from getting too close as The Beatles (left to right, Paul McCartney, George Harrison, Ringo Starr, and John Lennon) perform on stage at the Convention Hall, Las Vegas, in August 1964.*

The biggest danger, however, came from the ever-present crush of adoring fans. "On tour that year, it was crazy," George Harrison would later recall. "Not within the band. In the band, we were normal, and the rest of the world was crazy." Even the sequence of concerts, as they criss-crossed the country, seemed ridiculous.

The band would often rush from a gig—escorted by local police, of course—to the airport, fly to their next destination, grab a few hours sleep, then be smuggled into the next venue. Before each show, time had to be found to meet the local press, and to shake hands with mayors, sheriffs, senators, and their wives and children. Fans massed outside every venue The Beatles visited, trying to climb in windows or bribe security men, while backstage, with the jostling crowd of cops, photographers, stage staff, and The Beatles' own entourage, it was almost as chaotic. Even hotel rooms were not a safe

haven; fans tried to get into their rooms—one was caught hiding in a laundry basket, another got stuck in an air-conditioning shaft—and there was a constant stream of well-wishers and journalists waiting to meet the band. The Beatles often hid themselves away in the bathroom, the only place where they could find "a bit of peace and quiet."

Things didn't slow down much when The Beatles returned home. There was just a two-week gap before a UK tour began, which saw them play another 27 dates in a single month and, during that break they had to spend four days with George Martin at Abbey Road, laying down tracks for their end-of-year album release. Although the band had started recording the new album before taking off for America, they were still finishing it between dates on the British tour.

Above: *The Beatles having fun on the diving board of their Hollywood Hills hideout during the tour of Canada and the US in August 1964. (Left to right, Ringo Starr, John Lennon, George Harrison, and Paul McCartney.)*

"I Feel Fine" Facts
B-Side: "She's A Woman"
Recorded: October 18, 1964
Released: November 23, 1964
Label: Parlophone (UK), Capitol (US)
Writers: Lennnon/McCartney
Producer: George Martin
Chart Success: UK No. 1, US No. 1

Before the album appeared early in December, just in time for the Christmas market, two tracks from the sessions, "I Feel Fine" and "She's A Woman", hit the stores as The Beatles' eighth UK single. Released on November 23, it made the Number One spot a week later, and stayed there for five weeks.

The same day that "I Feel Fine" was released in Great Britain, Capitol Records in America put out two Beatles albums, *Something New* and *The Beatles Story*. Mixing tracks from *A Hard Day's Night* with songs yet to be released in the US, plus the German language version of "I Want To Hold Your Hand", *Something New* didn't really live up to its name. The other record released that day was a double-disc "narrative and musical biography" of The Beatles featuring interviews with all four, as well as Brian Epstein and George Martin.

Above : *The Beatles (left to right, Ringo Starr, George Harrison, John Lennon, and Paul McCartney) live at the Hollywood Bowl on August 23, 1964, in Los Angeles, California.*

Above (inset): *A ticket for The Beatles' concert at the Hollywood Bowl on August 23, 1964, in Los Angeles, California.*

***Something New* Facts**
Released: November 23, 1964
Label: Capitol (US)
Chart Success: US No. 2

Track Listing
Side 1
I'll Cry Instead
Things We Said Today
Any Time At All
When I Get Home
Slow Down
Matchbox

Side 2
Tell Me Why
And I Love Her
I'm Happy Just To Dance With You
If I Fell
Komm, Gib Mir Deine Hand

Including a live version of "Twist And Shout", recorded at the Hollywood Bowl on the recent US tour, *The Beatles Story* also featured 14 studio tracks already released in the US, and interviews with hysterical fans after the Hollywood concert.

Following the formula of *Please Please Me* and *With The Beatles*, the new UK album, *Beatles For Sale,* contained eight original songs and six covers. Also like *With The Beatles*, none of the tracks had been previously released. The original tracks included three that had been considered for a single, "Eight Days A Week", "No Reply", and 'I'm A Loser', until John had come up with "I Feel Fine". The American material ranged from the rhythm and blues of "Mr. Moonlight", to a Buddy Holly cover. At the time some reviewers felt that reverting to covers, after the all-original *A Hard Day's Night*, suggested the boys were exhausted, having to fit the recording sessions between almost constant touring. But The Beatles had a huge selection of cover songs from their club and dancehall days and it is more likely that the band wanted to preserve some typical songs on disc. As on *With The Beatles*, the front sleeve photography by Robert Freeman (but not in black-and-white) had the boys, their mop top haircuts longer now, staring straight at the camera without a smile: they were as serious as ever.

Once again, American fans would not get to hear the new album as released in the UK. The American version of the album was named *Beatles '65*, and only eight of the 11 tracks were taken from *Beatles For Sale*.

While their records topped the charts, as usual, Christmas 1964 saw The Beatles playing their second annual Christmas Show in London for a month, beginning on December 24. It was an easy gig after the frantic touring earlier in the year. Shortly after the show finished, on February 11, 1965, a second Beatle got married.

Ringo wed his long-time girlfriend, Liverpool hairdresser Maureen Cox, at a short civil ceremony in Caxton Hall Registry Office, London. Brian Epstein was best man and guests included George and John; Paul was on holiday in

Portugal. The press was full of speculation about how the marriage would affect The Beatles' popularity, with so many of their fans being adoring young girls, and George even went on to say "I don't think The Beatles' image could stand another marriage." When asked in an interview how it felt to be married to such a famous man, the new Mrs Starkey replied simply, "Very nice!"

Unfortunately for the happy couple, there was no time for a honeymoon. The Beatles were back in the studio on February 15, recording songs for their next single and album, which would be part of the soundtrack for their next movie, provisionally called *Beatles No 2*. By February 23, 1965, the band had started filming, on location in the Bahamas.

Above Left: *A poster advertising The Beatles' 1964 Christmas show at the Hammersmith Odeon, London.*

Top: *Ringo Starr pictured with his wife Maureen at a press conference the day after their wedding.*

Above Right: *The Beatles catch a flight to the Bahamas from London airport to begin work on "Help!".*

This spread: *Paul McCartney, Ringo Starr, John Lennon, and George Harrison clown around for the camera on a London rooftop in 1964.*

Beatles For Sale Facts

Recorded: August 11 – October 18, 1964
Released: December 4, 1964
Label: Parlophone (UK)
Writers: Lennnon/McCartney
(except songwriters as noted below)
Producer: George Martin
Chart Success: UK No. 1

Beatles For Sale Track-By-Track
Side 1
No Reply (2.15)
It is reported that John's inspiration for this track was "Silhouettes", a 1957 doo-wop anthem by The Rays.

I'm A Loser (2.31)
An early example of how John Lennon's songwriting was coming under the influence of Bob Dylan.

Baby's In Black (2.02)
The song that is said to have inspired The Rolling Stones' 1966 hit "Paint It Black".

Rock And Roll Music (2.02) (Chuck Berry)
John gives it his all on this Chuck Berry classic, and joins George Martin and Paul at the piano, all three playing at the same time.

I'll Follow The Sun (1.46)
There's a strong Buddy Holly influence on this song, which Paul originally wrote in 1959.

Mr. Moonlight (2.35) (Roy Lee Johnson)
A minor US R&B hit for Dr Feelgood and the Interns in 1962, and a big hit with Beatles fans at the Cavern.

Kansas City/Hey Hey Hey Hey (2.30) (Jerry Leiber & Mike Stoller/Richard Penniman)
Paul went into in full Little Richard mode for this a medley of two of Richard's songs.

Side 2
Eight Days A Week (2.43)
Like "A Hard Day's Night", the title is supposed to have come from Ringo complaining about hard they had been working.

Words Of Love (2.10) (Buddy Holly)
Although The Beatles played several Buddy Holly numbers in their early days, this is the only one they ever released on record.

Honey Don't (2.56) (Carl Perkins)
Ringo gets to sing on this reworking of an old Carl Perkins favorite.

Every Little Thing (2.01)
George plays country-style guitar on this song, which Paul was said to have written for his girlfriend, Jane Asher.

I Don't Want To Spoil The Party (2.33)
Like on several tracks on the album, this features thoughtful lyrics from John.

What You're Doing (2.30)
A track notable for its drum intro, which was influenced by The Ronettes' "Be My Baby", produced by Phil Spector in 1963.

Everybody's Trying To Be My Baby (2.34) (Carl Perkins)
Another Carl Perkins cover, this time with George taking the lead vocal.

Above, Left and Right: *Paul McCartney (left) and John Lennon (right) on stage during The Beatles' second US tour in 1964.*

Left: *George Harrison (left), John Lennon (center), and Ringo Starr (behind the drums) take a break during rehearsals.*

Chapter 10: Help!-1965

Made with the same team as *A Hard Day's Night* (Walter Shenson producing and Richard Lester directing), between February and April 1965, The Beatles' second movie was a more ambitious project than their first. This time, the budget was bigger, due to the commercial success of the first movie, so it was filmed in color and shot on locations ranging from the sunny shores of the Bahamas to the snowy slopes of the Austrian Alps. Unfortunately, however, *Help!* did not achieve the same critical acclaim as *A Hard Day's Night*.

Right: *A movie poster advertising The Beatles' film "Help!".*

Far Right: *The Beatles (left to right, George Harrison, Ringo Starr, Paul McCartney, and John Lennon) pictured in the snow in March, 1965, in Obertauern, Austria, during a break from filming "Help!".*

Nevertheless, like the first movie, it was a perfect setting for The Beatles' music and the musical sequences were like pop videos, long before pop videos existed. The plot that strung these musical set pieces together revolved around a fanatical Eastern religious sect that is chasing Ringo because he has a ceremonial ring stuck on his finger. With the pursuers closing in, the four Beatles have a series

of amusing adventures in the sea, sand, snow, and among British Army tanks on maneuvers.

Filming finished on April 14, the same day that a new single, "Ticket To Ride", one of the songs featured in the movie, was released.

Help! was an enjoyable film, but it was not as solid a piece of movie-making as *A Hard Day's Night*, and The Beatles knew it. John and Paul would later admit that the group had felt like guest stars, or even extras, in their own movie. Over the next two years, film project after film project was shown to them, but The Beatles turned them all down.

While The Beatles were filming the "ski-slope" sequences in Austria, yet another album of old recordings appeared in

"Ticket To Ride" Facts
B-Side: "Yes It Is"
Recorded: February 15, 1965
Released: April 9, 1965 (UK), April 19, 1965 (US)
Label: Parlophone (UK), Capitol (US)
Writers: Lennnon/McCartney
Producer: George Martin
Chart Success: UK No. 1, US No. 1

Above: (Left to right) John Lennon, George Harrison, Paul McCartney, and Ringo Starr during the filming of "Help!".

Right: *(Left to right) Paul McCartney , John Lennon, and Ringo Starr (George is hidden behind John) on a piste vehicle in the Austrian Alps during the making of "Help!".*

America. Capitol had finally acquired the rights to the tracks that Vee-Jay had released as *Introducing... The Beatles* early in 1964, and produced what amounted to a cut-down version of the group's UK debut LP, *Please Please Me*.

Perhaps not surprisingly, *The Early Beatles* failed to chart. The band was never far from the top of the US charts, however, and, in June, Capitol released *Beatles VI*, which included tracks from the British album *Beatles For Sale* and the upcoming UK *Help!* Album. In early July, it hit the Number One spot in *Billboard*.

The Early Beatles Facts
Released: March 22, 1965
Label: Capitol (US)
Chart Success: –

Track Listing
Side 1
Love Me Do
Twist And Shout
Anna
Chains
Boys
Ask Me Why

Side 2
Please Please Me
P.S. I Love You
Baby It's You
A Taste Of Honey
Do You Want To Know A Secret

Left: *(Left to right) Ringo Starr, Paul McCartney (in the background), John Lennon, and George Harrison climb out of a swimming pool during the filming of "Help!".*

Below: *American pop singer Tony Bennett (left) presents an award to The Beatles (left to right, Ringo Starr, George Harrison, Paul McCartney, and John Lennon) at the New Musical Express Poll Winners' Concert at Wembley, London, in April 1965.*

DID YOU KNOW?
Paul McCartney wrote the tune to "Yesterday" before he thought of any lyrics. The first version of the song was called "Scrambled Eggs", and featured the opening line "Scrambled eggs, oh baby how I love your legs."

***Beatles VI* Facts**
Released: June 14, 1965
Label: Capitol (US)
Chart Success: US No. 1

Track Listing
Side 1
Kansas City/Hey Hey
    Hey Hey
Eight Days A Week
You Like Me Too Much
Bad Boy
I Don't Want To Spoil The
    Party
Words Of Love

Side 2
What You're Doing
Yes It Is
Dizzy Miss Lizzy
Tell Me What You See
Every Little Thing

book was full of the same kind of nonsense poems and quirky pictures John had been producing since his schooldays at Quarry Bank. In those days he had usually been told that he was wasting his time, now he was hailed as the "literary Beatle." As with his previous book, John helped promote *A Spaniard In The Works*, mainly in UK radio interviews for highbrow arts programs, instead of the pop music shows that would usually want to talk to one of The Beatles.

That same June, while *Beatles VI* went on sale in the US, it was announced that each of The Beatles was to receive one of the highest civilian honors in Great Britain: the MBE (Membership of the Most Excellent Order of the British Empire), which would be presented to them by Queen Elizabeth II at Buckingham Palace later in the year.

Details of the Queen's Birthday Honors list were usually kept secret, but the restriction was lifted on the night of June 11, so that UK newspapers could carry the story the next day. The Beatles were at Twickenham Film Studios at the time, viewing a rough cut of *Help!,* and were surrounded by journalists from the world's media when they came out.

The press response was predictably excited. One newspaper was headlined, "She Loves Them! Yeah! Yeah! Yeah!" though enthusiasm quickly gave way to stories of war veterans returning their own medals in disgust that four long-haired musicians were being given such distinction. Despite such protests, it was an official recognition of The Beatles as national figures.

Two weeks after the MBE announcement, just before the group started a short European tour of dates in France, Italy, and Spain, John Lennon published his second book of humorous writings and drawings, *A Spaniard In The Works*.

A similar book had been published in April 1964. Called *In His Own Write*, the critics had loved it, and the second

The Beatles' European dates started on June 20, in Paris, and it came as a surprise to the band that every concert wasn't a sell-out. The fans were there in their thousands and, as usual, chaos reigned around every venue and hotel the boys visited. However, now there were not as many people welcoming the group or bidding them farewell at airports as two years earlier, either in the UK or the rest of Europe, and the street scenes never approached riot proportions. It seemed that the extreme Beatlemania of 1963 was fading. Many fans were perhaps realizing, as The Beatles already had, that it was pointless to pay to see a group perform for 25 minutes and not to hear a note of music.

The band had begun to accept that, for their live performances, they could never return to the comparative sanity that they enjoyed before they became famous in 1963. They could not enjoy friendly banter with the fans in the front row at the Cavern club, or turn up at a small dance hall with just enough equipment to fit into their six-seater van. Those days were long gone, and every gig now reminded them of the fact.

At the beginning of August 1965, the movie *Help!* was released worldwide, as was the soundtrack album. Again the US long player differed from that released in Britain, and included orchestral tracks by the George Martin Orchestra. On the record sleeve was a Robert Freeman photograph

Right: *The Beatles standing in a window at Twickenham Film Studios, Middlesex, England. (Left to right, John Lennon, Paul McCartney, Ringo Starr, and George Harrison.)*

Below: *A program for the Royal World Premiere of "Help!". The program is signed by all four of The Beatles on the rear cover.*

of The Beatles in their ski clothes, each holding their arms to make a letter in semaphore. It was intended that the four of them, standing side-by-side, would spell out "H-E-L-P", but the pattern didn't work to Freeman's liking, so, in fact, they were spelling out the letters N-U-J-V on the British cover, and N-V-U-J on the American version.

"Help!" Facts
B-Side: "I'm Down"
Recorded: April 13, 1965
Released: July 19, 1965 (US),
July 23, 1965 (UK)
Label: Parlophone (UK), Capitol (US)
Writers: Lennnon/McCartney
Producer: George Martin
Chart Success: UK No. 1, US No. 1

Help! Facts

Recorded: February 15 – June 17, 1965
Released: August 6, 1965
Label: Parlophone (UK)
Writers: Lennnon/McCartney (except songwriters as noted below)
Producer: George Martin
Chart Success: UK No. 1

Track-By-Track
Side 1
Help! (2.16)
John sings the title song from the movie, already released as a single on July 19, 1965.
The Night Before (2.33)
The first Beatle track to feature an electric piano, played by John.
You've Got To Hide Your Love Away (2.08)
This was the first time since "Love Me Do" that The Beatles brought in an outside musician, Johnnie Scott, who played flute.
I Need You (2.28) (George Harrison)
George sings lead on a song that he also wrote.
Another Girl (2.02)
The first time Paul McCartney played lead guitar on a Beatles album.
You're Going To Lose That Girl (2.18)
A classic Beatles track, which was recorded in just three hours during the last session before the band took off for the Bahamas to start filming *Help!*
Ticket To Ride (3.03)
Released as a single in April 1965, it was only included on the album because it featured in the movie.

Side 2
Act Naturally (2.27) (Voni Morrison/Johnny Russell)
Ringo sings a cover of a record by Buck Owens and The Buckaroos, the original having topped the *Billboard* Country Singles chart in 1963.
It's Only Love (1.53)
The song's original working title was "That's A Nice Hat", and was recorded under that name by the George Martin Orchestra.
You Like Me Too Much (2.34) (George Harrison)
Another track written by George, thought to be written about his girlfriend, Patti Boyd.
Tell Me What You See (2.35)
Among various percussion instruments featured on this track, John was said to have played washboard, an echo of his skiffle days with The Quarry Men.
I've Just Seen A Face (2.04)
The working title was "Aunty Jin's Theme", named for Paul's Aunt Jane. Again, George Martin would use that title in an orchestral version.
Yesterday (2.04)
The first solo track by a Beatle, "Yesterday" featured just Paul singing , backed by a string quartet. It would go on to be covered by hundreds of vocalists over the years.
Dizzy Miss Lizzy (2.51) (Larry Williams)
John belts out an old Cavern regular, originally written and recorded by Larry Williams, one of Lennon's favorite rock'n'roll singers.

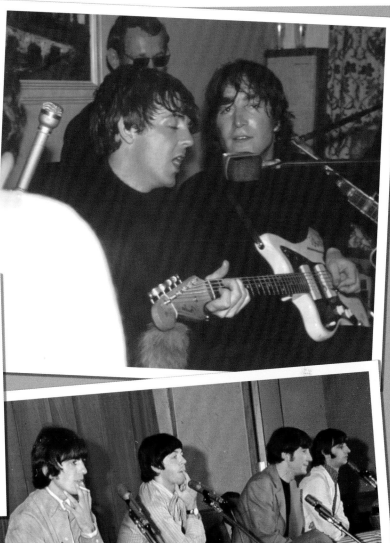

Right: *Paul McCartney (left) and John Lennon (right) in session during the photo-shoot for the "Help!" album cover.*

Below Right: *(Left to right) George Harrison, Paul McCartney, John Lennon, and Ringo Starr attend a press conference to promote the movie "Help!".*

Below: *The Beatles (left to right, George Harrison, Ringo Starr, Paul McCartney, and John Lennon) are presented with gold records to commemorate a sales milestone for the "Help!" album.*

Help! **Facts (US version)**
Released: August 13, 1965
Label: Capitol (US)
Chart Success: US No. 1

Track Listing
Side 1
The James Bond Theme (George Martin Orchestra)
Help!
The Night Before
From Me To You Fantasy (George Martin Orchestra)
You've Got To Hide Your Love Away
I Need You
In The Tyrol (George Martin Orchestra)

Side 2
Another Girl
Another Hard Day's Night (George Martin Orchestra)
Ticket To Ride
The Bitter End/You Can't Do That (George Martin Orchestra)
You're Going To Lose That Girl

This spread: *John Lennon, Ringo Starr, Paul McCartney, and George Harrison on location on Salisbury Plain, England (the usual site of army exercises) during filming of Help!. In the background are British service personnel who carried out routine exercises.*

►16

►17

Help! Movie Fact File

Directed: Richard Lester
Produced: Walter Shenson
Written: Charles Wood, Marc Behm
Music: The Beatles/George Martin /Ken Thorne
Cinematography: David Watkin
Edited: John Victor Smith
Distributed: United Artists
Released: July 29, 1965 (UK), August 11, 1965 (US)
Running Time: 90 minutes
Budget: £400,000 ($1,120,000)
Gross Revenue: £1,940,000 ($5,430,000)

Principal Cast List

John – John Lennon
Paul – Paul McCartney
George – George Harrison
Ringo – Ringo Starr
Clang – Leo McKern
Ahme – Eleanor Bron
Foot – Victor Spinetti
Algernon – Roy Kinnear
Superintendent – Patrick Cargill
Bhuta – John Bluthal
Doorman – Alfie Bass
Abdul – Warren Mitchell
Jeweller – Peter Copley
Lawnmower – Bruce Lacey

Above Left: *Ringo Starr plays drums on the set of "Help!".*

Above: *(Left to right) Ringo Starr, George Harrison, John Lennon, and Paul McCartney on a sledge during the filming of "Help!".*

Left: *(Left to right) George Harrison, John Lennon and his wife Cynthia, and Ringo Starr with his wife Maureen, arrive at the UK premiere of "Help!" at the London Pavilion Theatre, Piccadilly Circus, London.*

Plot

An Eastern religious cult, led by the high priest Clang, is performing the annual sacrifice of a young woman to the god Kieli when they realize that the girl is not wearing the sacrificial ring. She has sent it to Ringo Starr, who is unable to get it off his finger. Cult members begin tracking Ringo down to either take the ring by force or sacrifice him so their god won't be insulted. As the band is chased, John, Paul, and George decide to remove the ring from Ringo's finger and return it to the cult, thus avoiding death. One of the female members of the sect, Ahme, is attracted to the four Beatles, and Paul McCartney in particular, and works to sabotage the efforts of the rest of the murderous cult.

The cult's attempts to capture Ringo fail again and again, either through The Beatles' cunning or their own stupidity,

and the "Fab Four" seek help from a mad scientist, Professor Foot, who thinks the ring's power can help him rule the world. Meanwhile, a London police chief sets a trap, while the cult finally manages to capture Ringo and prepare to sacrifice him on the beach alongside the beautiful Ahme. Ringo is told the sect will attack the other Beatles if they attempt a rescue, and kill Ringo if he warns them. However, Ringo manages to untie himself and waves to John, Paul, and George to warn them away. With this act of courage, the ring falls from his finger. He then puts it on Clang's, saying "Get sacrificed! I don't subscribe to your religion!" and Ahme declares that Clang will be the next sacrifice, because he is wearing the ring. The movie ends the police arresting the cult members, and The Beatles running around to "Help!".

Chapter 11: Bigger than Elvis-1965

By the time the *Help!* movie was released in the United States, The Beatles had started a second North American tour. Through the last two weeks of August 1965, the group played in nine US cities, plus Toronto in Canada, and were met with the same hysteria as during the previous year's tour. All the concerts were in stadiums, some more famous for sports events than pop music. The tour opened on August 15, at the home of the New York Mets baseball team, Shea Stadium, in the borough of Queens, with a gig that would become legendary. The event was filmed by Ed Sullivan. Titled *The Beatles at Shea Stadium,* the resulting documentary was later broadcast on major networks around the world, and remains a unique record of the chaos and mass hysteria of The Beatles' American tours.

Beatlemania had remained at fever pitch in the US since the previous year. As before, fans besieged ticket outlets, surrounded hotels where the Fab Four stayed, and threw themselves at the stage—or as near to the stage as they could get—when the group performed. In an attempt to stop the band being mobbed, as they had been on the 1964 tour, organizers of the 1965 concerts arranged military-style operations to ensure The Beatles' safe passage to and from venues. In New York, the group was flown by helicopter from their hotel to the roof of the nearby World's Fair building, then driven in a Wells Fargo armored truck to the stadium, where a 2,000-strong security force was on hand to take

Right: *The Beatles (left to right, Ringo Starr, George Harrison, Paul McCartney, and John Lennon) perform to a screaming crowd at Shea Stadium, New York, on August 15, 1965.*

care of crowd control. The record-breaking audience of 55,600 was confined to the spectator areas of the stadium, behind wire fencing, with only the performers and security allowed on the actual field.

The show opened with sets from the support acts King Curtis, Cannibal and The Headhunters, Brenda Holloway, and Sound Incorporated, before The Beatles appeared on the field. When they arrived, the noise became deafening. Film footage of the event shows security guards covering their ears while teenage girls and grown women, scream, cry, and faint. Despite the heavy security, a number of fans managed to break through the fence, and rushed toward The Beatles on stage before they were chased, tackled, and physically restrained.

The Vox company, who supplied all The Beatles' sound equipment, provided specially-designed 100-watt amplifiers for the tour, which could reach a louder volume than ever before heard at a rock concert. However, even these were not loud enough to allow The Beatles' music to be heard over the fans' screams. Instead, the group used the stadium's public address system. This, too, was drowned out by piercing screams while The Beatles went though a half-hour set during which neither they nor their audience could hear what they were playing. At one stage, during "I'm Down", John Lennon began playing the electric keyboard with his elbows, knowing nothing could be heard.

Although it wasn't the first rock concert to be held in a big stadium (Elvis Presley had played at similar venues in the 1950s) the Shea concert broke all show business records. Promoter Sid Bernstein later said, "Over 55,000 people saw The Beatles at Shea Stadium. We took $304,000, the greatest gross ever in the history of show business."

Below: *Paul McCartney (2nd right) watches as a fan is carried off stage by security guards during the US tour in August 1965.*

During the last stage of the 1965 American tour, on August 27, while the band was in California, The Beatles met their original rock 'n' roll hero, Elvis Presley. Since 1961, Presley hadn't made a single live appearance, or any records of note. Instead, he spent much of his time in Hollywood, filming a series of light-hearted movies. The meeting, fixed by Presley's manager "Colonel" Tom Parker, took place at Elvis' mansion at 565 Perugia Way, Bel Air, Los Angeles. The Beatles arrived at 11pm and were greeted by Presley in his darkened living room. Epstein and Parker stood aside to watch the meeting.

Things didn't get off to a good start, Elvis was watching television with the sound off, and playing a bass guitar, while members of his entourage stood near at hand. The atmosphere was awkward and for a while there was little conversation. Eventually Elvis told The Beatles, "If you damn guys are gonna sit here and stare at me all night, I'm gonna go to bed." This seemed to break the ice. Guitars were produced and, for a while, The Beatles jammed with the King of Rock 'n' Roll.

Below: *The Beatles (left to right, Ringo Starr, John Lennon, George Harrison, and Paul McCartney) play to another screaming audience at Houston's Coliseum on August 19, 1965.*

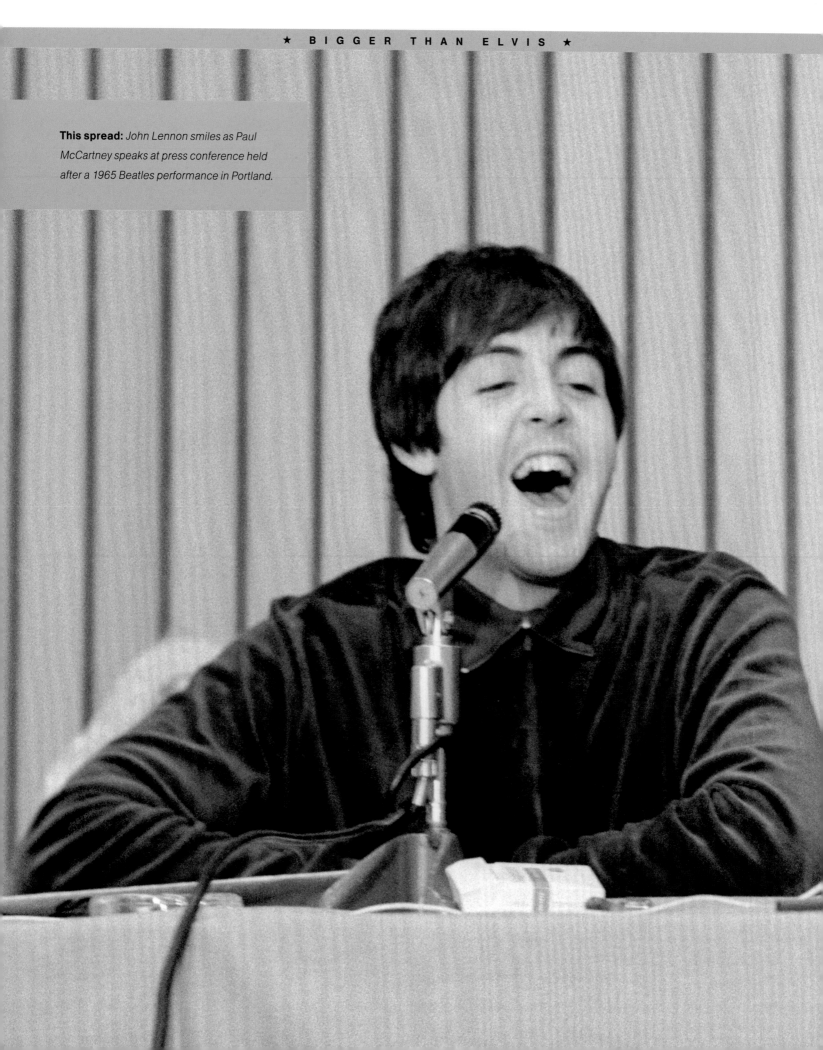

This spread: *John Lennon smiles as Paul McCartney speaks at press conference held after a 1965 Beatles performance in Portland.*

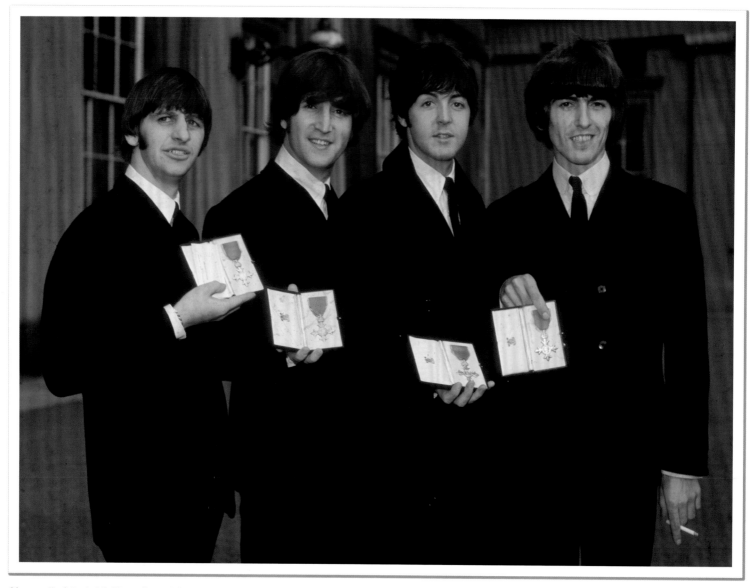

Above: (Left to right) Ringo Starr, John Lennon, Paul McCartney, and George Harrison outside Buckingham Palace, London, after receiving their MBEs (Member of the Order of the British Empire) from Queen Elizabeth II in October 1965.

By the time everyone stopped playing, conversation had became easier. The Beatles and Elvis discussed touring, their fans, and making movies. John asked Presley if he would ever get back to making rock 'n' roll records, and Elvis blamed his tight movie schedules for his absence from the recording studio. The Beatles and their party also played a few games of pool with Elvis' team of assistants, the so-called "Memphis Mafia", and met his wife, Priscilla, briefly. As the band left, The Beatles were given a complete set of Elvis Presley albums, gun holsters, gold leather belts, and a table lamp in the shape of a wagon.

With demand for anything to do with The Beatles running high, on September 25, 1965, America's ABC television network launched *The Beatles* animated cartoon series. Each episode was named for a Beatles song and had a storyline based on its lyrics. A total of 39 episodes were produced, shown in America from 1965 to 1967, and, with re-runs, the series lasted until 1969. The Beatles had nothing to do with the series, except to allow the use of their music and, as time went on (and their "mop-top" image changed), the band distanced themselves from it. In later years, however, they each admitted they enjoyed looking back at it.

Did You Know?

The Beatles had 21 singles at Number One in the US charts, more than any other act, while Elvis Presley had 17 US chart toppers.

The cartoon series was only shown on UK television briefly, but The Beatles still dominated the news in their home country. On October 26, 1965, they hit the headlines again, when they were presented with their MBEs by the Queen. Neither the country or the Royal household had never seen anything like the mayhem outside Buckingham Palace as the band arrived. While fans outside the ornate gates struggled with police to catch a brief glimpse of their heroes, inside the palace, the ceremony went well. About 50 members of the Queen's staff asked The Beatles for autographs and the band joked with Her Majesty as she pinned on their medals. After the ceremony, Paul McCartney quipped at a press conference, "She was just like a mum to us."

The Beatles were now a national institution, but the band was not about to stand still, content with their fame and fortune, which their next album release proved.

Above Right: *The Beatles pictured with British Prime Minister Harold Wilson after receiving their MBEs. (Left to right, Ringo Starr, John Lennon, Harold Wilson, George Harrison, Paul McCartney.)*

Right: *Beatles fans are held back by police outside Buckingham Palace as the members of the group arrive to receive their MBE medals.*

Chapter 12: Rubber Soul- 1965

After the 1965 series of concerts in America, The Beatles were growing tired of touring, and the chaos that went with it. They hated the fact that they couldn't hear themselves playing on stage, did not like living in hotel rooms, and resented not being able to speak truthfully to the ever-present members of the media. They had always joked around during on-tour press conferences but now wanted to speak out about more serious matters, such as the Vietnam war. Brian Epstein, however, strongly advised the band not to make their political opinions public.

Although they accepted their MBE awards with grace, The Beatles turned down Epstein's suggestion that they should play another Royal Command show in 1965. And, while agreeing to tour Great Britain in December, the band made it clear to Epstein that they did not want to go on with what they considered "pointless" one-night concerts much longer. They were selling records by the million, the band argued, tours or no tours, and the best place for them to be was not on stage but in the recording studio.

The 18 concerts that The Beatles played through early December (two shows in each of nine venues), were the last they would perform in their home country, though they were the only people who knew it at the time.

Their set featured the same 11 songs every night and, on Sunday, December 5, the band played their last concert in their home town, Liverpool. There were over 40,000 requests for tickets for the two Liverpool shows, though the venue,

Right: *(Left to right) Ringo Starr, Paul McCartney, John Lennon, and George Harrison discuss their concert at Shea Stadium, New York City, at a press conference.*

Above: *Paul McCartney on stage during The Beatles' last tour in 1965. Ringo Starr plays drums in the background.*

the Empire Theatre, had seating for only 2,550. The group's last British concert tour ended at the Capitol Cinema in Cardiff, Wales, on December 12, 1965.

And as the short tour began, as if to show what they were capable of in the studio, The Beatles released both their first double-A-side single, "We Can Work It Out" and "Day Tripper", along with a new album, *Rubber Soul*, on December 3, 1965.

DID YOU KNOW?
The *Rubber Soul* album cover was the first by The Beatles not to have the group's name on it. Two more (*Abbey Road* and *Let it Be*) would also not feature the name.

"We Can Work It Out" Facts
B-side: "Day Tripper"
Recorded: October 20, 1965
Released: December 3, 1965 (UK),
December 6, 1965 (US)
Label: Parlophone (UK), Capitol
(US)
Writers: Lennnon/McCartney
Producer: George Martin
Chart Success: UK No. 1, US No. 1

With its distorted image of the four Beatles, again photographed by Robert Freeman, *Rubber Soul* was a break from the past, in more ways than one. From now on, The Beatles' albums contained no more covers of the old R&B and rock 'n' roll hits they'd played since their days in Hamburg and Liverpool. And, unlike their previous albums, which were a mixed bag of songs with no connection to each other, *Rubber Soul* had a consistent sound and feel. In fact, the idea of the single-theme "concept album," which is often said to have started with *Sgt. Pepper's Lonely Hearts Club Band* in 1967, first appeared on *Rubber Soul* two years earlier.

As 1965 came to a close, the double-sided single, and the album, topped the charts everywhere that pop records were bought.

Despite worrying that the group's image could not "stand another marriage" when Ringo tied the knot in February 1965, George Harrison became the third Beatle to wed less than a year later, on January 21, 1966.

He married Pattie Boyd, with Paul McCartney as best man, then took a honeymoon in Barbados, where The Beatles had started filming *Help!* a year earlier.

Through the spring of 1966, when they weren't in the recording studio, the individual Beatles took some time off. George enjoyed his new life as a husband at his home, "Kinfauns" in Surrey, and John relaxed with Cynthia and his son, Julian, at his 27-bedroom home, "Kenwood", in nearby Weybridge. Ringo and Maureen also enjoyed some time to themselves at their house, "Sunny Heights", also in Weybridge, while Paul moved into a big home in St. John's Wood, London, not far from Abbey Road and the EMI Studios. Nevertheless, work was never very far from their minds. All four Beatles set up small recording studios in their homes, and used them to experiment with new ideas, which they brought to Abbey Road sessions for the other band members to hear.

Above: *George Harrison and Patti Boyd pictured at their wedding on January 21, 1966.*

Above: *George Harrison and his wife Patti on the beach during their honeymoon in Barbados.*

This spread: *Paul McCartney, George Harrison, John Lennon, and Ringo Starr performing at the Circus Krone-Bau in Munich on June 24, 196*

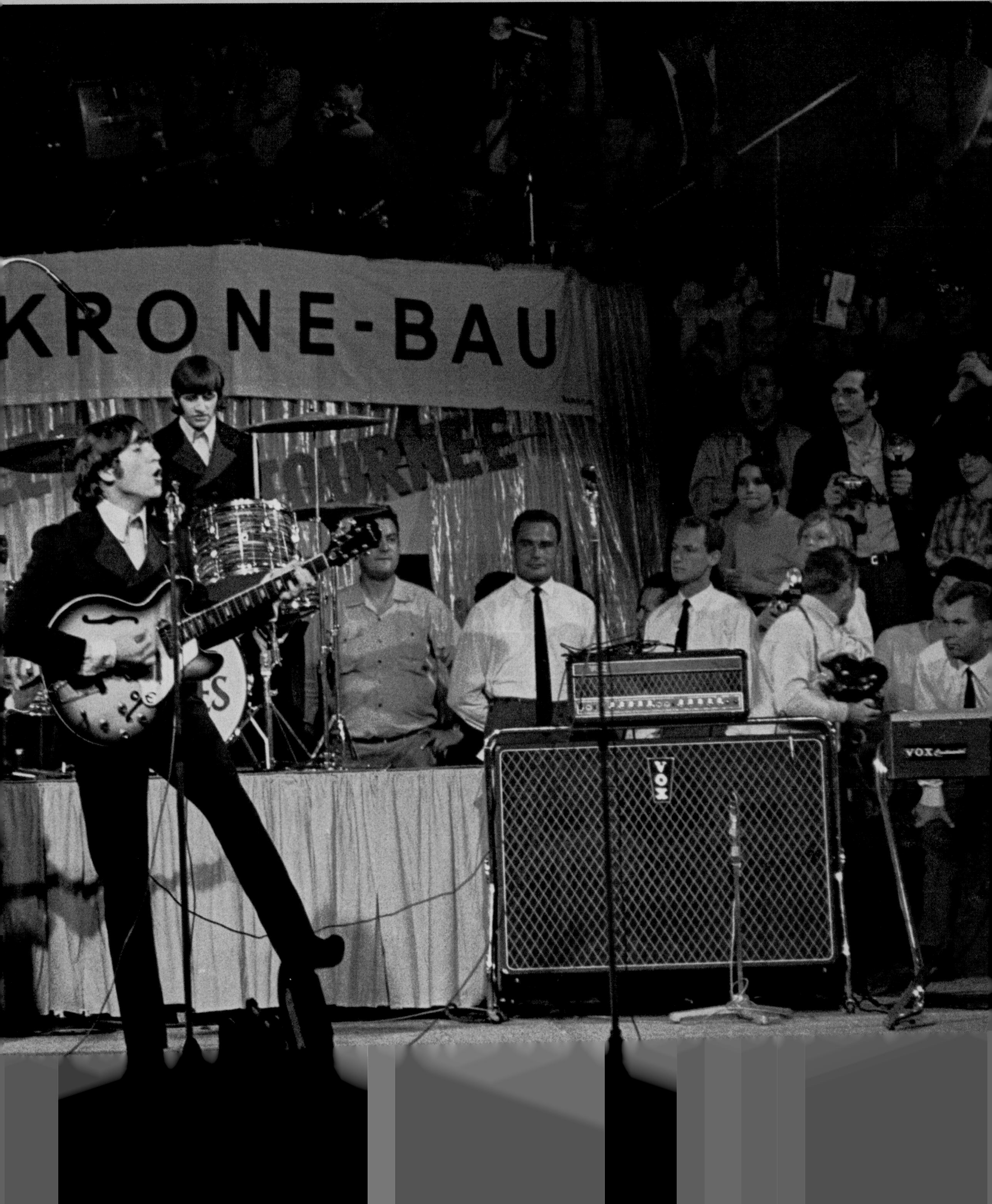
KRONE-BAU
VOX
VOX

This new working process produced The Beatles most radical album yet, the first hint of which reached the public at the end of May 1966, with the release of a new single that featured the tracks "Paperback Writer" and "Rain".

"Paperback Writer" Facts
B-side: "Rain"
Recorded: April 14, 1966
Released: May 30, 1966
Label: Parlophone (UK), Capitol (US)
Writers: Lennnon/McCartney
Producer: George Martin
Chart Success: UK No. 1, US No. 1

Both songs featured a boosted bass guitar, "the first time the bass sound had been heard in all its excitement," as their recording engineer, Geoff Emerick, would later recall, while "Rain" made use of revolutionary effects, including a backward vocal. Unusually for The Beatles, neither were love songs; one was about an aspiring author, the other about that great British obsession, the weather.

On June 6, 1966, the band broke more new ground when Ed Sullivan showed a film of The Beatles performing "Paperback Writer" and "Rain" on his show. "The boys can't be here now, so they've sent us this clip," he said. The age of the pop video was born, though in pre-video days such clips were called "promotional films". As George Harrison would later joke, "In a way, we invented MTV."

The two clips that Sullivan later presented on his show were shot on video, on May 28, by director Michael Lindsay-Hogg at the EMI studios in Abbey Road, with The Beatles miming to both songs. The next day, two short films promoting the same songs were shot in the grounds of a grand 18th Century British mansion, Chiswick House, in west London. There, Lindsay-Hogg filmed the group not just "performing", but walking and sitting among the greenery and statues in the gardens. Both clips were shot in color, though the BBC had to play them in black-and-white for its top music show *Top Of The Pops*.

On May 1, 1966, The Beatles played their final public gig in the UK, when they performed at the annual NME (*New Musical Express*) Poll Winners Concert, at London's Empire Pool, Wembley.

They played a short set that included "I Feel Fine", "Nowhere Man", "Day Tripper", "If I Needed Someone", and "I'm Down" to an audience of 10,000 fans.

Then, on June 24, they played the first dates of a world tour that began in Germany.

A film, made for German television, showed how unprepared The Beatles now were for live performances. The band didn't bother to rehearse as they knew they wouldn't be heard. It was shot on the opening night of the tour at the Circus-Krone-Bau in Munich, and at one point George introduced "Yesterday" as being a track from *Beatles For Sale*. Before they finished the set with "I'm Down", John, George, and Paul could be heard checking with each other about the lyrics, despite which, Paul still got the first three verses mixed up. The trip, which finished in San Francisco at the end of August, would be the last time The Beatles ever toured.

Above: *The Beatles (John Lennon left, Ringo Starr, 2nd left, George Harrison, right, Paul McCartney, 2nd right) collect their awards at the NME Poll Winners' Concert at Wembley, London, on May 1, 1966.*

Left: (Left to right) John Lennon, Paul McCartney, George Harrison, and Ringo Starr perform at the NME Poll Winners' concert on May 1, 1966.

Below: The Beatles (left to right, George Harrison, Ringo Starr, Paul McCartney, and John Lennon), with their manager Brian Epstein (far right), at a press conference at the Bayerischer Hof Hotel in Munich, where they were presented with an award for being "the best beat group in the world."

Above: The Beatles (clockwise from top right, Ringo Starr, George Harrison, Paul McCartney, and John Lennon) relax in the buffet car of a train, during their 1966 tour of Europe.

Rubber Soul Facts

Recorded: June 12, October 12 –
November 11, 1965
Released: December 3, 1965 (UK)
Label: Parlophone (UK)
Writers: Lennon/McCartney
(except songwriters as noted below)
Producer: George Martin
Chart Success: UK No. 1

Track-By-Track
Side 1
Drive My Car (2.25)
A great, up-beat, opening track with a strong R&B and
soul sound.
Norwegian Wood (This Bird Has Flown) (2.00)
The first Beatles recording on which George played sitar. He
discovered the Indian instrument after hearing one used on the
soundtrack of *Help!*
You Won't See Me (3.20)
One of The Beatles' longest tracks to date, with a playing time
of just over three minutes.
Nowhere Man (2.40)
A track that was rumored to be Bob Dylan's favorite Beatles
song.
Think For Yourself (2.16) (George Harrison)
A warning against lies; George would later say "I don't quite
recall who inspired that tune. Probably the government."
The Word (2.42)
A foretaste of later "message" songs such as "All You Need Is
Love".
Michelle (2.42)
Another Beatle song that has become an all-time standard.
With Paul's lines sung in French, this was an immediate hit
when released as an extended play single in France.

Side 2
What Goes On? (2.44) (Lennon/ McCartney/Starkey)
A reworking of a John Lennon song written that was written
in the days of The Quarry Men, the track was inspired by Carl
Perkins and featured Ringo on lead vocal.
Girl (2.26)
The last song recorded for the album, like 'Norwegian Wood'
and "In My Life" it showed the growing influence of American
folk-rock on the band.
I'm Looking Through You (2.20)
Ringo plays Hammond organ on this Buddy Holly-sounding
song.
In My Life (2.23)
One of John's most reflective songs, this was originally inspired
by a critic suggesting he should write about his childhood.
Wait (2.13)
Originally recorded for *Help!* but not used, "Wait" was brought
back for *Rubber Soul* and extra vocals added.
If I Needed Someone (2.19) (George Harrison)
Evidence that George's songwriting was improving with each
album, this track is easily as good as many Lennon–McCartney
numbers.
Run For Your Life (2.21)
Not one of the best Beatles songs, John later said he didn't like
this track.

Right: *(Left to right) Paul McCartney, Ringo Starr, George Harrison, and John Lennon pose for a publicity shot around the time that "Rubber Soul" was released.*

**Rubber Soul Facts
(US version)**
Released: December 6, 1965
Label: Capitol (US)
Chart Success: US No. 1

Track Listing
Side 1
I've Just Seen A Face
*Norwegian Wood
(This Bird Has Flown)*
You Won't See Me
Think For Yourself
The Word
Michelle

Side 2
It's Only Love
Girl
I'm Looking Through You
In My Life
Wait
Run For Your Life

Above: *Workers on a production line at the EMI factory in Hayes, Middlesex, England, package copies of "Rubber Soul".*

Chapter 13: Off the Road- 1966

On June 20, 1966, just a few days before The Beatles left London for their final tour, Capitol Records in the United States released another compilation album, featuring tracks taken from various UK releases. Called *Yesterday and Today*, it included songs that had been left off the US versions of *Help!* and *Rubber Soul*, as well as "We Can Work It Out", "Day Tripper", and three tracks from The Beatles next UK album, which was not yet finished.

***Yesterday And Today* Facts**

Released:
June 20, 1966

Label: Capitol (US)

Chart Success:
US No. 1

Track Listing
Side 1
Drive My Car
I'm Only Sleeping
Nowhere Man
Dr. Robert
Yesterday
Act Naturally

Side 2
And Your Bird
Can Sing
If I Needed
Someone
We Can Work It Out
What Goes On?
Day Tripper

Right: *(Left to right) John Lennon, Ringo Starr, Paul McCartney, and George Harrison perform on the British TV show "Top of the Pops" in June 1966.*

Above: *(Left to right) George Harrison, John Lennon, Paul McCartney, and Ringo Starr leave Heathrow Airport, London, for their final German tour in 1966.*

DID YOU KNOW?

When Capitol Records withdrew the controversial *Yesterday and Today* album covers, they pasted the new photograph on the already printed "butcher" sleeves before printing any more. These rare "paste up" covers now bring huge sums at auctions of Beatles' memorabilia.

For the cover, The Beatles sent Capitol a studio photograph taken by Robert Whittaker. In the picture, all four of the band were dressed in white butchers' coats, posing with raw meat and the heads and limbs of baby dolls. It was later suggested, by Ringo, that the group had thought up the idea as a protest at their US label's constant "butchering" of their UK releases but nothing was said. The picture had been used widely in the UK, in press adverts for "Paperback Writer" and, when the US album first appeared, the American record buyers did not seem to be offended by the image; the record shot up the *Billboard* charts as usual.

Soon after releasing the album, however, Capitol had a change of heart, and withdrew what they felt was a "controversial" cover, re-issuing the album in a new sleeve and pasting a new photo over covers that had already been printed. The company president, Alan W. Livingstone, issued a statement: "...to avoid any possible controversy or undeserved harm to The Beatles' image or reputation, Capitol has chosen to withdraw the LP and substitute a more generally acceptable design." When asked what the artistic relevance of the offending cover was, Paul McCartney replied, "It's as relevant as Vietnam."

The cover controversy was just one of the group's problems as the tour progressed. From the start, it was clear that The Beatles were not having a good time.

After three dates in Germany during the last week of June 1966, the band admitted to reporters that they didn't enjoy playing live any more, because they couldn't hear what they were doing. Then they headed for Japan, where things began to go seriously wrong.

In the Japanese capital, Tokyo, The Beatles had been booked to play at the Budokan Hall. The three concerts at the venue were sold out, but the hall was also a center for martial arts and regarded, by some,

Above: *(Left to right) Paul McCartney, John Lennon, Ringo Starr, and George Harrison at a 1966 press conference in Japan.*

Right: *The Beatles (left to right, Paul McCartney, George Harrison, John Lennon, and Ringo Starr) on stage at the Budokan Hall in Tokyo on June 30, 1966.*

Above: *John Lennon speaks at a July 1966 press conference at London Airport after The Beatles' return from Manila.*

as a sacred monument. Thousands of demonstrators took to the streets in protest against a pop group "desecrating" the shrine and it took 35,000 security police to control rioting during the four days of The Beatles' stay. Apart from playing the concerts, the group was not allowed to leave the hotel.

After Japan, The Beatles headed for Manila, in the Philippines. On July 4, 1966, they played at the vast Rizal

Football Stadium in front of an estimated crowd of 100,000, the largest audience of their entire career. However, an ugly situation was developing. Because of an administrative mix-up, the group failed to turn up at a children's party hosted by Imelda Marcos, wife of the country's president. Brian Epstein had politely turned down the invitation, but the message had either not reached Imelda Marcos, or

Above: *The Beatles and manager Brian Epstein (left to right, Brian Epstein, George Harrison, Ringo Starr, John Lennon, and Paul McCartney) arrive back in London, in July 1966, following their tour of Germany, Japan, and the Philippines.*

had been ignored. Local television reported the "snub," and showed footage of children crying with disappointment because The Beatles had not arrived.

The Manila media blew the issue into a national crisis, to the point that The Beatles' security guards were withdrawn and the band had to run through angry crowds at the airport. Several of their party were punched and kicked, or were harassed by government troops. Before The Beatles were allowed to leave, Brian Epstein was made to give back all the money the band had earned in the country.

The next leg of the tour, another series of dates in North America, wasn't due to start until August 12, in Chicago. Before the band arrived in the country, an unexpected anti-Beatles backlash broke out across the United States. The trouble had its roots in London. In March 1966, a journalist named Maureen Cleave had interviewed John Lennon for the London *Evening Standard* newspaper. Cleave, a long-time supporter and friend of The Beatles, asked John about his views on God and religion, and quoted his reply in the paper: "Christianity will go. It will vanish and shrink.

This spread: *Ringo Starr, Paul McCartney, John Lennon, and George Harrison at a 1966 press conference at the Warwick Hotel, New York*

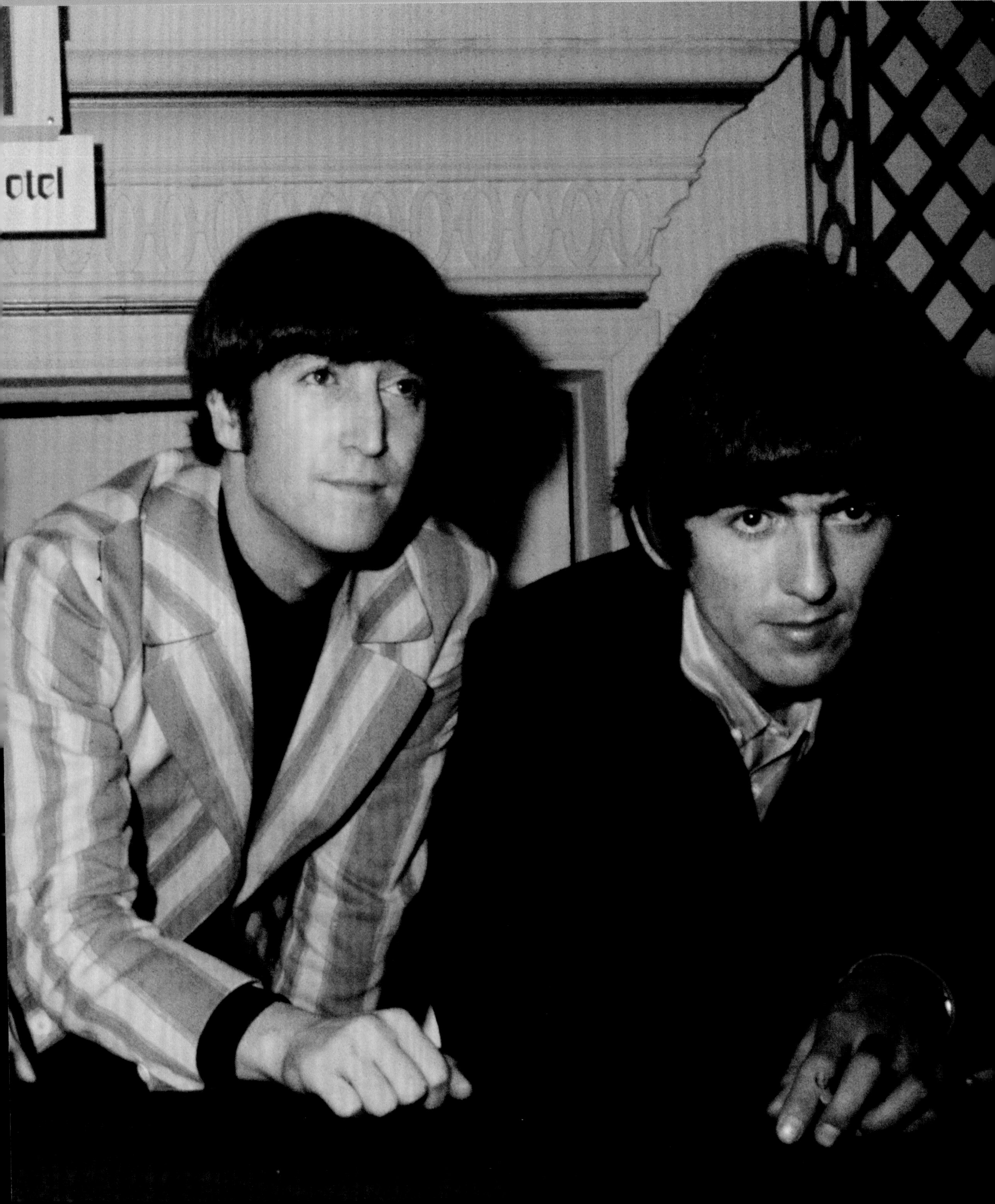
otel

Above: *John Lennon (left) and Ringo Starr (right) take a break from their hectic 1966 tour schedule.*

I needn't argue about that; I'm right and I will be proved right. We're more popular than Jesus now; I don't know which will go first—rock 'n' roll or Christianity. Jesus was alright [sic], but his disciples were thick and ordinary. It's them twisting it that ruins it for me."

As with the "butcher" photographs, the quote passed without comment in the UK. Similarly, there were no complaints when part of the interview was published in the *New York Times Magazine* on July 3. However, when the American teen magazine *Datebook* printed an excerpt at the end of July, the outcry across the United States was deafening. Newspapers called for a boycott of the tour, and radio stations, especially in the South, arranged bonfires at which listeners could burn Beatles' records and fan pictures.

The group received hate mail and death threats, and the Ku Klux Klan began marching outside concert halls where the group was due to appear.

Brian Epstein and the group considered canceling the trip but eventually decided to go ahead, and used the first press conference in Chicago to address the issue. There, John explained that he had not been speaking against God or Jesus, but simply stating a fact: that pop music had become more popular with young people than religion.

> *"They've got to buy them before they can burn them..."* — George Harrison in response to the burning of Beatles albums in America.

Fortunately, the controversy about John's comments did not seem to have much of an impact on American fans. The US tour was as chaotic as previous tours of the country and, at the height of the uproar, in early August, their next single climbed the charts on both sides of the Atlantic, as usual.

On one side was "Yellow Submarine", which was written almost as a playground song for children to sing along with; on the other was "Eleanor Rigby", which, according to critics, set new standards in popular song-writing. Both were taken from the album *Revolver*, which was released at the end of August, as the US tour came to an end.

"Yellow Submarine" Facts
B-side: "Eleanor Rigby"
Recorded: May 26, June 1, 1966
Released: August 5, 1966 (UK),
August 8, 1966 (US)
Label: Parlophone (UK), Capitol (US)
Writers: Lennnon/McCartney

The tensions on the road, from Japan to Manila to America, had convinced The Beatles that this would be their last tour. As if to confirm their decision, on August 19, at a concert in the Mid-South Coliseum, Memphis, a firecracker exploded on the stage during a performance. For a moment, all four Beatles thought someone was shooting at them. The show they played 11 days later, on August 29, 1966, at Candlestick Park in San Francisco, was their last public performance.

Above Right: *(Left to right) George Harrison, John Lennon, Paul McCartney, and Ringo Starr at a press conference before a live performance at Dodger Stadium, Los Angeles, on August 28, 1966.*

Right: *A poster advertising The Beatles' August 28, 1966, concert at Candlestick Park, San Francisco.*

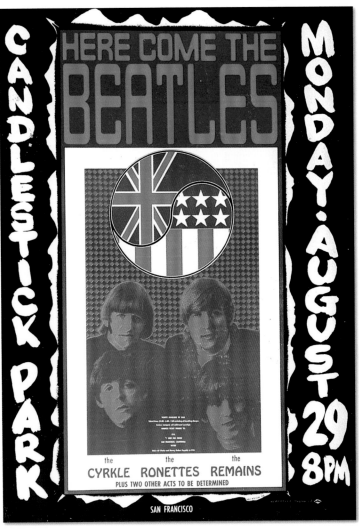

Chapter 14: Revolver-1966

The Beatles released *Revolver* in early August, 1966, and the album marked a great leap forward in the band's musical progress. Recorded during lengthy studio sessions, from April through to May, it showed that what the band was making in the studio was very different to what they had been playing on stage. All the ideas that the individual Beatles had been working on in their home studios were developed as finished tracks at the Abbey Road studios, and the sheer variety of the finished album was astonishing. While the songs on *Rubber Soul* had a common feel to them, the collection on *Revolver* was the opposite. As the "trailer" single "Yellow Submarine" and "Eleanor Rigby" suggested, no two tracks were similar. Even the cover artwork, designed by their old friend from the Hamburg days, Klaus Voorman, was completely different to anything on their previous record sleeves. The four Beatles' portraits were drawn in fine lines, their hair longer than before, and scattered with small photographs of The Beatles of the past, dating from 1962 to 1965, as if to say "The Beatles have changed."

To celebrate Lennon and McCartney's achievements as song writers, on August 6 the BBC produced a one-hour radio documentary called *The Lennon and McCartney Songbook*, which featured the two Beatles reviewing 15 versions of their songs by artists including Ella Fitzgerald, Peggy Lee, and The Mamas and The Papas. The show was recorded at Paul's house in London, and the fact that acts like Lee and Fitzgerald were covering Beatles songs proved that the group had been accepted by the "easy listening" mainstream, many of whom were usually snobbish about pop music.

Right: *(Left to right) Paul McCartney, John Lennon, Ringo Starr, and George Harrison pictured in August 1966, leaving Heathrow Airport for their final tour of the US.*

Above: *The Beatles (left to right, George Harrison, Paul McCartney, Ringo Starr, and John Lennon) perform on August 23, 1966 at Shea Stadium, New York.*

As the new album climbed the charts worldwide through August 1966, The Beatles played the final dates of their last tour, and then went their separate ways until the end of November.

Paul McCartney, with a little help from George Martin, wrote the score for a movie, *The Family Way*. The music was not written for "rock" instruments, as might have been expected, but a classical line-up of brass and strings.

Toward the end of September, John Lennon flew to Almeria in southern Spain to begin shooting *How I Won the War*, an anti-war film being made by the director of both Beatles movies, Richard Lester. Lennon played the part of Corporal Gripweed, a supporting role.

Above: *(Left to right) John Lennon, George Harrison, and Paul McCartney during a Beatles concert at a packed Shea Stadium, New York.*

more about the instrument. There, he studied under the world-renowned sitar master, one of the few Indian musicians famous in the West, Ravi Shankar.

When he arrived in India, George checked into the Taj Mahal Hotel in Bombay under the alias Sam Wells, but news that a Beatle was in town soon leaked out and George was chased by the press everywhere he went. To resolve the problem he held a press conference, then moved to another hotel.

Ringo, not having much else to do with his band mates otherwise occupied, relaxed at his Surrey mansion with his family, and visited John on location in Spain. Lennon was probably glad of the company; he would

Above: *John Lennon in a still from the movie "How I Won The War".*

The film was set in World War II, which meant that John needed a radical change of image. The first thing to go was his long hair, and the army-regulation "short back and sides" haircut he was given made news headlines around the world. He was also provided with old-fashioned, wire, round-framed "granny glasses." Unlike the haircut, which he soon grew back, John liked the new spectacles. They quickly became part of the John Lennon image and fashionable around the world. *How I Won The War* was an odd "art house" movie and not an obvious box-office hit but, with John Lennon's name prominent in the cast list, it was more successful than it might otherwise have been.

Meanwhile, George Harrison, who had been exploring Indian music since he had first discovered the sitar while The Beatles were making *Help!*, traveled to India to learn

Above: *George Harrison (left) at a 1967 press conference with Ravi Shankar (right).*

This spread: *John Lennon talks with Ringo Starr during a break in filming on "How I Won the War", 1966.*

Above: *John Lennon makes a guest appearance in a Christmas special of the British TV show "Not Only...But Also", November 1966.*

DID YOU KNOW?

In November 1966, John Lennon appeared on the BBC comedy Show "Not Only... But Also", with Peter Cook and Dudley Moore, playing the part of a men's lavatory attendant.

later admit that spending seven weeks in the desert, most of the time just standing around, was not his idea of fun. Filming started early in the day and evenings were spent in a drab rented house nearby. However, the lack of distractions meant that he did a lot of song writing, including a number that would become one of The Beatles' all-time classics when it was released as a single early the following year.

With all four Beatles taking a substantial time away from the band for the first time in years, rumors started to circulate worldwide that the group had broken up. In Britain, the *Sunday Times* newspaper printed an article that read almost like an obituary. It discussed why The Beatles might be splitting up and wondered what life would be like without the group. The BBC also hinted at the group's break-up in news bulletins and, as The Beatles didn't comment, their silence made the end of the band seem even more likely. In fact, the four musicians weren't sure what the future held, and certainly didn't feel obliged to respond to media speculation. Normally, Brian Epstein would have quashed the rumors immediately but, by now The Beatles manager was often in hospital, suffering from depression, which had resulted in a suicide attempt.

When filming for *How I Won the War* finished, John returned to London and, on November 6, 1966, met the woman who would change his life forever: Yoko Ono. The link between the two was Paul McCartney, who had become increasingly involved in the London "underground" arts scene. By the fall of 1966, he was also helping to finance several arts projects, including the *International Times* alternative newspaper and the Indica bookshop and art gallery in the St. James's area of London. It was at an Indica art show that John met the Japanese artist.

Yoko, who at that time lived in New York City, was well known on the Sixties modern art scene as a "conceptual artist", staging "happenings" and performances. It was at one such event that the founder of Indica, John Dunbar, introduced Lennon to Ono.

Above: *John Lennon with Yoko Ono in 1967.*

"There was a sort of underground clique in London," Lennon would later recall. "John Dunbar, who was married to Marianne Faithfull, had an art gallery in London called Indica, and I'd been going around to galleries a bit on me off days in between records, also to a few exhibitions in different galleries that showed sort of unknown artists or underground artists."

Lennon had heard about "this amazing woman" who staged happenings, and went to the gallery preview the night before her exhibition opened. He was fascinated by works such as a single apple that was on sale for $400/£200, exclaiming, "Two hundred quid to watch the apple decompose," and, most of all, by a ladder that led up to a painting on the ceiling. The painting was a black canvas with a spyglass hanging from a chain. Lennon immediately climbed the ladder and peering through the spyglass to read, in tiny letters, the word "yes".

When introduced by Dunbar, Yoko had no idea who John was. According to a later interview with Lennon, she'd only heard of Ringo, "which means 'apple' in Japanese," and had no interest in The Beatles or their music. When they met, Yoko handed John a card which said "breathe" on it.

Although John was naturally suspicious of "arty" people and events, he was immediately attracted to Ono's outrageous sculptures and performance art, as well as her simple attitude to life. "Whether it's art or music," she told him, "you do what you do, and don't have to justify it in any way to anyone—it simply is what it is." Lennon agreed with her completely.

Top, Above, and Above Right: *Paul McCartney (top), John Lennon (above), Ringo Starr (above right, center), and George Harrison (above right, right) arrive at the EMI studios in Abbey Road in November 1966.*

Over the next few months, John and Yoko met several more times at art events, and began to write to each other regularly. That, however, was all that happened between them for some time.

In October, 1966, Brian Epstein informed EMI that there would be no tracks for a new Beatles album in time for Christmas, so the company decided to release the first Beatles "greatest hits" collection, *A Collection of Beatles Oldies*. The back cover added the slogan, "But Goldies!" but, in fact, the 16-track album did have one new song for UK fans: John Lennon's cover of the Larry Williams track "Bad Boy", which had been issued in America in 1965. For the first time, all the Beatles recordings since 1962, except for their two German-language songs, were now available on both sides of the Atlantic.

At the end of November, having led almost totally separate lives since the final concert in San Francisco, all four Beatles came together to begin new recordings. Most of the tracks they now worked on would end up on their next album, *Sgt. Pepper's Lonely Hearts Club Band*, but among the new songs there was one that John brought to the session that he had written while filming in Spain. It was called "Strawberry Fields Forever", and when released, in February 1967, with "Penny Lane", it was hailed by many as the greatest single in the history of pop music.

Revolver Facts

Recorded: April 6 – June 21, 1966
Released: August 5, 1966 (UK)
Label: Parlophone (UK)
Writers: Lennon/McCartney (except songwriters as noted below)
Producer: George Martin
Chart Success: UK No. 1

Track-By-Track
Side 1
Taxman (2.36) (George Harrison)
George's protest about high taxes, named UK politicians of the time, "Mr. Wilson" and "Mr. Heath".
Eleanor Rigby (2.11)
One of The Beatles' finest lyrics and with a beautiful, haunting, melody, a leading UK critic said this track signaled that pop music "had come of age."
I'm Only Sleeping (2.58)
John Lennon's tribute to the joys of staying in bed.
Love You To (3.00) (George Harrison)
George was the only Beatle to play on this track. He was joined by an Indian tabla player and studio musicians.
Here, There and Everywhere (2.29)
A ballad written by Paul for his girlfriend, Jane Asher, it is thought that The Beach Boys' "God Only Knows" was a big influence for the song.
Yellow Submarine (2.40)
A modern day nursery rhyme, and inspiration for the animated film of 1968.
She Said, She Said (2.39)
Based on a conversation with actor Peter Fonda, this was originally a very aggressive song by John, but was later rewritten.

Side 2
Good Day Sunshine (2.08)
This track followed a trend for "sunny" songs in 1966, such as the Lovin' Spoonful's "Daydream" and "Sunny Afternoon" by The Kinks.
And Your Bird Can Sing (2.02)
Although Beatle fans searched for deep meaning in this song, John Lennon insisted it was a simple track, written to fill a gap in the album.
For No One (2.03)
Only Paul and Ringo play on this track, which has a French Horn solo by classical musician Alan Civil.
Dr. Robert (2.14)
The doctor in the title was a friend of The Beatles, well known on the New York art scene.
I Want To Tell You (2.30) (George Harrison)
Not one of George's best songs, this track documents the difficulty he often had in saying what he really meant.
Got To Get You Into My Life (2.31)
The Beatles also offered this song to a group known as Cliff Bennett and The Rebel Rousers. Their cover single, produced by Paul, made the UK Top 10 a week after *Revolver* was released.
Tomorrow Never Knows (3.00)
The Beatles' most experimental track to date, this mystical-sounding song, which doesn't include the words "tomorrow never knows," was originally called "Mark I", until Ringo came up with the title.

Revolver Facts (US version)
Released: August 8, 1966
Label: Capitol (US)
Chart Success: US No. 1

Track Listing
Side 1
Taxman
Eleanor Rigby
Love You To
Here, There and Everywhere
Yellow Submarine
She Said, She Said

Side 2
Good Day Sunshine
For No One
I Want To Tell You
Got To Get You Into My Life
Tomorrow Never Knows

Above: *Paul McCartney arrives at EMI studios, Abbey Road, for a rehearsal with The Beatles during the recording of "Revolver", in June 1966.*

Left: *John Lennon signs autographs for fans as he arrives for rehearsals at the EMI studios in London, June 1966.*

Chapter 15: Sgt Pepper's Lonely Hearts Club Band-1967

As 1966 came to an end, The Beatles' UK record label, Parlophone, released *A Collection of Beatles Oldies*, on December 10, the "greatest hits" album that proved how far the group had come since their first single release just four years earlier. On December 16, The Beatles' fourth special Christmas Record was distributed exclusively to members of their fan club, a gesture they would continue until Christmas 1970.

"Strawberry Fields Forever"
Facts
B-side: "Penny Lane"
Recorded: December 29 – 30, 1966,
January 4 – 12, 17, 1967
Released: February 17, 1967 (UK),
February 13 (US)
Label: Parlophone (UK), Capitol (US)
Writers: Lennnon/McCartney
Producer: George Martin
Chart Success: UK No. 2, US No. 1

The Beatles released "Strawberry Fields Forever" as a single in February 1967. Considered a masterpiece by critics, it was named for a Salvation Army children's home close to where John Lennon had lived as a boy in Allerton, Liverpool.

Above: *(Left to right) Ringo Starr, John Lennon, Paul McCartney, and George Harrison pose for a group portrait in 1967.*

Above: *Ringo Starr films a scarf waved by John Lennon during sessions for "Sgt. Pepper", February 15, 1967.*

John had written three versions of the track on his return from Spain after the filming *How I Won the War* and, in the studio, he, George Martin, and the other Beatles pieced the different versions together in late December 1966 and January 1967. It was a groundbreaking track that used every new piece of recording technology that was available in the mid Sixties, including the mellotron—an early electronic keyboard that imitated other instruments—and tricks like cymbals recorded backward.

Eventually, two versions of the song emerged in the recording studio, a rock version and, later, an orchestral one, which was arranged by George Martin. After John added his vocals, the later version was marked as the final one, until Lennon decided the song should begin with the electric rock version and end with the orchestral. Martin spotted a problem, however, because the two versions were in different keys, but by slowing one down and speeding the other up, Martin was able to match both the key and speed of the recordings. The end product was like nothing ever heard on a pop single.

DID YOU KNOW?
In January 1967, an interview with Paul McCartney was used in a TV documentary about the new hippie "underground" counter-culture in London, called *It's So Far Out, It's Straight Down.*

The other side of the single was equally memorable and, again, named for a Liverpool landmark: Penny Lane. Unlike the Lennon song, which only referred to Strawberry Fields in the title, the Paul McCartney song described details of the street for which it was named. Including classical wind and brass instruments, the elegant feel of "Penny Lane" was given a final touch with a piccolo trumpet, played by David Mason, who Paul had seen playing on a TV concert a few days earlier.

For the single, The Beatles wanted two promotional film clips. These were produced by Tony Bramwell, who the band had known since the Liverpool days when he was an assistant road manager to Neil Aspinall, and directed by Peter Goldmann, who made TV pop shows in Sweden. Early in January, Goldmann arrived in England and started looking round for suitable locations, as well as watching The Beatles recording at Abbey Road. He chose Knole Park, near Sevenoaks in Kent, and Stratford in East London. In Knole Park, a large wooded area about 20 miles south-east of London, he shot two sequences for "Strawberry Fields", and one for "Penny Lane." Inspired by Richard Lester's work on *A Hard Days Night*, the band didn't attempt to mime a "performance", but acted out a series of sequences that seemed to reflect the music. It was an attempt to capture the "atmosphere" of the tunes, an approach repeated by later pop "videos" through the Seventies, Eighties, and even today.

The urban area of Stratford was used as a substitute for the area around Penny Lane in Liverpool. Here, the group walked the streets and rode white horses. Goldmann and the crew, without The Beatles, later traveled to Liverpool to shoot some of the landmarks mentioned in the song, including the barber's shop and the bus shelter in the middle of the roundabout, which they cut with the sequences filmed with the group. Finally, more footage was filmed at Knole Park. This time the band sat at a dinner table and were served with their instruments by "servants" in wigs.

Originally, it was intended that both tracks would go on The Beatles' next album but, when EMI reminded the group that a new single was overdue, they agreed to release "Strawberry

Above: *The Beatles on a bench in London, May 1967. (Left to right, John Lennon, George Harrison, unidentified man, Paul McCartney, Ringo Starr.)*

Fields Forever" and "Penny Lane" as a double-A-side single. One of the first rock records to feature English rather than American place names in its lyrics, it was named by more than one music writer as the greatest pop single of all time as soon as it came out. Nevertheless, though it reached Number One spot in the US charts, it only hit Number Two in the UK, and was The Beatles' first single not to top the charts in their home country since their debut, "Love Me Do", in 1962.

As The Beatles continued recording their new album, more records were being broken. In March 1967, the UK music paper *Disc and Music Echo* reported that there were no less than 446 versions of "Yesterday", recorded by various artists, on the market. At the beginning of May, EMI announced that the total world sales of The Beatles' records, including singles and albums, had reached 200 million.

Also in May, Paul McCartney met his future wife, Linda Eastman. Linda, whose mother was heiress to the American Lindener Department Store fortune, was a professional photographer at the time. She was in the UK on an assignment to take photographs of "Swinging Sixties" musicians in London, for a book to be called *Rock and Other Four Letter Words*. The two met in a late-night London club, the Bag O'Nails, where they were watching a performance by the British R&B star Georgie Fame, and later went on to the Speakeasy club to hear the psychedelic hit-makers of "A Whiter Shade of Pale", Procol Harum. They met again, four days later, at the launch party for the *Sgt. Pepper* album, which took place at Brian Epstein's home in Belgravia.

However, though they were immediately attracted to each other, it would be some time before the couple began seeing each other regularly. After her assignment was finished, Linda went back to New York City and didn't meet up with Paul again until he and John Lennon were in the city to announce the formation of The Beatles' Apple company in May, 1968.

Left: *Paul McCartney talking to Linda Eastman at the press launch of "Sgt.Pepper" in May 1967. The couple married two years later.*

Above: *(Left to right) George Harrison, Ringo Starr, John Lennon, and Paul McCartney, May 1967.*

By the time recording sessions came to an end, early in April, a "concept" had emerged for The Beatles' new album. Paul had the idea that the "band" in one of his songs, "Sgt. Pepper's Lonely Hearts Club Band", should represent The Beatles, and the album would be the 20-year-old Pepper Band giving an open-air concert on a bandstand in a park. The album would start with sounds of the band tuning up, with audience noise in the background, and end with the "Sgt. Pepper" theme repeated. Although *Rubber Soul* had, in fact, been more of a "concept" album, with a common sound running through it, *Sgt. Pepper* is often considered the first, because of the Pepper Band's "performance" linking the tracks in this way.

One of the most radical moments on *Sgt. Pepper* came on the final track, "A Day In The Life". Paul McCartney had the idea of filling the empty space after John's final chorus with an orchestral climax, with each musician playing from his lowest to highest note, though not necessarily at the same speed, and becoming louder as they played. George Martin booked 40 musicians from top London classical orchestras, and each was given a prop, including false noses, masks, and pieces of a gorilla costume, in order to create a carnival atmosphere.

As Martin and McCartney took turns in conducting, the assembled musicians created a crescendo for the middle of the song, and a longer one for the end. This arrangement was

Above: *Paul McCartney conducts a 40-piece orchestra during sessions for the album "Sgt. Pepper's Lonely Hearts Club Band", February 15, 1967.*

influenced by experimental classical music, in which Paul was interested, and was totally out of the ordinary for a pop music record. There was, however, a problem with how to finish the arrangement. Ending suddenly on the top note would have been an anti-climax, and The Beatles' first idea was to finish with all four of the band humming the final chord. This was recorded, but did not seem a powerful enough way to end the track. Instead, the humming was replaced with the same chord played on three pianos and a harmonium. The crash of the chord was overdubbed four times, and lasted an incredible 53 seconds, almost a fifth of the length of the whole track, and nearly half the length of "Please Please Me". It was an incredible climax to a remarkable song, and an equally amazing album.

Since *Rubber Soul*, The Beatles had taken tight control over the cover art of their albums and, for *Sgt. Pepper,* they were determined to have something special on the sleeve. Lennon and McCartney contacted a friend, the famous pop artist Peter Blake, and told him that they needed a group portrait of the fictional "Pepper" band. Blake suggested that the band could be surrounded by the audience, made up of people The Beatles admired or thought important. The four Beatles gave Blake a list of musicians, writers, film stars, comedians, sportsmen, and other key figures, then Blake set about making life-size cardboard cutouts of each.

The celebrity crowd included Hollywood stars such as Marlon Brando and Mae West, Indian gurus, writers including Edgar Allan Poe, H.G. Wells, and George Bernard Shaw, as well as fellow rock musicians Dion and Bob Dylan: over 50 characters in all, including the former Beatles bass player Stuart Sutcliffe. In front of the assembled cutouts was a bass drum with the "Sgt. Pepper" logo painted on it in bright fairground-style lettering. Behind the drum stood The Beatles themselves, in colorful silk military uniforms, with moustaches and holding brass band instruments. To their left were four dummies (from the famous Madame

Above: *The Beatles (clockwise from top left, Ringo Starr, George Harrison, John Lennon, and Paul McCartney) pose for the cameras on May 22, 1967.*

Tussauds waxwork museum) of The Beatles during the early "mop top" period.

Another new development on the *Sgt. Pepper* album sleeve was the inclusion of song lyrics. Now a normal feature of pop and rock albums, it was only after *Sgt. Pepper* that singers and bands regularly started to include lyrics on album covers and dust sheets.

As soon as the album came out, on June 1, 1967, the cover attracted almost as much attention as the music. With its double "gatefold" sleeve and sheet of cut-out "Pepper"

Left: *A British Royal Mail stamp, released in January, 2007, featuring the cover of The Beatles' album "Sgt. Pepper's Lonely Hearts Club Band".*

items, including badges, uniform stripes, and a moustache, it set a new standard in rock album packaging. The final bill for the cover came to over £2,800/$5,600, equivalent to £37,500/$75,000 today. In 1967, it was a staggering sum and was estimated to be 100 times the average cost of an album cover at the time.

Sgt. Pepper had taken some 700 hours to record, and an estimated £50,000/$100,000 to produce. On its release, the album shot to the top of the charts all over the world. It stayed at the Number One slot in the UK for 27 weeks, and for 19 in the USA. The critics loved it, with even classical music reviewers raving, and history would judge it as the artistic high point of The Beatles' career.

Sgt. Pepper's Lonely Hearts Club Band Facts

Recorded: December 6, 1966 – April 21, 1967
Released: June 1, 1967 (UK), June 2, 1967 (US)
Label: Parlophone (UK), Capitol (US)
Writers: Lennon/McCartney (except songwriters as noted below)
Producer: George Martin
Chart Success: UK No. 1, US No. 1

Track-By-Track
Side 1
Sgt. Pepper's Lonely Hearts Club Band (1.59)
The opening track, complete with sounds on an orchestra tuning up, introduces the fictitious band.

With A Little Help From My Friends (2.46)
Of all his vocals on Beatles' albums, this may be Ringo's best.

Lucy In The Sky With Diamonds (3.25)
This track was inspired by a painting by John's son, Julian, of classmate Lucy O'Donnell. She had asked him to draw a picture of her on a black background with stars. Julian insisted these were diamonds in the sky, and not stars. The lyrics also reflect John's love of Lewis Carroll's children's book *Through The Looking Glass*.

Getting Better (2.47)
Sg. Pepper was experimental in many ways, and this track featured a droning sound made by an Indian tamboura, played by George.

Fixing A Hole (2.33)
Although given all kinds of meanings by fans and critics, "Fixing A Hole" is simply a song about Paul repairing his farmhouse in Scotland, and what he was feeling at the time.

She's Leaving Home (3.24)
Inspired by a newspaper article Paul read about a girl running away from home, this track has a similar feeling to "Eleanor Rigby". George and Ringo don't appear; Paul and John just sing with a backing of harp and strings.

Being For The Benefit Of Mr. Kite (2.36)
John based the lyrics of this track on an old English circus poster he'd found. Only Paul plays his usual instruments (bass guitar and lead guitar), while John plays Hammond organ, and George Martin a Wurlitzer fairground organ. Ringo and George, plus The Beatles' two road managers, Mal Evans and Neil Aspinall, all play harmonica parts.

Side 2
Within You, Without You (5.03) (George Harrison)
Another Indian-inspired track from George, he and Aspinall both play tambouras, alongside four session musicians on other Indian instruments, eight violins, and three cellos. John, Paul, and Ringo don't appear.

When I'm Sixty-Four (2.38)
A complete contrast to the previous track, Paul's jaunty song was written for his father, who had just turned 64.

Lovely Rita (2.43)

Paul wrote this track after getting a ticket from a female traffic warden in London, but used the American expression "meter maid," probably because it sounded better.

Good Morning, Good Morning (2.35)

The horn section on this track was recorded by Sounds Incorporated, an instrumental group The Beatles had known since their Hamburg days. After being signed by Brian Epstein, the band toured the world as The Beatles' opening act.

Sgt. Pepper's Lonely Hearts Club Band (reprise) (1.20)

A re-run of the opening track, with slightly amended lyrics, it was George Martin's idea to use this to bring the album to a close.

A Day In The Life (5.03)

A combination of two songs, one by John Lennon and the other by Paul McCartney. During his parts, John refers to, among other things, the death of a friend in a car crash and his own part in the movie *How I Won The War*, while Paul's middle part describes, in typically bright style, taking a bus and having a smoke. The song attracted controversy because of implied drug references, but it was the 53-second ending that particularly startled listeners when it first appeared. The build-up featured a 41-piece orchestra and finished with the crash of three pianos and a harmonium.

Top: *(Left to right) Ringo Starr, John Lennon, Paul McCartney, and George Harrison, at a press call to promote "Sgt. Pepper".*

Above: *(Left to right) John Lennon, George Harrison, Ringo Starr, and Paul McCartney dressed in psychedelic clothing while promoting "Sgt. Pepper" in 1967.*

Chapter 16: All You Need Is Love -1967

June 1, 1967, the day that *Sgt. Pepper* was released, marked the beginning of the "Summer of Love". The hippie youth culture of "flower power" and the influence of psychedelic drugs were being discussed by the mainstream media for the first time, and the four Beatles were seen as the popular face of the new culture. As George Martin wrote in his book *Summer of Love,* many years later, "With *Sgt. Pepper* The Beatles held up a mirror to the world."

When *Sgt. Pepper* was released, the BBC immediately banned the final track, "A Day In The Life", from being played on air because of an apparent drug reference in the song, which John brought to a close with the message, "We'd love to turn you on." At the time, to "turn on" meant to take drugs in youth slang. Two weeks after the album's release, Paul admitted to the press that he'd taken the mind-expanding drug LSD four times. He went on to explain that he had been asked about it by a reporter, and was faced with a choice of whether to lie or to tell the truth. Paul added, "I decided to tell the truth, but if I'd had my way I wouldn't have told anyone, because I'm not trying to spread the word about this."

Drugs or no drugs, "love" was in the air in the summer of 1967, and The Beatles provided the soundtrack for the time. The group was invited to take part in *Our World*, a two-hour television special devised by the BBC and broadcast on June 25, which made history as the first live satellite broadcast to link nations around the globe.

Right: *The Beatles play "All You Need Is Love" on "Our World", the first worldwide satellite broadcast, June 25, 1967. (Left to right, Paul McCartney, John Lennon, Ringo Starr, George Harrison.)*

Representing the UK, The Beatles assembled a group of session musicians, plus a crowd of friends and family, to join a live, on-air recording of their new single, "All You Need Is Love", watched by an estimated 400 million viewers in 24 countries.

The day before the show, The Beatles gathered at the EMI studios in Abbey Road, where the broadcast was to be filmed. First, they gave a press conference to over 100

Top: *A psychedelic felt-tip drawing by John Lennon called "Strong".*

Above: *(Left to right) Paul McCartney, George Harrison, Ringo Starr, and John Lennon pictured before their performance of "All You Need Is Love" on the "Our World" satellite link up.*

urnalists and photographers, then the group began recording backing rhythm track for the next day's historic session. hey also rehearsed their slot with the BBC camera crew, 13 dditional musicians, and a conductor.

The Beatles were to appear twice on *Our World*, first in a ief five second slot for the opening credits, then on the main slot for exactly six minutes and 11 seconds. As they ran rough their number, it was clear everything had to be just ht. Although they had a pre-recorded a backing track, Paul's ss guitar, Ringo's drums, and the orchestra, were to be live,

along with the vocals. There was no room fo

When the time arrived for the broadcas George, and Paul all sat on high stools, with his drum kit, surrounded by a large group of were sitting on the floor. There was a party a with balloons and placards painted with slo "All You Need Is Love", "Love, Love, Love", a You Need". The orchestral musicians wore f dress, while The Beatles' friends and relativ hippie-style clothes.

Above: *(Left to right) Paul McCartney, John Lennon, Ringo Starr, and George Harrison during their performance of "All You Need Is Love" on the "Our World" satellite link-up.*

Right: *Paul McCartney (left) and John Lennon (right) during The Beatles' performance of "All You Need Is Love" on the "Our World" satellite link up.*

This spread: *Paul McCartney, John Lennon, Ringo Starr, and George Harrison pictured in 1967 holding signs that read "All you need is love" in four different languages.*

Among the crowd were Rolling Stones Mick Jagger and Keith Richards, Marianne Faithfull, Eric Clapton, Pattie Harrison, Keith Moon, Jane Asher, Mike McCartney, The Hollies' Graham Nash, and Beatles biographer Hunter Davies.

The session went exactly as planned, with no mistakes and the assembled guests singing along to the chorus perfectly. When the UK slot was over, the cameras were switched off and some of the crowd danced around the studio.

From its opening lines of "Love, love, love" to the closing fade-out, "Love is all you need", "All You Need Is Love" captured the mood of the times. Released with "Baby You're A Rich Man" on the flip side, a reference to the "beautiful people" and hippie trend-setters who hung out with The Beatles, the single shot to Number One in the charts around the world immediately after it was released.

But before *Sgt. Pepper* and "All You Need Is Love" were released, The Beatles had been back in the studio recording material for two new projects.

The first was an idea dreamed up by Paul McCartney during a trip to America in April 1967.

> ***"All You Need Is Love" Facts***
> **B-side:** "Baby You're A Rich Man"
> **Recorded:** June 14, 23 – 25, 1967
> **Released:** July 7, 1967 (UK),
> July 17, 1967 (US)
> **Label:** Parlophone (UK), Capitol (US)
> **Writers:** Lennnon/McCartney
> **Producer:** George Martin
> **Chart Success:** UK No. 1, US No. 1

Above: *Paul McCartney (5th from right) pictured during the filming of "Magical Mystery Tour" in September 1967.*

Left: *The "Magical Mystery Tour" bus stuck on a bridge in Dartmoor, England, September 1967.*

Above: *(Left to right) John Lennon, Paul McCartney, George Harrison, and Ringo Starr pictured at Plymouth Hoe, England, in September 1967, during the filming of "Magical Mystery Tour".*

His plan was for an hour-long television film, directed by the group, for which The Beatles would hire a bus, fill it with actors, friends, and family as extras, and drive around the English countryside with a camera crew. Each Beatle would think up scenes to stage, for which they would write some lines, while leaving plenty of room for ad-lib improvisation. There would also be slots for the band to play their latest songs. Paul had already written the title song before he put the idea to John, George, and Ringo. The film was to be called *Magical Mystery Tour*, and Paul's early notes detailed scenes

with a stripper, one set in a laboratory, and another in an army recruiting station. He also suggested a cast list that included a driver, a "small man," and "a fat woman." Before filming started, The Beatles began recording music for the project, starting with the title song.

At the same time, through May and early June of 1967, The Beatles recorded material for the soundtrack of the second new project, a cartoon feature film called *Yellow Submarine*, which was to go into production later that year. Although none of the band was particularly interested in the

Above: *An Italian film poster advertising The Beatles' film "Yellow Submarine", which was released in 1968.*

project, which was being produced without their direct involvement, they put aside some new songs for the movie.

Brian Epstein had little involvement in these new activities, particularly the proposed *Magical Mystery Tour*. Since the band had given up touring the previous year, there were no dates for him to fix, agents to deal with, or on-the-road press conferences to arrange. In the recording studio, The Beatles had assumed almost total control over what they were doing. George Martin played his part in the production room, but Brian's influence in that area had been small since the days of "Love Me Do" and "Please Please Me". On one occasion, when Brian offered an opinion on something going on in the studio, John Lennon replied, "We'll look after the music Brian, you look after the accounts." Both Epstein and The Beatles had grown up since the days of the Cavern lunchtime sessions, one-night stands in dusty dance halls, and early evening spots on local television. The Beatles and their manager were still close friends and Brian shared the bands enthusiasm for all the trappings of the new pop culture—the drugs and "good vibrations" of 1967 "flower power"—but the four Beatles were not reliant on him any more, a simple fact that Brian was increasingly aware of.

The "Summer of Love", was already well underway by the time the band finished in the studio and recorded "All You Need Is Love". "Peace and love" was the motto of the movement, but the new hippie culture wasn't only about feeling good. There was a growing interest among the young, especially in the United States, in Eastern ideas and religion, including Buddhism, Hinduism, and various forms of yoga and meditation.

Above: *(Left to right) John Lennon, George Harrison, and Paul McCartney, recording voices for "Yellow Submarine", July 1968.*

Top: *The Beatles and friends with the Maharishi Mahesh Yogi, September 4, 1967. (Left to right) Paul McCartney, Jane Asher, Patti Harrison, Ringo Starr, Ringo's wife Maureen, John Lennon, George Harrison, and Maharishi Mahesh Yogi.*

Above Left: *(Left to right) Paul McCartney, George Harrison, and John Lennon, backstage with the Maharishi Mahesh Yogi after a lecture on transcendental meditation at the Hilton Hotel, London, August 25, 1967.*

Above Right: *Paul McCartney and his girlfriend Jane Asher leave a transcendental meditation course in Bangor, North Wales, after hearing of the death of The Beatles' manager, Brian Epstein.*

It was no surprise that George Harrison, whose interest in Indian music had been reflected in every Beatles album since *Rubber Soul*, was part of the trend. Just as his fellow Beatles had accepted George's Indian instruments in their recordings, so all three now followed him in exploring ideas from the East.

Harrison had become interested in the teachings of an Indian guru who was visiting Britain. The Maharishi Mahesh Yogi already had a following in America and elsewhere in the Western world. The four Beatles met the guru in August, and he told them of his method of Transcendental Meditation. A famous photograph taken at the time pictures The Beatles, Cynthia Lennon, Maureen Starkey, Pattie Harrison, and Jane Asher, plus Paul's brother Mike, sitting at the Maharishi's feet.

Intrigued by the guru's teachings, George and the other Beatles arranged to go to a seminar he had organized in the North Wales town of Bangor. However, any peace they might have found was shattered by news that arrived while they were there. On August 27, 1967, Brian Epstein died.

DID YOU KNOW?

John and Paul both wrote songs for the Our World program, for which John's "All You Need Is Love" was chosen. It was rumored that Paul's submission was "Your Mother Should Know".

Above: *John Lennon and his wife Cynthia arrive at the memorial service of The Beatles' manager, Brian Epstein.*

Chapter 17: Dark Days 1967-1968

Brian Epstein, who had been The Beatles' manager and mentor since the beginning of 1962, was found dead at his London home at 24 Chapel Street, Belgravia. His death was ruled "accidental suicide" from an overdose of barbiturates by a coroner. On learning the news, John, Paul, George, and Ringo were stunned, and when interviewed by reporters at the meditation seminar in Bangor, Lennon and Harrison, with tears in their eyes, could only repeat what the Maharishi had told them about the human soul moving on after death. Away from the cameras, The Beatles went into a state of near panic, sensing this could mean the end of them as a group. "The Beatles were finished when Eppy died," John Lennon later recalled. "I knew, deep inside me, that that was it. Without him, we'd had it."

Brian Epstein's funeral was held in Liverpool on August 30, 1967. It was attended by close family members only, with none of The Beatles present. Six weeks later, on October 17, all four Beatles attended a memorial service, at the New London Synagogue.

Unable to face the issue of how to replace Epstein or, indeed, whether to replace him at all, the band threw themselves into the *Magical Mystery Tour* project, for which they had, so far, only recorded two songs. Filming for the TV show was scheduled to begin on September 1, and they needed to have all the tracks finished and recorded by that date. The finished two were the title song, plus Paul's "nostalgia" number "Your Mother Should Know". The tracks still to be recorded included an instrumental named "Flying", Paul's "Fool On The Hill", a song written by George called "Blue Jay Way", and a track by John Lennon that would become a Beatles masterpiece. "I Am The Walrus" was full of

Right: *Three of The Beatles—(left to right) Ringo Starr, George Harrison, and John Lennon—in Bangor, North Wales. The band had just heard that Brian Epstein had died.*

the nonsense lyrics that had reviewers and fans looking for hidden meanings when there were none, and ended with the old British playground rhyme, "Oompah, oompah, stick it up your jumper," as well as the sound of radio being tuned across various stations.

The filming of *Magical Mystery Tour* was not as straightforward as recording the songs, however. None of the band had any experience of directing a film, and trying to do so with a bus full of people traveling across southern England was a recipe for disaster. There was no formal script, or any other of the detailed plans that usually go into making a film. Apart from friends and relatives, the

Left: *This page, from one of John Lennon's schoolbooks, was an influence on the song "I am the Walrus".*

Above: *Paul McCartney emerges from the "Magical Mystery Tour" bus to sign autographs in September 1967.*

Left: *John Lennon beside a swimming pool in Newquay, England, during the filming of "Magical Mystery Tour", September 1967.*

Above: *George Harrison pulls a funny face during the filming of "Magical Mystery Tour" in September 1967.*

cast consisted of actors and actresses picked almost at random from the pages of *Spotlight*, the annual UK catalog of available talent. There was no proper film crew either, just three cameramen. The choice of locations, in the English West Country of Devon and Cornwall, was based solely on the fact that Paul and George had once visited them on a hitchhiking holiday, in 1957. And filming in country locations wasn't always easy: on one occasion, the bus became stuck because no-one had thought to check that a tiny bridge over a stream was wide enough for it to drive over.

All four Beatles directed different sections of the film with varying degrees of success. One of John's was called "Happy Nat the Rubber Man" and featured the UK comic actor Nat Jackley chasing a bikini-clad girl around the pool of the hotel where they were staying. Ringo took part in an ad-lib sequence in which he and his "aunt" have a furious argument, while George's scene was of himself meditating, wearing a jacket that was far too big, in a cornfield.

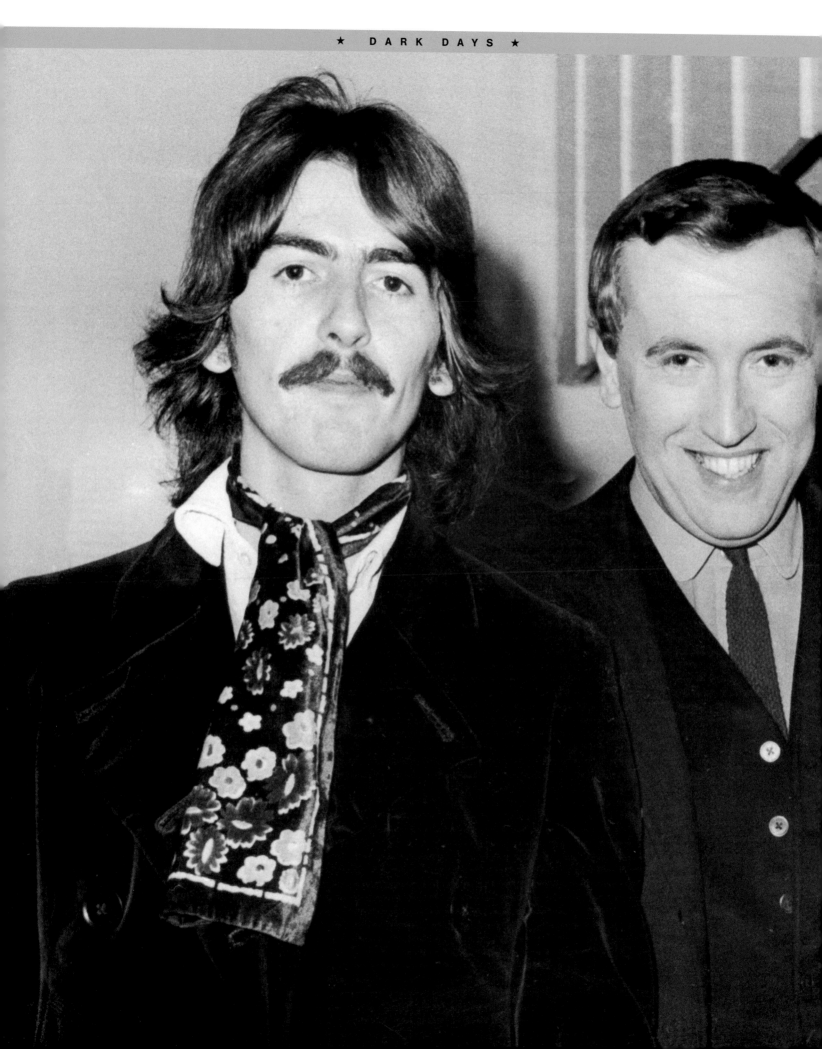

This spread: *John Lennon and George Harrison pictured during a 1967 television appearance with British interviewer David Frost.*

It was planned that the "indoor" scenes would be shot at the famous Shepperton film studios, just outside London, but, again, The Beatle's lack of foresight became obvious. They failed to book the studio facility and couldn't get a place there. Instead, the band hired West Malling Air Station for a week. This was a large deserted air base, to the south-east of London, that had been used during World War II as a base for the United States Army Air Force. Within its grounds were a number of huge concrete walls that had been built to protect planes on the ground from enemy bombs. It was in front, and on top, of one of these walls that The Beatles filmed the "I Am The Walrus" sequence. For most of the indoor scenes they used an empty aircraft hangar at West Malling.

These scenes included moments such as the "magician's laboratory" sequence, "Aunt Jessie's Dream" (in which John shoveled piles of spaghetti onto Jessie's dining table), George's "Blue Jay Way" scene in swirling fog, and the spectacular "Your Mother Should Know" ballroom

Below: *The Beatles (left to right, Ringo Starr, Paul McCartney, John Lennon, George Harrison) perform "I am the Walrus" at West Malling, England, September 24, 1967.*

finale. This sequence had all four Beatles in white suits and shoes, walking down a glistening staircase while over 150 professional ballroom dancers floated around them. It was one scene in the film that could have easily gone wrong but, miraculously, didn't.

Although everyone on the bus had a good time, the resulting footage was often amateurish and disconnected, with only the song sequences holding the show together. After it was shown in the UK, on BBC Television on December 26, 1967, *Magical Mystery Tour* received bad reviews from critics, even the music writers most sympathetic to The Beatles, who usually thought the group could do no wrong.

To be fair though, the BBC had screened the film on a black and white channel, which didn't help. The whole point of many of the scenes was their color effects, and the film was never intended to be shown in black and white. Because of the bad press, and despite the fact that it had been watched by 15 million viewers in the UK, a million-dollar deal for American TV rights was dropped. In January 1968, too late in many respects, the BBC broadcast the film again on their new color channel, BBC 2.

Above: *Ringo Starr (2nd left) and Paul McCartney (2nd right) attend a party to launch "Magical Mystery Tour" on December 22, 1967. With them are Ringo's wife Maureen and Paul's girlfriend Jane Asher.*

Above Right: *John Lennon arrives at a fancy dress party to launch the "Magical Mystery Tour" film in December 1967.*

The music from *Magical Mystery Tour* was much more successful than the film. On November 27, 1967, "I Am The Walrus" was released as a single, as the flip side to "Hello Goodbye", and topped the charts in the US and UK. On the same day, Capitol Records in the USA released all the film's songs on one side of an album, the other side featuring all three singles from 1967. In Great Britain, *Magical Mystery Tour* was released as a double EP: two 7-inch discs that featured only the film material without the previously released singles. Both formats immediately went to Number One in their respective charts.

A song that wasn't featured in *Magical Mystery Tour* was "Hello Goodbye", though it had been released as a single alongside "I Am The Walrus". With no footage available to help promote the track, on November 10, the group assembled on the stage of London's Saville Theatre to shoot a short film. In front of an empty auditorium, they shot enough material for three different clips. The first had the band in their *Sgt. Pepper* uniforms (the only time they had worn them since the cover photograph in March), against a psychedelic backdrop and surrounded by dancing girls in Hawaiin-style grass skirts. The second featured The Beatles in normal clothes against a rural background, but still with the "Hawaiian" dancing girls. The third was a mixture of outtakes from the first two clips, with some extra shots of John dancing the twist.

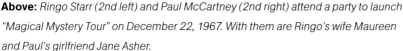

"Hello Goodbye" Facts
B-side: "I Am The Walrus"
Recorded: October 2, 19 – 20, 25, November 2, 1967
Released: November 24, 1967 (UK), November 27, 1967 (US)
Label: Parlophone (UK), Capitol (US)
Writers: Lennnon/McCartney
Producer: George Martin
Chart Success: UK No. 1, US No. 1

This spread: *George Harrison and John Lennon, sporting Indian attire, with Mike Love of the Beach Boys, stroll happily through a street in Shankaracharyyanagar, India in February 1968.*

All three were directed by Paul McCartney, and the first to be seen in the USA was the clip with the band in Sgt. Pepper outfits, which was aired on the *Ed Sullivan Show* on November 26, 1967. None were shown in the UK, because the Musicians Union banned miming on film. Oddly, this meant that The Beatles could make promotional films in which the band didn't pretend to play, as for the famous "Paperback Writer" and "Strawberry Fields" clips, but not miming to their own records.

In mid February 1968, John and Cynthia Lennon joined George and Pattie Harrison on a trip to Rishikesh in Northern India, in order to continue their meditation studies at a three-month long "guide course" with the Maharishi at his Shivananada Ashram center. Also at the camp were the American actress Mia Farrow, her sister Prudence, British folk-rock singer Donovan, and Mike Love of The Beach Boys. The Lennons and Harrisons were joined few days later by

Ringo and his wife Maureen, Paul, and Jane Asher. The trip brought The Beatles association with The Maharishi to an abrupt end, however. Ringo was the first to leave, after just 11 days, complaining about the food and saying it was "Just like Butlins" (the UK family holiday camps where he played, before his Beatle days, with Rory Storm and The Hurricanes).

The other Beatles stayed a few weeks longer but left suddenly, on John Lennon's insistence, after the Maharishi was suspected of making advances to Mia Farrow. Nevertheless, despite their suspicions about the guru, The Beatles continued to say publicly how beneficial they found meditation, and George Harrison would follow a similar path for the rest of his life. While they may not have found the peace they were seeking, the India trip had been productive for The Beatles. The band returned with a number of new songs that would form the basis of *The Beatles*, a double-disc album that they began recording in May 1968.

Above: *John Lennon (left) and George Harrison (center) leave Heathrow Airport, on February 15, 1968, for two months of transcendental meditation at Rishikesh, in the Himalayas, with the Maharishi Mahesh Yogi. Accompanying them are their wives Cynthia (2nd left) and Patti (right), as well as Patti's younger sister Jenny (2nd right).*

"Lady Madonna" Facts

B-side: "The Inner Light"
Recorded: February 3,6, 1968
Released: March 15, 1968 (UK),
March 18, 1968 (US)
Label: Parlophone (UK), Capitol (US)
Writers: Lennnon/McCartney
(B-side, Harrison)
Producer: George Martin
Chart Success: UK No. 1, US No. 4

Soon after their return from India, a new Beatles single was released. Recorded just before they had left for Rishikesh in February 1968, "Lady Madonna" hit the shops in the middle of March. A boogie-style track written by Paul, it featured an Indian-influenced song of George's on the B-side, "The Inner Light".

Above: *The Beatles and their wives at Rishikesh in India with the Maharishi Mahesh Yogi, March 1968. (Ringo Starr, front row 3rd left, Paul McCartney, front row center left, George Harrison, front row center right, John Lennon, front row 3rd right.)*

Above: *(Left to right) unknown, John Lennon, Mike Love of The Beach Boys, Mahareshi Mahesh Yogi, George Harrison, Mia Farrow, unknown, Donovan, Paul McCartney, Jane Asher, and unknown at the Rishikesh in India, March 1968.*

DID YOU KNOW?
"The Inner Light", the B-side to "Lady Madonna", was the first George Harrison composition to feature on a Beatles single.

Magical Mystery Tour Facts

Recorded: December 6, 1966 – April 21, 1967
Released: November 27, 1967 (US), November 19, 1976 (UK), six-track double EP comprising all of Side 1, December 6, 1967 (UK)
Label: Parlophone (UK), Capitol (US)
Writers: Lennon/McCartney (except songwriters as noted below)
Producer: George Martin
Chart Success: US No. 1, EP version UK No. 2 (singles chart)

Track-By-Track
Side 1

Magical Mystery Tour (2.48)
There are echoes of "Penny Lane" and "Lovely Rita" on the opening track, which features three trumpets and Paul playing piano.

The Fool On The Hill (3.00)
Paul backs his own vocals on piano, recorder, and flute.

Flying (2.16) (Lennon/McCartney/Harrison/Starkey)
The only track ever to be composed by all four Beatles, and the only instrumental track the band recorded after "Cry For A Shadow" from their Hamburg days.

Blue Jay Way (3.50) (George Harrison)
George's song is based on the story of The Beatles' publicist Derek Taylor getting lost in fog in Los Angeles, while trying to find Blue Jay Way, where George was staying.

Your Mother Should Know (2.33)
Another Paul song in the old-fashioned style of "When I'm Sixty-Four".

I Am The Walrus (4.35)
Often thought of as John Lennon's masterpiece, this track was inspired by his admiration for writer Lewis Carroll, and harked back to the nonsense verses John had written since his schooldays. The lyrics are pure nonsense, written to confuse all those who were looking for deep meanings in everything he wrote.

Side 2

Hello Goodbye (3.24)
Released as a single with "I Am The Walrus," at the same time as *Magical Mystery Tour* album came out.

Strawberry Fields Forever (4.05)
Along with its B-side "Penny Lane", this track has been named by numerous critics as the greatest pop single of all time. Strawberry Fields was a Salvation Army orphanage close by where John grew up in Liverpool.

Penny Lane (3.00)
Paul's song reflects on the Liverpool he grew up in, and features contributions from John, who also lived near Penny Lane.

Baby You're A Rich Man (3.07)
Like "A Day In The Life," this track was, in fact, two songs joined together: Paul's "Baby You're A Rich Man", and John's "Beautiful People".

All You Need Is Love (3.57)
First heard during the *Our World* worldwide TV broadcast for which it was recorded live, the international flavor of the show was underlined by using snippets of the French national anthem, the old English ballad "Greensleeves", and Glenn Miller's US wartime favorite "In The Mood".

Above: *(Left to right) John Lennon, George Harrison, Ringo Starr, and Paul McCartney on the tour bus, during the filming of "Magical Mystery Tour" in September 1967.*

Left: *The rear end of the "Magical Mystery Tour" bus.*

Chapter 18: The Beatles-1968

With The Beatles back from India by March 1968, the band began work on a new business venture. They had recently announced the formation of a new record label, which would be the label for all their new releases, though still a part of the giant EMI company. At the end of April, the new enterprise, called Apple Corps Ltd, set up offices in London and began operations. To launch Apple, John and Paul flew to New York to appear on television talk shows, saying that their new company would not just be their own record label, but a production outlet for all sorts of creative ventures. Through Apple, The Beatles intended to sign musical artists and fund projects in other branches of the arts.

DID YOU KNOW?
The first Apple business meeting to be held in the United States, on May 12, 1968, was on board a Chinese "junk" boat, sailing around the Statue of Liberty.

Right (main picture): *John Lennon (front left) and Paul McCartney (behind, 2nd left) pictured at the Apple headquarters with Apple employees in 1968.*

Right: *John Lennon (left) and Paul McCartney (right) at London Airport on May 16, 1968, after a trip to the US to promote The Beatles' new company, Apple Corps.*

Left: *(Left to right) Paul McCartney, Mary Hopkin, and arranger Richard Newson pictured with the Aida Foster Children's Choir recording Hopkin's song "Those Were the Days" for the Apple label, July 26, 1968.*

Above: *Paul McCartney in the Apple offices with Mary Hopkin. Hopkin is holding a copy of her debut album, "Post Card", which was produced by McCartney.*

Above: *The 40-foot psychedelic mural on the wall of the Apple boutique, which was opened by The Beatles on Baker Street in London.*

Many of the projects that Apple funded were short-lived and lost The Beatles large sums of money. Some of the artists they supported were sincere hopefuls, while others were opportunists, or even con men. On the musical side, a world The Beatles understood, things went better. Over the next two years they signed an amazing variety of artists, including the American singer-songwriter James Taylor, Liverpool vocalist Jackie Lomax, a world-famous jazz outfit called the Modern Jazz Quartet, and US soul musicians Billy Preston and Doris Troy.

In terms of sales, Apple's biggest success came in August 1968, with the Welsh folk singer Mary Hopkin. Her debut single, "Those Were The Days My Friend", which was produced by Paul McCartney, went to the top of the UK charts and made Number Two in the American *Billboard* list. It eventually sold four million copies worldwide.

The biggest disaster for Apple was the store they opened in London's Baker Street in early December 1967. The idea was to sell trendy items; Paul McCartney described it as "a beautiful place where beautiful people can buy beautiful things." In reality, though, it was a clothes store, and became known as the "Apple Boutique". Decorated inside and out with swirling psychedelic designs, the store was managed by John's old friend from the Quarry Men, Pete Shotton, and George Harrison's sister-in-law, Jenny Boyd. The Apple Boutique was a very laid-back place to work, an attitude that led to members of staff helping themselves to goods, as well as a large amount of shoplifting. By the middle of 1968, the shop had made a loss of nearly $500,000/£250,000, a fortune in those days and, on July 30, it closed.

Above: *Crowds gather outside the Apple boutique to witness its last day of business before finally closing in July 1968.*

Above: *George Harrison (left) with Brian Jones (center) of The Rolling Stones and Brian's girlfriend Anita Pallenberg (right) at George's house in Esher, Surrey, England in 1968.*

The next day staff were told that they could give away all remaining stock, on the basis of one item per person. Hundreds of people arrived to claim their free gift from The Beatles, and the police were called to keep order. The store was emptied within a couple of hours and even the shelves and the rugs on the floor were taken. The next day, the *Daily Mail* newspaper quoted Paul McCartney as saying, "We always make our mistakes in public."

Meanwhile, The Beatles forged ahead with the new material they had written in India. Work began in May 1968, when the band gathered at George's home in Esher, Surrey, to rehearse and make test "demo" discs of 23 new Lennon, McCartney, and Harrison songs, as well as one that Ringo had written that the rest of the band thought good enough to record.

At the end of May, they took the demos to Abbey Road and began professional recording sessions, which continued until October, when 33 new songs were completed.

During the sessions, it became increasingly clear that The Beatles had now begun to make music as individuals instead of as a group. John arrived at the studios to record one of "his" songs, as did Paul and George. Sometimes, one Beatle would be working on a song in one Abbey Road studio while another Beatle was down the corridor working on another song. Although the band members worked together when necessary, many tracks did not even feature all four members of the band. Since *Revolver*, it had become obvious that particular songs were Paul's, or John's, or George's, but now the separation seemed more complete. During lengthy sessions through the summer of 1968, tensions within the band, which had been mounting since the death of Brian Epstein, surfaced again and again. There were frequent disagreements over the way certain songs should be recorded, to the point that an Abbey Road engineer, Geoff Emerick, who had been on George Martin's team since *Revolver*, resigned because of the "poisonous" atmosphere. The situation became so bad that Ringo Starr walked out, on August 22, convinced he wasn't needed in The Beatles any longer. In many ways, he was right; for the two weeks that Ringo was absent, Paul played the drums on various tracks.

Nevertheless, the group persuaded Ringo to return by September 4, in time to make a promotional film for the next single, "Hey Jude", which they had recorded at the end of July.

When it was released at the end of August, "Hey Jude" and its flipside, "Revolution", hinted at a new direction in The Beatles' music. Gone were the special effects and electronic trickery of their recent releases. Apart from some minor orchestral parts in "Hey Jude",

Right: *Paul McCartney with British pop singer Cilla Black in a recording studio, January 1968. McCartney had written the song "Step Inside Love", which was to be the theme song for Black's new television show.*

The Beatles recorded the songs as a straight rock band, a hint of what was to come on the new album, which was due out in November. The single eventually sold over six million copies worldwide, becoming the biggest hit of The Beatles' career. On September 14, less than three weeks after its release, *New Musical Express* in the UK reported that gross sales figures had topped two million dollars.

Despite the tensions in the studio, "Hey Jude" was one of the most memorable of The Beatles' songs. At seven minutes,

Below: *Cynthia Lennon outside the Royal Courts of Justice, in London, where she was starting divorce proceedings against John, November 8, 1968:.*

"Hey Jude" Facts

B-side: "Revolution"
Recorded: July 31, August 1, 1968
Released: August 30, 1968 (UK),
August 26, 1968 (US)
Label: Apple (UK), Capitol (US)
Writers: Lennon/McCartney
Producer: George Martin
Chart Success: UK No. 1, US No. 1

Right: *(Left to right) Eric Clapton, John Lennon, Julian Lennon, Yoko Ono, and Brian Jones of The Rolling Stones at a press conference at Internel Studios in Stonebridge Park, Wembley, England, for The Rolling Stones' "Rock & Roll Circus" project.*

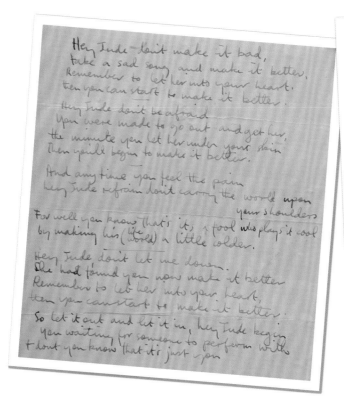

Above: *The lyrics for "Hey Jude", handwritten in 1968 by Paul McCartney.*

Above: *John Lennon behind a tape recorder with a cup of tea at the Apple Recording Studio, Saville Row, England, in 1969.*

it ran longer than any other single or album track by the group, with the catchy "nah nah nah nah-nah-nah naa-naaaah" ending lasting a full four minutes. "Revolution" was a John Lennon track that addressed politics in a way The Beatles had never done before. 1968 had seen student demonstrations spill onto streets around the world. Although John agreed with many of the students' aims and, like them, was especially opposed to the Vietnam War, the song was a warning against violent protest.

Paul McCartney wrote "Hey Jude" as a message to five-year-old Julian Lennon. At the time, the young lad was having to deal with his parent's separation, prompting Paul to write lines such as, "take a sad song and make it better". In May 1968, John Lennon and Yoko Ono had finally become partners, and Cynthia had left her husband after returning from a holiday to find the couple together in her home.

John and Yoko became inseparable and made the first of several experimental albums together, *Unfinished Music No 1:*

Two Virgins, which was released on Apple and featured a naked photograph of the couple on its cover. The album appeared on November 11, just three days after John and Cynthia's divorce was granted. Cynthia would later admit, "John had at last found his soul mate. Yoko did not take John away from me, because he had never been mine. He had always been his own man and had always done his own thing, as I had learned to do."

On July 17, 1968, John, Paul, and George attended the British premiere of the animated cartoon film *Yellow Submarine*. Although one of John's ideas, the four Beatles had little involvement in the movie's production, except for contributing the soundtrack songs and appearing briefly in a cameo sequence at the end of the movie. The band's voices were all provided by actors. Spectacular to look at, the movie's animated graphics were in the "psychedelic" style of the time.

The soundtrack album, not released until January 1969, had one side of Beatles' songs with the other featuring George Martin's orchestral arrangements. Despite the small number of actual Beatles' tracks, the album reached Number Three in the UK album charts, and Number Two in the US.
The *Yellow Submarine* movie did not appear in America until November 13, 1968, and was eclipsed by the release, two weeks later, of the long-awaited new Beatles' album. Called *The Beatles*, the double-disc collection arrived in a plain white cover, in total contrast to their previous album, *Sgt Pepper*. The record quickly became known as the "White Album" by fans, and came with a poster-collage by the famous UK artist Richard Hamilton, who had also provided the idea for the sleeve, as well as four individual photo portraits of the group.

Like "Hey Jude" and "Revolution", the other songs on *The Beatles* took a simple "no-frills" approach and reactions to the album were mixed. It had been 18 months since the release of *Sgt. Pepper*, and the new album had been much anticipated. Many fans and reviewers felt that some of the songs had an "unfinished" feel, and even George Martin would later admit that he would have preferred only half the songs on it to be released as a single album. However, despite the views of some, *The Beatles* didn't disappoint in terms of sales. As was normal for a Beatles album of completely new tracks, it topped the charts worldwide.

Top Right: *George Harrison and his wife, Patti, arrive at the London Pavilion for the world premiere of "Yellow Submarine", in July 1968.*

Above Right: *(Left to right) Paul McCartney, Ringo Starr, and George Harrison, hold a cardboard picture of John Lennon at the premiere of "Yellow Submarine" in July 1968.*

Left: *(Left to right) Yoko Ono, John Lennon, and Paul McCartney at the premiere of "Yellow Submarine", at the London Pavilion, in July 1968. John and Paul are holding apples, the symbol of their newly formed company, Apple Corps.*

Below: *George Harrison with a Blue Meanie at the press screening of "Yellow Submarine".*

Buttons: *A set of pin-backed buttons promoting "Yellow Submarine" and featuring cartoon versions of The Beatles. (Clockwise from the top, Paul McCartney, Ringo Starr, John Lennon, and George Harrison.)*

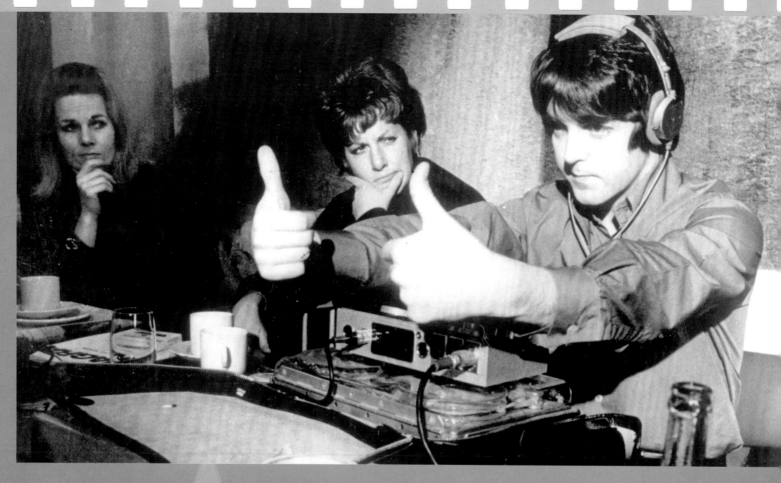

Above: *Paul McCartney gives the thumbs up during production of The Beatles' movie "Yellow Submarine", February 1, 1968.*

Yellow Submarine Movie Facts

Directed: George Dunning
Dennis Abey (live action sequence)
Produced: Al Brodax
Written: Lee Minoff, Al Brodax, Jack Mendelsohn, Erich Segal
Music: The Beatles, George Martin
Cinematography: John Williams
Edited: Brian J. Bishop
Distributed: United Artists

Released: July 17, 1968 (UK), November 13, 1968 (US)
Running Time: 90 minutes
Budget: $500,000/£250,000
Gross Revenue: Not available

Principal Voices
John – John Clive
Paul – Geoffrey Hughes
George – Peter Batten, Paul Angelis
Ringo – Paul Angelis
Old Fred, Young Fred – Lance Percival
Lord Mayor, Nowhere Man – Dick Emery

Above: *An image from "Yellow Submarine", directed by George Dunning and Dennis Abey.*

Above: *A poster advertising The Beatles' film "Yellow Submarine".*

Plot

The Blue Meanies have taken over Pepperland, draining it of all its color and music, firing anti-music missiles, hitting people with green apples, and turning the inhabitants to stone with the pointed finger of a giant white glove. The only survivor, the Lord Admiral, escapes in the Yellow Submarine and goes to Liverpool to enlist the help of The Beatles. After traveling through strange worlds, including the Sea of Time, Sea of Monsters, and Sea of Green, and meeting various bizarre characters on the way, The Beatles, armed only with music, love, and witty remarks, drive out the Blue Meanies and restore Pepperland to tranquility.

In the live sequence at the end, the real Beatles, having returned home, show off their souvenirs. George has the submarine's motor, Paul has "a little love," and Ringo still has half a hole in his pocket. John sees "newer and bluer Meanies within the vicinity of this theater," and announces that there is only one way to go out: "Singing!"

The Beatles Facts

Recorded: May 30 – October 14, 1968
Released: November 22, 1968 (UK),
November 25, 1968 (US)
Label: Apple (UK), Capitol (US)
Writers: Lennon/McCartney (except as noted)
Producer: George Martin
Chart Success: UK No. 1, US No. 1

Track-By-Track
Side 1
Back In The U.S.S.R. (2.45)
Heavily influenced by both Chuck Berry's "Back In The USA" and
the music of The Beach Boys, this track was a great
rock 'n' roll number with which to open the two-disc package.
Dear Prudence (4.00)
A song dedicated to Prudence Farrow, sister of the actress Mia
Farrow, who was in India at the same time as The Beatles.
Glass Onion (2.10)
This track features nonsensical John Lennon lyrics that refer to
other songs, including "Strawberry Fields", "Lady Madonna", and
'I Am The Walrus".
Ob-La-Di, Ob-La-Da (3.10)
Taken from a Nigerian phrase meaning "life goes on", this
reggae-style song, written by Paul, was later covered by the
Scottish group Marmalade, who had a UK chart topper with it.
Wild Honey Pie (1.02)
Paul McCartney was totally solo on this track, playing guitar and
drums, as well as singing all the vocals.
The Continuing Story Of Bungalow Bill (3.05)
A catchy, sing-along, track that has vocal contributions from
Yoko Ono and Ringo's wife, Maureen.
While My Guitar Gently Weeps (4.46) (George Harrison)
One of George Harrison's most memorable tracks, lead guitar
was played by his friend Eric Clapton.

Happiness Is A Warm Gun (2.47)
John's title for this track came to him after George Martin
showed him an advertisement in a gun magazine.

Side 2
Martha My Dear (2.28)
Paul was again influenced by older styles of pop music for this
track, which was named for his Old English Sheepdog, Martha.
I'm So Tired (2.01)
Written by John about Yoko Ono, this track has a similar theme
to "I'm Only Sleeping" on Revolver.
Blackbird (2.20)
Another solo performance from Paul.
Piggies (George Harrison) (2.04)
In a similar style to "Taxman" on *Revolver*, George hits out at
greedy people making money from The Beatles.
Rocky Racoon (3.33)
Written by Paul while The Beatles were in India, this track was
about a drunken doctor who had treated him there.

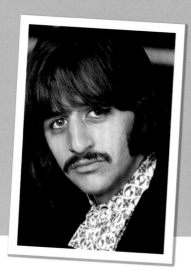

Don't Pass Me By (3.52) (Starkey)

Written years earlier, in 1963, this was the first time a Ringo-only composition featured on a Beatles album. George Harrison plays a violin on the track, which was another first.

Why Don't We Do It In The Road? (1.42)

Another solo track from Paul, who played guitar, bass guitar, piano, and drums, as well as singing.

I Will (1.46)

A short track with Paul, again, doing most of the work, though this time with Ringo on drums, bongos, and maracas.

Julia (2.57)

This beautiful song, dedicated to John's dead mother, features Lennon playing solo.

Side 3

Birthday (2.40)

The only song on the entire double album co-written by John and Paul, "Birthday" was written for George's wife, Patti, and has Patti and Yoko Ono on backing vocals.

Yer Blues (4.01)

John Lennon parodies the late-Sixties boom in blues music that swept the UK.

Mother Nature's Son (2.46)

Paul, and assorted session musicians, praise life in the country.

Everybody's Got Something To Hide Except Me And My Monkey (2.25)

This track was a bitter response from John to a cartoon drawing that showed Yoko as a monkey on his back, draining him of talent.

Sexy Sadie (3.15)

A Lennon song about the Maharishi, who had shocked the band when he made a pass at Mia Farrow.

Helter Skelter (4.30)

This track is one of the wildest "jam sessions" The Beatles ever put out on record, and features John playing saxophone. The recording was originally 25 minutes long, and would have covered a whole side of an album.

Long, Long, Long (3.08) (George Harrison)

A dirge-like, slow number from George, that is said to have been inspired by Bob Dylan's "Sad Eyed Lady Of The Lowlands".

Side 4

Revolution 1 (4.13)

An almost acoustic, slower, version of the "Hey Jude" B-side, in which John reflects on the violent protest that swept the western world in 1968.

Honey Pie (2.42)

A 15-piece band accompanies Paul McCartney on a track that was influenced by the music of the Twenties and Thirties.

Savoy Truffle (2.55) (George Harrison)

Written by George, this track was dedicated to his friend Eric Clapton and is about his love of desserts and candy.

Cry Baby Cry (2.34)

John worked on this song in India with the UK folk-rock singer Donovan. It has a fairytale quality, similar to "Lucy In The Sky With Diamonds", and was partly inspired by the children's nursery rhyme, "Sing A Song Of Sixpence".

Revolution 9 (8.15)

The nearest a Beatles track gets to the kind of experiment in noise that John and Yoko had been trying. Paul didn't want to include it; not because he didn't approve but because he had been interested in similar things for some years and felt he should have been involved.

Good Night (3.14)

A Ringo "solo" track, on which he was accompanied by a 30-piece orchestra, harp, and choir.

This Spread: *Portraits of The Beatles (clockwise from top left, John Lennon, Paul McCartney, George Harrison, Ringo Starr) from the artwork of "The Beatles", commonly known as the "White Album".*

Yellow Submarine Facts

Recorded: May 12, 1967 –February 11, 1968
October 22 – 23,1968 (George Martin Orchestra)
Released: January 17, 1969 (UK),
January 13, 1969 (US)
Label: Apple (UK), Capitol (US)
Writers: Lennon/McCartney (except as noted)
Producer: George Martin
Chart Success: UK No. 3, US No. 2

Track-By-Track
Side 1
Yellow Submarine (2.40)
Already released on *Revolver*, and as a single, "Yellow Submarine" serves here as the title track of the movie.
Only A Northern Song (3.23) (George Harrison)
George wasn't pleased at having to write a song for the movie, and made his feelings clear on this track about The Beatles' publishing company, Northern Songs.
All Together Now (2.08)
Paul, like the rest of The Beatles, resented having to come up with new songs for the movie, and this track was recorded in just six hours.
Hey Bulldog (3.09)
Originally, this track mentioned a bullfrog in the lyrics, but as Paul was barking like a dog during the warm-up to recording it, the band decided to call it "Hey Bulldog" instead.
It's All Too Much (6.27) (George Harrison)
A long track by Beatles standards, this was not recorded for the *Yellow Submarine* project, but was passed over to the movie to make up the number of tracks.
All You Need Is Love (3.47)
This is a different, and slightly longer, version of the song to the one recorded for the *Our World* TV show, though it has the same rhythm track as backing.

Side 2
Pepperland (Martin) (George Martin Orchestra)
Sea of Time (Martin) (George Martin Orchestra)
Sea of Holes (Martin) (George Martin Orchestra)
Sea of Monsters (Martin) (George Martin Orchestra)
March of the Meanies (Martin) (George Martin Orchestra)
Pepperland Laid Waste (Martin) (George Martin Orchestra)
Yellow Submarine in Pepperland (Lennon/McCartney) (George Martin Orchestra)

Left: *John Lennon and Yoko Ono at the Apple offices, Savile Row, England, in 1969.*

Below Left: *George Harrison (left) and Eric Clapton (right) performing in 1969.*

Below: *Paul McCartney at the Apple offices, Savile Row, England, in 1969.*

Chapter 19: Abbey Road -1969

When recording sessions for *The Beatles* came to an end in October 1968, the four Beatles began exploring projects of their own. With their own label, Apple, the band members found they were able to work outside of the group while seeming as united as ever, to the outside world, at least. John Lennon had been first to release a record on the Apple label, with his and Yoko's experimental album but, in December, George Harrison followed suit by releasing the soundtrack music he had recorded for a fantasy-psychedelic movie called *Wonderwall*. He had written it, he said, "as a mini-anthology of Indian music because I wanted to help turn the public on to Indian music." George also worked on an album of synthesized electronic music, called *Electronic Sound,* which he released in May 1969 on the Apple off-shoot label, Zapple. The only other Zapple release was John and Yoko's second experimental record, *Unfinished Music No. 2: Life With the Lions*, which also appeared in May 1969.

Right: *The Beatles perform their last live public concert on the rooftop of the Apple building.*

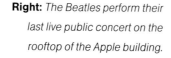

DID YOU KNOW?

The first concert appearance of a Beatle outside the group was n March 1969 when John Lennon played with Yoko Ono, at Cambridge University in England, for a recital of experimental music that became one side of their album *Unfinished Music No2: Life With The Lions*.

that premiered in New York in December 1968. The film had an all-star cast, including Marlon Brando and Richard Burton, but received bad reviews and was banned in several countries because of its X-rated content. In February 1969, Ringo took on another, bigger, role; this time alongside the famous British comedian-actor Peter Sellers in the movie *The Magic Christian*.

Only Paul McCartney, it seemed, had concerns about where The Beatles were going as a group. Missing the unity and sense of purpose of the band's early days, he suggested to his band mates that they stage a limited number of concerts. Paul said that though they had produced some amazing work in the studio, the process was very private, and in danger of becoming sterile. Playing to a live audience, he argued, might help give the band a new creative drive.

Ringo, meanwhile, had become interested in film acting. He'd already had a cameo role in *Candy*, a bizarre comedy

Above: *Paul McCartney leaves the Apple headquarters in his car in 1969.*

Left: *Ringo Starr (left) on the set of "The Magic Christian" with co-star Peter Sellers (right).*

The other Beatles were not enthusiastic, though George Harrison hinted in interviews he gave in September 1968 that the band might take over a concert venue and perform for a month or more. In October, Paul told reporters that once the group had finished work on *The Beatles*, they were going to work up some new songs and perform them live. There was even mention of a three-day charity event in December at London's Roundhouse venue. Nothing happened, however, and a new date was suggested for an event in January, at which The Beatles would film rehearsals of new material, then play a one-off concert in a spectacular location, which would also be filmed. Various places were suggested, including a Roman amphitheater in North Africa, the Sahara Desert, and a Mediterranean cruise liner. Director Michael Lindsay-Hogg, who had made the promotional clips for "Paperback Writer", "Rain", "Hey Jude", and "Revolution", was hired to work on the project.

On January 2, Lindsay-Hogg's crew began filming the band's rehearsals at Twickenham Film Studios, just west of London. The film, and the recording The Beatles made of the rehearsal, would later provide a unique record of the group's working methods. There was a huge amount of new material for them to run through since the last time they had played live and, between trying out songs from their final two albums, *Abbey Road* and *Let It Be*, The Beatles played old rock 'n' roll numbers.

It was still planned that the rehearsal footage would be followed by a live concert film, to be shown on television and, as the band chatted and joked between numbers, there was talk about the prospect of the concert. There were also tensions and arguments. On one occasion, on January 10, George Harrison walked out, not just from the session, but from The Beatles. For five days he was effectively no longer a Beatle.

Left:

Paul McCartney plays the drums in the Apple studio, in 1969, while US folk-rock singer Donovan claps along.

When the band got together to resolve the problems, George insisted on scrapping the idea of a live concert. Instead, he wanted the rehearsals at Twickenham to form the basis for a new album. The film now took on a new aspect; it would be a TV program about the making of a new Beatles album. The film crew moved to the new Apple Studios, which The Beatles had opened in the basement of their Savile Row headquarters and, over 10 days of sessions, most of the material that would become *Let It Be* was recorded. The group's idea for the new album was to get back to their roots, playing completely straight with no overdubbing or technical trickery. The proposed title for the album, at that stage, said it all. It would be called *Get Back*.

In order to "fill out" the sound a little, without the use of overdubs, George brought in Billy Preston to play keyboards on most of the sessions. The Beatles had known the American musician since 1962, when he was in Little Richard's band and shared the bill with them at the Star Club in Hamburg. Preston's presence seemed to calm some of the friction within the band, as George would later explain: "People behave nicely when you bring a guest in because they don't really want anybody to know that they are so bitchy. Straight away it just became a one hundred percent improvement in the vibe in the room."

So, it was as a five-piece group that The Beatles made their final "live" appearance, not in an exotic location as had been planned, but on the windswept roof of their Apple offices. It was January 29, 1969 and, as crowds watched from the street below in the crisp winter cold, The Beatles taped 45 minutes of live performance before they were ordered to stop by the police.

Above Left: *Yoko Ono and John Lennon share a quiet moment at a piano in the Apple Studio.*

Left: *Keyboard player Billy Preston, whose calming presence helped to ease the tensions between The Beatles during the recording of "Abbey Road".*

Right: *(Left to right) Yoko Ono, John Lennon, and George Harrison relax in the Apple offices.*

Two days later, the group were back in the basement studios to finish three more songs, after which they handed all the recordings over to George Martin and fellow producer Glyn Johns. The band wanted the finished songs mixed with chatter and snippets of jamming between the tracks but, though Johns presented a sequence in this style in March, the band eventually rejected it.

Plans for the album were still going ahead in April, when Apple released "Get Back" and "Don't Let Me Down" from the sessions as a single, claiming in advertisements that the recordings were "The Beatles As Nature Intended" and promising the *Get Back* album for the summer. The Beatles even had a cover picture taken by Angus McBean, the photographer who had shot the cover of their debut album, *Please Please Me*, with the group standing in exactly the same positions as on the 1963 sleeve, leaning over a balcony at the EMI London headquarters. However, The Beatles could not agree on final approval of Glyn Johns' sequence, though test pressings had been made and widely distributed in the record trade, and the project came to a halt for the rest of the year.

"Get Back" Facts

B-side: "Don't Let Me Down"
Recorded: January 30, 1969
Released: April 11, 1969 (UK),
May 5, 1969 (US)
Label: Apple (UK), Capitol (US)
Writers: Lennnon/McCartney
Producer: George Martin
Chart Success: UK No. 1, US No. 1

Above: *Paul McCartney puts a protective arm around his wife, Linda, as they struggle through crowds gathered outside Marylebone Register Office, following their marriage on March 12, 1969.*

Above: *John Lennon and Yoko Ono receive the press at their bedside in the Hilton Hotel, Amsterdam, March 1969.*

On March 12, 1969, Paul McCartney married Linda Eastman in a civil ceremony at Marylebone Registry Office in London. His former girlfriend Jane Asher had broken off their engagement the previous July.

Eight days later, John Lennon and Yoko Ono also got married. After the ceremony in Gibraltar, they flew to Amsterdam to stage the first of their famous "Bed-Ins". As part of their campaign for world peace, the two stayed in bed, in Room 902 of the Hilton Hotel, for one week, and invited journalists to conduct bedside interviews. "When we got married," John explained later, "we knew our honeymoon was going to be public anyway, so we decided to make a statement. We sat in bed and talked to reporters for seven days. It was hilarious."

On April 1, the couple staged another "happening", this time appearing before the press in Vienna, Austria, inside a large bag. Then, on May 26, John, who had now officially changed his name to John Ono Lennon, and Yoko held another "Bed-In", at the Hotel La Reine Elizabeth in Montreal, Canada.

John and Yoko's peace campaigning didn't stop at publicity stunts. On June 1, they recorded "Give Peace A Chance" in their Montreal hotel room. Although the song was credited to Lennon and McCartney, it was John's first solo record away from The Beatles. "Give Peace A Chance" was released on Apple, by The Plastic Ono Band, on July 7, 1969, and became an instant anthem at rock concerts and peace demonstrations around the world. John and Yoko's exploits

"The Ballad of John and Yoko" Facts

B-side: "Old Brown Shoe"
Recorded: April 14, 1969
Released: May 30, 1969 (UK),
June 4, 1969 (US)
Label: Apple (UK), Capitol (US)
Writers: Lennnon/McCartney
(B-side, Harrison)
Producer: George Martin
Chart Success: UK No. 1, US No. 8

were also the subject of a Beatles single, when John and Paul recorded "The Ballad of John and Yoko" on April 14. It topped the British charts when it was released at the end of May.

Although the recordings for the *Get Back* project had yet to appear on record, The Beatles continued through the summer of 1969, preparing other tracks for release. On August 8, at 11.35 in the morning, the band gathered on the road crossing outside the Abbey Road studios for a shoot with photographer Iain Macmillan, giving a clue to the title of their next album. Macmillan was allowed only 10 minutes to take the photo, in order not to hold up traffic. Since then, the photo has become one of the most enduring of all Beatles' images.

Right: *John Lennon and Yoko Ono pictured during the filming of a promotional film for "The Ballad of John and Yoko".*

The sessions for *Abbey Road* finished with "I Want You (She's So Heavy)" on August 20, 1969; the track was the last ever recorded by all four Beatles together in a studio. After the simpler approach of both *The Beatles* album and the not-yet-released *Get Back* tracks, *Abbey Road* was a return to the high-tech studio techniques and ambitious arrangements that The Beatles' had used from *Rubber Soul* to *Magical Mystery Tour*. As well as a four-song medley on the second side, highlights included two Beatles' classics, John Lennon's "Come Together" and the song that signaled George Harrison's "coming of age" as a songwriter, "Something". Both were released on a single at the end of October.

Although it was not the final new Beatles album to appear—that would be when the *Get Back* tracks became available as *Let It Be* half a year later—when *Abbey Road*

was released on September 26, 1969, it was a fitting close to the band's remarkable recording career.

"Something" Facts

B-side: "Come Together"
Recorded: May 2, 5, July 11, August 15, 1969
Released: October 31 (UK), October 6, 1969 (US)
Label: Apple (UK), Capitol (US)
Writers: Harrison (B-side, Lennnon/McCartney)
Producer: George Martin
Chart Success: UK No. 4, US No. 3

Above: *Paul and Linda McCartney enjoy a private joke as they attend the British premiere of the film "Midnight Cowboy" in September 1969.*

Abbey Road Facts

Recorded: February 22 – August 20, 1969
Released: September 26, 1969
Label: Apple (UK), Capitol (US)
Writers: Lennon/McCartney (except as noted)
Producer: George Martin
Chart Success: UK No. 1, US No. 1

Track-By-Track

Side 1

Come Together (4.16)

This famous track began as a request for John Lennon to write a campaign song for Timothy Leary, the writer, psychologist, and promoter of psychedelic drugs, who was running for Governor of California against Ronald Reagan. It was based around Leary's campaign slogan, "Come together, join the party," and when Leary decided not to run, John changed the lyrics and style of the song.

Something (2.59) (George Harrison)

George's lyrics were inspired by Pattie Harrison, and the music by Ray Charles, who also recorded the song a few years later.

Maxwell's Silver Hammer (3.24)

In keeping with the lyrics, Ringo can be heard banging an anvil with a hammer.

Oh! Darling (3.28)

Paul's song recalls the style of early rock'n'roll "doo-wop" ballads from the Fifties.

Octopus's Garden (2.49) (Richard Starkey)

Ringo was inspired to write this track after refusing a meal of octopus in Sardinia. A local then told him how the creatures collect anything shiny, making their own "octopus's garden" under the sea.

I Want You (She's So Heavy) (7.49)

Apart from "Revolution 9", this is the longest track recorded by The Beatles. It is actually two songs joined together.

Side 2

Here Comes The Sun (3.40) (George Harrison)

George wrote this beautiful and gentle track while sitting in Eric Clapton's garden, on a day off from recording.

Because (2.45)

A track written by John after listening to Beethoven's Moonlight Sonata. When the piece had finished, he suggested to Yoko that he could write something with the same chords, except running backward.

You Never Give Me Your Money (3.57)

The first in a medley of four separate songs, this track reflects Paul's views of the business meetings that were going on within The Beatles at the time.

Sun King (2.31)

John claimed that this song had come to him in a dream, which might explain why the lyrics are a mixture of French, Spanish, Italian, and nonsense-style English.

Mean Mr. Mustard (1.06)

Based on a newspaper story that John read, the track is about a miser who hid all his money so everyone would think he was poor.

Polythene Pam (1.13)

One of the inspirations for John's song was an early Liverpool Beatles fan, Pat Hodgetts, who was known as Polythene Pat because she liked to eat polythene.

Right: *The lyrics for "Maxwell's Silver Hammer", handwritten by Paul McCartney.*

Below Right: *Paul McCartney plays the drums during a 1969 recording session in the Apple Studio.*

She Came In Through The Bathroom Window (1.58)

This track was written about the mania of The Beatles' early American tours, when girls would do anything to get into the group's hotel rooms. One fan climbed up a drainpipe and "came in through the bathroom window" to Paul's suite.

Golden Slumbers (1.31)

The words to this song were taken from a 400-year-old poem by Thomas Dekker, which Paul discovered while visiting his father's home near Liverpool.

Carry That Weight (1.37)

Paul's lyrics tell of the pressure of fame and fortune, without the protection they once had when Brian Epstein was alive.

The End (2.04)

Fittingly, for the final album they made, Ringo plays his only drum solo on any Beatles record.

Her Majesty (0.23)

The last track, on the last album the Beatles made, was a ditty about the Queen, which Paul McCartney recorded alone.

Chapter 20: Let It Be -1970

Throughout 1969 The Beatles were still having hit records, but their business affairs were in a mess, a situation that had been caused by the death of their manager, Brian Epstein, and the formation of the Apple company. In January, John Lennon revealed the truth about the band's finances to the UK music paper *Disc and Music Echo*, and the story was picked up immediately by the news media worldwide. "Apple is losing money," John said. "If it carries on like this, we'll be broke in six months." He went on to describe how the company had attracted many hangers-on, and said that money was pouring out more quickly than even The Beatles' earnings could maintain.

Paul McCartney was slightly more optimistic, but suggested hiring a top New York law firm, Eastman and Eastman, to help untangle the financial mess. Although the company Paul wanted to hire had a long history in the music and publishing business, the other Beatles were hesitant because the head of the company, Lee Eastman, was about to become Paul's father-in-law.

Eventually, however, all four signed up to the arrangement, though Lennon, Harrison, and Starr still had their doubts. On John's suggestion, the three began talking to New Yorker Allen Klein. Klein was a tough-talking music manager who had negotiated millions in overdue royalties for The Rolling Stones. After reading Lennon's view of the Beatles' finances,

Eastman and Eastman
39 West 54th Street
New York
New York 10019

18th April 1969

Attention Lee Eastman, Esq.

Dear Mr. Eastman,

This is to inform you of the fact that you are not authorized to act or to hold yourself out as the attourney or legal representative of "The Beatles" or of any of the companies which the Beatles own or control.

We recognize that you are authorized to act for Paul McCartney, personally, and in this regard we will instruct our representatives to give you the fullest co-operation.

We would appreciate your forwarding to

ABKCO Industries Inc.
1700 Broadway
New York
N.Y.

all documents, correspondence and files which you hold in your possession relating to the affairs of the Beatles, or any of the companies which the Beatles own or control.

Very truly yours,

John Lennon

Richard Starkey

George Harrison

This Spread: *(Clockwise from top left) John Lennon and Yoko Ono at London's Heathrow Airport on their way to Majorca in November 1969. Ringo Starr on board the cruise ship Queen Elizabeth II with his wife, Maureen, and their two children in May 1969. A legal letter signed by John Lennon, Ringo Starr (Richard Starkey), and George Harrison in April 1969 informing Lee Eastman that they were not happy for him to represent The Beatles. George Harrison (left) with Ravi Shankar (right) at a press conference in 1970 to promote the first ever British Indian Festival. Paul and Linda McCartney in 1969, a week before the birth of their daughter, Mary.*

This spread: *John Lennon and Yoko Ono pictured at a press conference given from their bed in a hotel in Amsterdam in March 1969.*

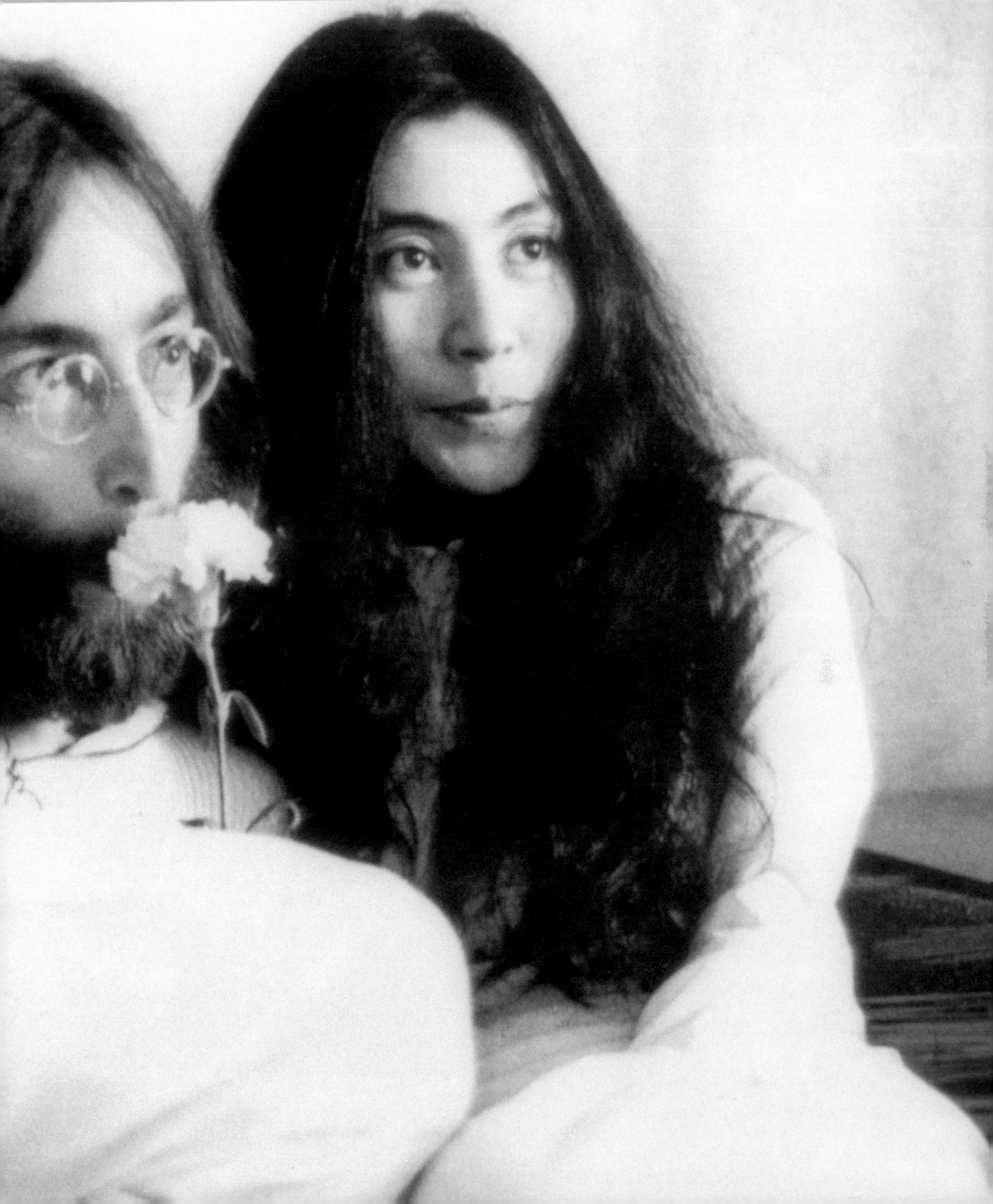

Above: *George Harrison and his wife, Pattie, pictured on their way to Nice, France, for a holiday in September 1969.*

he rushed to London to offer his services. John was impressed by Klein's no-nonsense approach, in contrast to the polite manners of the Eastmans, and signed him on as his personal representative after just one meeting. George and Ringo soon did the same, and the three Beatles, opposed by Paul McCartney, appointed Klein as the group's business manager.

In July 1969, The Beatles terminated their relationship with Brian Epstein's company, NEMS. NEMS was then put up for sale and, as it claimed a 25% commission on all the band's record royalties, it was in The Beatles' interest to buy NEMS. The Epstein family later said they would have preferred to sell it to The Beatles rather than an outside bidder, but were anxious about the managerial struggle going on within the band. Instead, they sold NEMS to an investment

Below: *Allan Klein (left) with John Lennon (center) and Yoko Ono (right) at the Apple headquarters in Savile Row, London, in April 1969.*

company though, soon after, Klein managed to buy The Beatles out of their NEMS contract.

With business arrangements between The Beatles and NEMS now seemingly settled, Klein turned his attention to EMI and re-negotiated The Beatles contract, nearly doubling their record royalties. He also reached an agreement with EMI that The Beatles would release at least two albums a year until 1976.

The arrangement was almost wrecked when John Lennon told Klein and the other Beatles that he wanted a "divorce" from the group, but Klein persuaded him not to ruin the deal by making his wish to leave the band public. Instead, in interviews, Lennon gave the impression that though he was now more interested in personal projects, he would still play with The Beatles as and when required.

In mid-September 1969, just a couple of weeks before the release of Abbey Road, rumors that Paul McCartney was dead began to circulate in America . The gossip started in Des Moines, Iowa, in a high school magazine article, and spread like wildfire after a local radio station interviewed a fan who claimed to have found "hidden clues" in various songs and photographs of the band that revealed that Paul had died.

The gossip quickly became a widespread urban myth, which alleged that Paul had been killed in a car accident in 1966 and replaced by a look-alike named William "Billy" Shears, the name of the fictitious leader of the Sgt. Pepper band. "Clues" were said to have been hidden on records, and could be revealed by playing discs backward.

One such piece of "evidence" suggested that John says "I buried Paul" in a slow, deep voice over the final refrain of "Strawberry Fields Forever". This was dismissed by Lennon, who asserted that he had actually said "cranberry sauce".

Above: *Paul McCartney attends a film premier in September 1969, at the height of the rumors of his death.*

The most famous claim, however, was made soon after *Abbey Road* appeared. In the cover photograph, Paul McCartney was the only one crossing the road in bare feet, and some said that this was symbolic of a corpse. When the story appeared in the *Chicago Sun-Times* on October 21, newspapers and journals began to take it more seriously and, early in November, *Life* magazine finally ended the stories with an article called "The Case of the Missing Beatle: Paul is Still With Us".

John Lennon, meanwhile, was paying more attention to his "other interests" than The Beatles. In September 1969, he and Yoko played a "Rock 'n' Roll Revival" concert in Toronto, Canada, with the Plastic Ono Band. Alongside Eric Clapton on guitar, Klaus Voorman on bass, and Alan White on drums, they played a set that included old songs like "Blue Suede Shoes"

and "Money", as well as John's 1968 song "Yer Blues" and a yet-to-be-released number called "Cold Turkey". They also performed a new song, "Give Peace A Chance", and two of Yoko Ono's experimental pieces. The concert was released on Apple as a live album, *Live Peace in Toronto*, on December 12.

John made the news in November 1969, when he returned his MBE award to Buckingham Palace as a protest

Below: *Yoko Ono (right), John Lennon (2nd right), and Eric Clapton (2nd left, seated) pictured the day after the Plastic Ono Band headlined the Toronto Rock 'n' Roll Revival show at Varsity Stadium, Toronto, September 1969.*

against Britain's involvement in a war in the African region of Biafra. However, the impact of this political gesture was lessened by John joking to the press that it was also a protest at the solo single "Cold Turkey" slipping down the UK charts. As Christmas approached, John and Yoko were once more promoting their peace efforts, this time by paying for huge billboards to be put up in 11 major cities around the world, each declaring, "War Is Over! If You Want It. Happy Xmas from John & Yoko." Two years later, the slogan would feature on John's hit single with the Plastic Ono Band, "Happy Xmas (War Is Over)".

The third solo single by John Lennon to appear on the Apple label, "Instant Karma (We All Shine On)", was recorded in a single day at the end of January 1970, and released on February 20. It reached Number Three in the US charts and Number Five in the UK.

Like Lennon, the other Beatles also began concentrating on their own projects. In late January, 1970, Paul began work on his first solo album,

Above: *John Lennon and Yoko Ono, on the steps of the Apple building in London, holding one of the posters that they distributed to the world's major cities as part of a peace campaign protesting against the Vietnam War.*

Right: *(Left to right) John Lennon, Yoko Ono, Mal Evans, and Klaus Voorman perform "Instant Karma" on the British TV show "Top of the Pops" in December, 1970.*

Left: *Ringo Starr with his wife, Maureen, at an airport in February 1970. Ringo's badge refers to the film "The Magic Christian" in which he starred alongside Peter Sellers.*

McCartney, at Abbey Road, using the alias "Billy Martin." It was released in April, and topped the *Billboard* chart in America. Ringo's movie with Peter Sellers, *The Magic Christian,* opened in February 1970, just as the drummer returned to the studio to start work on his own solo album, *Sentimental Journey,* which was also released in late April. George, too, worked through 1970 on his solo debut, which would appear as the album *All Things Must Pass,* with a chart-topping single "My Sweet Lord", at the end of November. By now it was becoming clear to the public that, as a band, The Beatles had almost come to an end.

However, The Beatles had yet to decide what to do with the studio and film material from the *Get Back* project. Director Michael Lindsay-Hogg had completed a first version of the film, which was now called *Let It Be.* When The Beatles watched it, they saw that they had not finished recording two of the songs they had been working on, George's "I Me Mine" and John's "Across The Universe". For the Lennon song, the band decided to use a recording made back in 1968 while, for "I Me Mine", George, Paul, and Ringo met up for the last-ever studio session by The Beatles as a group, on January 3, 1970.

The four Beatles were still not happy with either the sequence or the feel of the recordings, so George and John decided to invite the legendary American producer Phil Spector to take over the project. As with the choice to appoint Allen Klein, Paul claimed he was not consulted about Spector and, as the producer began work early in April with Ringo adding drum tracks, McCartney announced publicly that he would be leaving The Beatles because of "personal, business, and musical differences."

Almost immediately after, the title track from the album, "Let It Be", was released and hit Number One in the US charts. It was followed early in May by the *Let It Be* album and the movie, which premiered in New York on May 13.

Paul McCartney was outraged by some of Spector's work on the album, particularly the more orchestral arrangement bowed out in the first year of the Seventies. It had been just eight years since they had made their first single and only six since they took America, and the rest of the world, by storm. In that time they changed popular music, and the music business, forever.

DID YOU KNOW?

Recorded in February 1968, "Across The Universe" first appeared on a compilation album of various artists called *No One's Gonna Change Our World*, a charity release in aid of the World Wildlife Fund, before The Beatles included it on *Let It Be* in 1970.

of "A Long And Winding Road", which Paul insisted had been done without his approval. It was to prove the final straw. On December 31, 1970, Paul McCartney began legal procedures in the London High Court, charging Allen Klein with mismanagement of Apple funds, requesting appointment of a receiver for Apple, and beginning proceedings to dissolve The Beatles partnership.

With the aptly titled *Let It Be*, the group that came together as Liverpool teenagers in the late Fifties and helped to define the Sixties,

"Let It Be" Facts

B-side: "You Know My Name (Look Up The Number)"
Recorded: January 25 – 26, 1969
Released: March 6, 1970 (UK), March 11, 1970 (US)
Label: Apple (UK), Capitol (US)
Writers: Lennon/McCartney
Producer: George Martin
Chart Success: UK No. 2, US No. 1

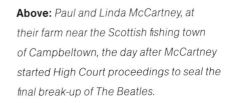

Above: *Paul and Linda McCartney, at their farm near the Scottish fishing town of Campbeltown, the day after McCartney started High Court proceedings to seal the final break-up of The Beatles.*

Left: *Allen Klein speaking at a press conference given at Apple headquarters in April 1970, where it was announced that Paul McCartney was leaving The Beatles.*

Let It Be Facts

Recorded: February 1968, January 1969,
March – April 1970
Released: May 8, 1970 (UK) May 18, 1970 (US)
Label: Apple (UK), Capitol (US)
Writers: Lennon/McCartney (except
songwriters as noted below)
Producer: George Martin/Phil Spector
Chart Success: UK No. 1, US No. 1

Track-By-Track
Side 1
Two Of Us (3.33)
This track was written by Paul while he was enjoying some time away from the studio with Linda Eastman, and is widely believed to be his reaction to Yoko Ono claiming all John's attention.

Dig A Pony (3.55)
The first of four tracks recorded live at the rooftop session on January 30, 1969, the lyrics sound as if they were made up on the spot and include references to The Rolling Stones and the early Beatles name of Johnny and The Moondogs.

Across The Universe (3.51)
This track originally appeared, in 1969, on a World Wildlife Fund charity album *No One's Gonna Change Our World*. For *Let It Be*, Phil Spector added an orchestra and choir.

I Me Mine (2.25) (George Harrison)
The last song ever recorded by The Beatles, though John was not present at the session.

Dig It (0.51) (Lennon/McCartney/Starkey/Harrison)
This track lasted less than a minute on the album, though the original recording lasted 12 minutes.

Let It Be (4.01)
The lyrics for one of The Beatles most famous songs were written by Paul at a time when there were tensions within the group.

Maggie Mae (0.39) (traditional: arrangement Lennon/McCartney/Harrison/Starkey)
This track is an old Liverpool song that The Beatles played as a "warm-up" number before starting the recording session.

Side 2
I've Got A Feeling (3.38)
Recorded at the rooftop session, this repeated the Beatles' technique of blending two songs together, in this case Paul's "I've Got A Feeling" and John's "Everybody's Had A Hard Year".

One After 909 (2.52)
The writing of this track dates from the days of The Quarry Men, and was recorded on the roof of the Apple offices.

The Long And Winding Road (3.40)
A song that was inspired by a road that winds through moorland near Paul's farm in Scotland. McCartney's disgust at Phil Spector adding an orchestra and choir to what was supposed to be a simple arrangement was the deciding factor in Paul leaving The Beatles.

For You Blue (2.33) (George Harrison)
A straightforward blues number written by George, and featuring John playing steel guitar.

Get Back (3.09)
The most famous of the "rooftop" tracks, "Get Back" was released as a single and topped the charts in Britain and the United States a year before the *Let It Be* album appeared.

Right: *Paul McCartney plays the bass guitar in the studio, 1970.*

Below: *George Harrison (right) in the studio with producer Phil Spector (left) in 1970.*

Let It Be Movie Facts

Directed: Michael Lindsay-Hogg
Produced: Neil Aspinall, The Beatles (executive)
Music: John Lennon, Paul McCartney, George Harrison, Ringo Starr
Cinematography: Anthony B. Richmond
Edited: Tony Lenny
Distributed: United Artists
Released: May 13, 1970 (US), May 20, 1970 (UK)
Running Time: 81 minutes

Principal Cast: The Beatles, Billy Preston, Mal Evans, Yoko Ono, George Martin

Above Left: *George Harrison plays an acoustic guitar in the studio in 1970.*

Above: *Paul McCartney sings into a microphone during the recording of "Let It Be".*

Above Right: *British comedian Spike Milligan, and wife Patricia Ridgeway, join hands with the police to keep surging crowds back at the premiere of "Let It Be" at the London Palladium, Piccadilly Circus.*

Plot:

The documentary was shot as a "fly on the wall" view of The Beatles at work. The first sequence, shot on a sound stage at Twickenham film studios, shows the band in rehearsal, each song being developed bit by bit. They discuss ways to improve numbers, not always agreeing—there's an awkward moment, for instance, when Paul suggests they lose George's guitar part on "The Two of Us," with George replying "...I won't play at all if you don't want to me to play."

The action then moves to their studio in the Apple offices, where they begin recording the new material, and during breaks "jamming" on old rock'n'roll classics. Various vistors appear throughout the rehearsal and recording sessions,

including their road manager Mal Evans (striking the hammer on "Maxwell's Silver Hammer"), Yoko Ono, Linda's daughter Heather, plus keyboard player Billy Preston.

Finally The Beatles—with Billy Preston—assemble on the roof of the Apple building for the famous open-air concert, in which they play "Get Back", Don't Let Me Down", "I've Got A Feeling", "One After 909", and "Dig A Pony". The camera cuts to the street below, capturing the reaction of the gathering crowd. The impromptu gig ends with John Lennon's comment, which also closes the *Let It Be* album, "I'd like to say 'thank you' on behalf of the group and ourselves, and I hope we passed the audition!"

Chapter 21: After The Beatles – John Lennon

Even the official announcements about the break-up of The Beatles couldn't convince fans that the group was finished. For the next decade there were rumors of reunions of one kind or another. The Beatles' own idea, for a once-and-for-all concert, never went away as far as many of their fans were concerned. Somehow it seemed inconceivable that the group that had provided the soundtrack for so many people's lives could simply dissolve. It was only when John Lennon was murdered on the fateful evening of December 8, 1980 that the story of The Beatles finally ended.

Out of all of The Beatles, prior to the group's final disbandment, John Lennon had been the one most actively involved in "outside" activities—mainly in collaboration with Yoko Ono. After the split he was free to pursue his "other interests" as he pleased. But cutting the ties with the band he'd been involved in for the past 12 years—the whole of his adult life—was bound to have an emotional impact, as it inevitably did on all four former Beatles.

Right: *John Lennon and Yoko Ono pictured at the Cannes Film Festival, May 18, 1971. John is carrying a copy of Yoko's art book Grapefruit in his jacket.*

In the same period, he and Yoko had been involved in various failed attempts to gain custody of Yoko's daughter, Kyoko from her first husband, Tony Cox, and in early 1970 the couple went through "primal scream" therapy sessions in Los Angeles, which were designed to vent their anger by releasing emotional pain from early childhood. Conducted by Dr Arthur Janov, the therapy involved two half days a week for four months, after which John felt no need to continue and returned to London to start work on his highly personal solo album *John Lennon/Plastic Ono Band*, which was released in December 1970.

No doubt spurred by the therapy, in "Mother" and " My Mummy's Dead" he confronted his feelings of childhood rejection, in "Working Class Hero" he uttered a four-letter expletive which led

to the song being banned by the BBC, and on the track "God", Lennon listed things he didn't believe in, including the line "don't believe in Beatles." The album went on to make the #11 spot in the UK charts and #10 in America, establishing—for the moment at least—John Lennon as the "angry" ex-Beatle.

"Working Class Hero" in particular hinted at John taking an increasingly political stance, which he confirmed with the single "Power o the People," recorded early in 1971 and released in the March. Despite its radical lyrics, the single made the Top 10 on both sides of the Atlantic and earned a gold disc in the US, selling over a million copies.

Left:
John Lennon and Yoko Ono in a Spanish hotel with Yoko's former husband, Tony Cox and his wife, in May 1972.

Right:
John Lennon performing with Chuck Berry on US TV show "The Mike Douglas Show" in 1971.

Left: *John Lennon and Yoko Ono pictured in their Ascot home in 1971.*

on Paul McCartney in "How Do You Sleep?" This, Lennon claimed, was in response to lyrics on Paul's album, *Ram* that were directed at him and Yoko. Early releases of the album also included a postcard featuring John holding a pig, mocking a similar pose by Paul with a sheep on the cover of *Ram*. By the time *Imagine* was released, topping the album charts worldwide, John and Yoko Ono had moved permanently to New York City. They first lived in the St Regis Hotel on Fifth Avenue, then after a few weeks moved to a street-level apartment in Greenwich Village, in

From the late summer of 1969, John and Yoko had been living in a luxurious country house, Tittenhurst Park, where he had built his own recording studio. It was here, through June and July 1971, that he laid down the basic tracks for what many would consider his post-Beatles masterwork, *Imagine*.

Much of the final album was re-recorded and mixed at the Record Plant studios in New York, and on its release in the Fall was acclaimed as an instant classic. Its title track became a universal anthem of peace, love, and equality—although "imagine no possessions" seemed ironic to many, with its promotional film shot at a grand piano in the Lennons' spacious mansion. Other songs reflected John's tougher side, including the confessional "Jealous Guy" and "Crippled Inside," the anti-war "I Don't Wanna Be A Soldier," and his thinly veiled attack

October 1971. It was a period of great peace for Lennon, who in the UK was constantly hounded as an ex-Beatle by the press and paparazzi; he found he could walk the streets of the Village virtually undisturbed. He became a part of the neighborhood very quickly, cycling around, visiting local shops, and enjoying a freedom he hadn't experienced since the early 1960s; he declared that NYC was on a par with his naive Liverpool as his natural home.

Almost as soon as John and Yoko had moved to New York they got involved in the radical political scene, befriending anti-war activists and taking part in various demonstrations and fundraising rallies. In December 1971 they released the single "Happy Xmas (War Is Over)", an anti-war song. Featuring vocals by John, Yoko and the children of the Harlem Community Choir, on its release it failed to make it into the *Billboard* charts. It wasn't released in the UK until the following November due to a publishing dispute, where it hit the #4 spot, and has continued to be a seasonal hit every Christmas since.

The message of the single, however, along with the Lennons' high-profile political activity, was noted by the US administration of Richard Nixon, who early in 1972 began a four-year attempt to have the radical ex-Beatle deported. It was only after many appearances at deportation hearings (at one stage John was ordered to leave the US within 60 days) and Nixon's resignation in 1974, that the order was finally overturned in 1975. And when Jimmy Carter was inaugurated as President in January 1977, John and Yoko attended the Innaugural Ball.

Right: *John Lennon and Yoko Ono pictured in 1971 giving some of their hair to Black Power leader, Michael X. In exchange they are receiving the shorts worn by Cassius Clay when he fought Henry Cooper. The hair and shorts were sold in a Peace Auction.*

Left: *John Lennon flashing a peace sign as he and Yoko Ono appear at the New York office of Immigration and Naturalization in May 1972 to fight deportation proceedings.*

This spread: *John Lennon pictured at President Jimmy Carter's Inaugural Ball in January 1977 with Yoko Ono and Muhammad Ali.*

While the authorities were preparing their case against John in the early months of 1972, he was back in the studio, recording the most directly political album of his career. Unlike when he was a Beatle, having to worry about the group's image, now Lennon could voice his opinion on any issues he liked, and on *Some Time In New York City* he did just that. Released in June 1972, the album, made with a New York rock 'n' roll outfit called Elephant's Memory, featured songs about all manner of political topics including women's liberation, the war in Vietnam, Britain's troubles in Northern Ireland—and, of course, Lennon's problems with the US immigration department. Though full of messages, none of the songs on the album had the impact of anything on *Imagine*; Lennon himself later admitted, "It became journalism, not poetry." The album made #11 in the UK album chart, but only just scraped into the US Top 50 at #48.

Despite their legal tussles, John and Yoko continued to appear at political events and benefit shows for various causes. On August 30, 1972, Lennon gave two concerts with Elephant's Memory at Madison Square Garden, in aid of patients at a New York school mental facility—they would be his last full-length concert appearances.

Apparently devastated at the commercial failure of the *New York City* album, it would be over a year before John worked in the studio again, during which time the Lennons moved from their Greenwich Village address, relocating in May 1973 to the more secure Dakota Building at West 72nd Street overlooking Central Park.

In July and August he was back at the Record Plant recording *Mind Games*; released in November 1973, it was warmly received by fans and critics, reaching #13 in the UK and #9 in the US, where it went gold. The title song, which began life in 1969 and can be heard in The Beatles' *Let It Be* sessions, was released as a single at the same time, making the Top 30 in both Britain and America.

It was during the recording of *Mind Games* that John Lennon and Yoko Ono decided to separate, and soon after, John moved to California in the company of their personal assistant, May Pang. Pang had worked for the Lennons for three years, and when they decided to split, it was on Yoko's suggestion that she move in with

Above: *John Lennon and Yoko Ono performing on stage in 1973.*

Left: *Harry Nilsson, May Pang and John Lennon, at the Smothers Brothers Comeback Show in 1974.*

Below: *John Lennon out on the town in Los Angeles during his "lost weekend" period in 1974.*

John. It was the beginning of an 18-month period without Yoko at his side, which Lennon would later refer to as his "lost weekend."

In Los Angeles, May Pang encouraged Lennon to establish a more regular contact with his son, Julian, whom he hadn't seen for years. And at the same time he also reconnected with Ringo Starr, Paul McCartney, the ex-Beatles road manager Mal Evans, and the singer Harry Nilsson, who had counted The Beatles among his biggest fans.

John announced he was planning to produce Nilsson's next album, *Pussy Cats*, and Pang rented a beach house for the musicians involved, including Lennon, Nilsson, and Ringo Starr. It was the start of a riotous period of drunken excess on the part of Lennon and Nilsson, during which the two rock stars hit the headlines more than once.

With The Who drummer Keith Moon also in tow, they started fights, wrecked bars, and caused general mayhem around the LA club scene. "It was Keith Moon, Harry, me, Ringo, all living together in a house, and we had some moments" John confessed in a BBC interview in 1975 "... I hit the bottle like I was 18 or 19, and I was acting like I was still at college."

In June 1974 John returned to New York with May Pang, to finish work on *Pussy Cats* and begin recording his next album, *Walls and Bridges*. The album, released in October, achieved two significant milestones in the record books—it was John's only *Billboard* chart topper as a solo artist during his lifetime, and included his only #1 single in his lifetime, a duet with Elton John "Whatever Gets You Thru The Night." It was as a result of the single's success that John made a surprise appearance at Elton John's Thanksgiving concert at Madison Square Gardens—he'd promised to appear if the single topped the charts, which he doubted it would. John and Elton performed the song, along with the Beatles classics "Lucy In The Sky With Diamonds" and "I Saw Her Standing There."

On their return to New York, Lennon and May Pang had rented an apartment—including a room set aside for Julian to visit—and by the end of the year were considering buying a house together. In January 1975, however, John and Yoko suddenly got together again, and his affair with Pang became the year-and-a-half "lost weekend."

This spread: *John Lennon with Yoko Ono, during a 1973 press conference.*

During this time with May Pang, Lennon recorded *Rock 'n' Roll*, a collection of oldies of the kind The Beatles played in Liverpool and Hamburg, produced with Phil Spector. Featuring classics from the 1950s and early 1960s by the likes of Little Richard, Buddy Holly, and Fats Domino, it featured a cover photo of a leather-clad Lennon in a Hamburg doorway, taken back in the early 1960s by one of the art student "exi" crowd, Jurgen Vollmer—who also played bass on the sessions.

Above: *John Lennon and Yoko Ono pictured during a recording session of Lennon's last album* Double Fantasy.

Right: *John Lennon with his arms around his wife Yoko Ono and Roberta Flack at the 1975 Grammy Awards.*

Below: *John Lennon and Yoko Ono pictured together in 1980.*

On its release in February 1975, *Rock 'n' Roll* became another hit for Lennon, reaching #6 in both the UK and US, where it soon went gold. The single from the album, "Stand By Me," was also a US Top 20 hit that Spring.

After the *Rock 'n' Roll* sessions, apart from co-writing and playing on David Bowie's first US #1 "Fame" in January 1975, Lennon retired from music altogether. For the next five years, he more or less vanished from the public eye; he became a self-styled "house husband," as he and Yoko raised their son Sean, who was born on John's 35th birthday, 9 October 1975. They spent time in Ono's native Japan, but otherwise lived in Dakota.

During this time John Lennon was still writing songs and in 1980, he and Yoko Ono released *Double Fantasy*. It was an album of songs based on their married life together, arranged as a dialogue between the couple. Recorded through August and September 1980, and previewed by the single "(Just Like) Starting Over," the album was released in November.

Above: *Part of the crowd, estimated at over 100,000 people, that gathered in Central Park, New York to hold a vigil for John Lennon on December 14, 1980.*

John threw himself back into the public arena, giving interviews and plugging the album at every opportunity. With tracks such as "(Just Like) Starting Over", "Woman" (both of which were hit singles), and "Beautiful Boy", the album reflected a new, relaxed John Lennon, at peace with himself, his family, and the world.

He and Yoko had been working on some further tracks (later to be released on *Milk and Honey*), when they returned home to their New York apartment at around 10.50pm on December 8, 1980. As they approached the dark security entrance to the Dakota Building, Mark David Chapman shot John Lennon four times in the back. Earlier that evening John had signed a copy of *Double Fantasy* for the deranged fan, who it was later revealed was a schizophrenic, and had been stalking the former Beatle since October.

John was taken by ambulance to the emergency unit of the Roosevelt Hospital nearby, but was pronounced dead on arrival at 11.07pm. The world was stunned by the news of the assassination, as Yoko Ono issued a statement the next day announcing that there would be no funeral, ending with the plea: "John loved and prayed for the human race. Please pray the same for him." It was just two months after John Lennon's 40th birthday.

Lennon's body was cremated at Ferncliff Cemetery in Hartsdale, New York, on 10 December and Yoko Ono was rumored to have scattered his ashes in Central Park, where she later set up the Strawberry Fields memorial. Mark Chapman pleaded guilty to second-degree murder and was sentenced to 20 years to life; he is still in prison, having been refused parole several times.

Chapter 22: After The Beatles - Paul McCartney

While The Beatles were officially still together, Paul McCartney had recorded his first solo album. With Paul playing all the instruments—bass, drums, acoustic guitar, lead guitar, piano, Mellotron, organ, and toy xylophone—*McCartney* really was a solo effort, the only additional help came from his wife Linda on some backing vocals.

Recorded through late 1969 and early 1970, the album included songs that Paul had written during the previous couple of years, originally intended for Beatles albums and one, the instrumental, "Hot As Sun," that he had written back in the days of The Quarrymen. Released in mid-April, 1970, a week after The Beatles had announced he was leaving the group, the album certainly benefitted from the focus of media attention on the break-up of the band; it quickly hit #1 in the US *Billboard* chart and made the #2 position in the UK.

As the situation with the other Beatles reached crisis point, Paul and Linda (who, like Yoko Ono, received some of the "blame" for the band's break-up) went on a long holiday, spending much of their time on Paul's farm on the Mull of Kintyre in Scotland. It was there, often with Linda's input, that Paul wrote the songs that would appear on his next album, *Ram*. Recorded in New York between January and March 1971, it was released in May, the only album to be credited jointly to Paul and Linda McCartney (although Linda, again, only supplied backing vocals).

Right: *Paul McCartney pictured on stage during a 1972 US television appearance.*

Above: *Paul McCartney and his wife Linda appearing at the Grammy Awards ceremony on March 16, 1971. McCartney accepted the composer's award for The Beatles' "Let It Be".*

Right: *McCartney and his wife Linda, arriving at Britain's High Court of Justice on February 19, 1971 to officially break up the Beatles' partnership.*

A worldwide hit, *Ram* topped the chart in Britain and reached #2 in America; and earlier in the year, a single cut at the same sessions, "Another Day," was an international hit. Despite some bad press from The Beatles' bust-up, Paul McCartney felt he was back where he belonged—topping the charts around the world.

The other place where Paul felt he belonged, and had been absent from since the mid-1960s, was on stage playing in front of a live audience. So partly with that in mind, in August 1971, he and Linda formed Wings, a four-piece group comprising of Paul on bass, Linda on keyboards, drummer Denny Seiwell who'd played on *Ram*, and the former Moody Blues guitarist, Denny Laine. They quickly began recording their debut album, with the intention of making it as raw and instant-sounding as possible—five of the eight songs were actually recorded in one take. After a November launch party publicly announcing the formation of Wings, *Wild Life* was released in December 1971. It only received (by an ex-Beatle's standards) a lukewarm reaction from both press and public, just scraping into the Top 10 in the United States (at #10) and making #11 in the UK.

At the end of the year, McCartney added guitarist, Henry McCullough, to the Wings line-up and made preparations to go on the road. During the final days of The Beatles, Paul had suggested the group did some low-key live gigs, harking back to their early days around the dance halls and clubs in Liverpool, but the other three had dismissed the idea. Now he had chance to make it happen with his own band and in February 1972, Wings embarked on a series of impromptu gigs at British universities. The idea was to travel in a van and turn up at venues unannounced, performing for whoever happened to be around. The first date was a lunchtime show at Nottingham University in the UK; with an admission price of 40 pence (less than a dollar), the proceeds were split equally between each member of the band. Although it was the first tour to feature an ex-Beatle since The Beatles broke up, Wings deliberately played no Beatle songs during the concerts, to show it was a brand new band in its own right.

Although Paul McCartney rarely expressed strong political views in the way that John Lennon did, with the first Wings single he did just that. Written in response to the "Bloody Sunday" shooting of protesters by British troops in Northern Ireland, and released on February 25, 1972, "Give Ireland Back to the Irish" was promptly banned by all British radio and television stations. But despite the lack of airplay, the single made the UK Top 20—and, significantly, it topped the chart in the Republic of Ireland.

Above: *Paul and Linda McCartney pictured with their band, Wings in December 1971.*

Above: *Paul McCartney relaxing before a US TV performance in 1972.*

was to make some live recordings to be included on a future album, but that never happened. The band, with their road crew and the McCartney children—who now included baby Stella, born in September 1971—travelled in a brightly painted double-decker bus for the "Wings Over Europe" tour. One downside was when Paul and Linda were arrested and fined for possession of marijuana in Sweden; McCartney joked that it would "make good publicity," but the arrest would cause him a lot of trouble trying to get visas for future tours.

Before and after the European trip, beginning in March 1972 in Los Angeles and ending in London in October, McCartney and Wings were busy in the studio laying down tracks for their next album, *Red Rose Speedway*. It appeared in May 1973 to a mixed reception, but nevertheless topped the chart in *Billboard*; and its spin-off single, "My Love" became McCartney's second US #1, when it was released before the album in the March.

But McCartney's finest hour with the group would be Wings' triumphant third album, *Band on the Run*, and their hit theme tune from a James Bond movie, "Live and Let Die". Recorded in October 1972, the song from the Bond film soundtrack was a huge hit when it was released the following June. Produced by George Martin, it made the Top 10 in the US (at #2) and UK and was the first James Bond theme song to be nominated for an Academy Award.

The second Wings single, released in May, was almost as controversial, but for very different reasons. In complete contrast to "Give Ireland Back to the Irish," it was a gentle version of the traditional nursery rhyme "Mary Had A Little Lamb," with Paul singing and his children, nine-year-old Heather (Linda's firstborn whom he had adopted) and two-year-old Mary, joining in on the chorus. Criticized and even ridiculed by the rock music critics, the single sold moderately well, but confirmed a widespread view that McCartney was 'going soft'.

Through July and August 1972, Wings took to the road again. This time it was for 26 dates across Europe, taking in France, West Germany, Switzerland, Denmark, Finland, Sweden, Norway, Holland, and Belgium. As well as promoting the two previous singles, the idea

Above: *Linda and Paul McCartney with baby daughter, Stella and the rest of Wings arriving in Helsinki in August 1972.*

Right: *Paul McCartney surrounded by lights during a 1972 US TV performance.*

Below: *Performing "Live and Let Die" on US TV in 1972.*

Right: *McCartney playing live with Wings in May 1976 in Los Angeles.*

Band on the Run was Wings' most successful LP, and is still the most celebrated of Paul McCartney's post-Beatles albums. It was the top-selling studio album in the UK in 1974 and restored McCartney's standing with the critics. At first, sales were slow after its release in December 1973, but by the spring of '74 it was topping the charts around the world; sales were boosted by the hit singles "Helen Wheels" (which featured on the US version of the album but not the UK), "Jet", and the title track, a US chart-topper. The album actually made the US #1 spot on three separate occasions.

McCartney realized, after the overwhelming success of *Band on the Run*, that it was time to take Wings on a major world tour. Staged in six separate legs, from September 1975 through to October 1976, the "Wings Over the World Tour" took in the UK, Australia, Europe and the United States (where it was known as the "Wings Over America Tour"), and was a huge promotional vehicle for the group's next two albums, *Venus and Mars* and *Wings at the Speed of Sound*.

Recorded over the first four months of 1975, *Venus and Mars* was released in May and topped the charts in many countries, including the USA, although it didn't enjoy the universal acclaim of *Band on the Run*. It formed a major part of the group's repertoire on the first two legs of the world tour, where they visited twelve cities in the UK followed by five in Australia before the end of 1975.

Wings was now made up of the permanent trio of Paul, Linda, and Denny Laine plus the American drummer, Joe English and the Scottish guitarist, Jimmy McCulloch (although on the tour they also took with them a four-piece brass section). It was this line-up that went into the Abbey Road studios early in 1976 to record *Wings at the Speed of Sound*.

Above: *Paul and Linda McCartney and their daughter, Mary, pictured in 1976 whilst on tour with Wings. Linda and Mary can be seen holding a copy of the bands album, Wings at the Speed of Sound.*

Right: *Paul McCartney and wife, Linda pictured during an interview whilst on tour in Paris in 1976.*

Another chart topper, it spawned two hit singles, "Silly Love Songs" (another US #1) and "Let 'Em In", and boosted the set list for the next stages of the world tour as it made its way across Europe and North America.

While they were on the American leg of the world tour, Wings recorded several concerts which became the basis for a triple-disc live album, *Wings Over America*, released in December 1976. It became the fifth Wings album in a row to top the American charts, and went on to sell over seven million copies.

April 1977 saw McCartney involved in an unusual release, a non-vocal orchestral version of the music on *Ram* which had been recorded at Abbey Road in June 1971, a month after the release of *Ram*. Paul decided to release the six-year-old recordings under the name of Percy "Thrills" Thrillington, with the album titled *Thrillington*. The only mention of his own name being after the liner notes where he was described as a friend of Percy. It wasn't until a journalist mentioned it at a 1989 press conference that Paul finally admitted that he was, in fact, Percy Thrillington. The nature of the album—and the fact that Paul's part in it was kept a secret—ensured it would only sell in limited numbers, but it was an early hint of an interest in orchestral music which would bear fruit later in his career.

Paul McCartney's most successful release of 1977 was another unlikely venture, a single which involved the local Scottish pipe band from Campbeltown, near his farm on the Mull of Kintyre. Written as a tribute to the beautiful location, the atmospheric, "Mull of Kintyre" was released in November 1977, in time for the lucrative Christmas market. It shot up the charts in Britain and elsewhere and became McCartney's biggest post-Beatle hit, selling over two million copies in the UK alone. While it topped the charts in a number of countries around the world, it didn't do well in the United States, where it only reached #33 in the *Billboard* listings.

Above: *Paul McCartney, Linda and daughter, Heather seen relaxing on a beach in April 1976.*

Left: *Paul McCartney performing with Wings in 1977.*

Below: *Wings (left to right) Paul McCartney, wife Linda, and Denny Lane, eat fish and chips from newspaper on boat trip down the River Thames on March 22, 1978 to launch their album London Town. Behind them is Tower Bridge.*

Above: *Paul McCartney dressed in 1920s style for a TV performance of the Wings single, "Goodnight Tonight" that was released at the same time as the Back To The Egg album.*

Although they had been recording off and on since February 1977, both in London and in a yacht moored off the Virgin Islands, Wings didn't release an album throughout all of 1977. The first delay came when Paul called a halt to the sessions after Linda discovered she was expecting another baby. Then American drummer, Joe English, decided he was homesick and returned to the USA; he was followed by guitarist, Jimmy McCulloch, who left to join The Small Faces in the September. For the first time since *Band of the Run* in 1973, the group was back down to the core trio of Paul, Linda and Denny Laine.

September 1977 also saw the birth of James McCartney, and while "Mull of Kintyre" stormed the UK charts in November, the next album was still on hold. Eventually the tracks were completed in January 1978, and *London Town* was ready for a release at the end of March.

Preceded by a US chart-topping single, "With A Little Luck," *London Town* fared well enough in the charts, making #2 in the US where it went platinum.

But it marked the beginning of a downturn for Wings' musical fortunes as the 1970s came to a close. The group's next album would be their last, with Laurence Juber taking over as their final lead guitarist, and Steve Holley the last drummer. Recorded over nearly a year, between June 1978 and April 1979, *Back To The Egg* was released in June, failing to make the Top 5 in either the UK or US.

After the release of *Back To The Egg*, Wings were inactive for much of 1979, as Paul worked on a new solo album, *McCartney II*. Recorded in his home studio in Scotland, the tracks relied heavily on synthesizers and other studio gadgetry, but that didn't stop the record doing well in the stores, topping the UK chart and making the #3 spot in the US when it was released in May 1980. There were also two chart singles from the collection, "Waterfalls" and the US #1, "Coming Up".

Through the Fall of 1979, Paul had been rehearsing with Wings for their next tour, a UK trek which would turn out to be their last. The tour climaxed with a series of concerts featuring an all-star "Rockestra" line-up of celebrity musicians, in aid of UNICEF and Kampuchean refugees. The concerts included established artists such as McCartney and The Who, as well as younger new wave acts like The Clash and The Pretenders; it would mark the final live appearance of Wings.

There were plans for a new Wings world tour, but these were abandoned after Paul was arrested at Tokyo airport on January 16, 1980 as the band arrived for some Japanese concerts.

Above: *Linda and Paul McCartney pictured together in Cannes, May 1980.*

He was jailed for nine days for possession of marijuana and other members of the band were questioned, but not charged. But the damage was done; the tour was cancelled, along with any other immediate plans for Wings.

Through 1980, Wings continued to rehearse some new tunes for a future album, but in December came the tragedy of John Lennon's assassination; Paul was, naturally, devastated and he cancelled any further sessions until February 1981, when he restarted the project as a solo album to be dedicated to John. Soon after that, Juber and Holly left the group and in April it was announced that Denny Laine had also departed, and that Wings had officially disbanded.

When the sessions resumed, with ex-Beatles' producer George Martin at the controls, Paul gathered together some famous names to guest on various tracks, including rock 'n' roll legend Carl Perkins, soul superstar Stevie Wonder, and Ringo Starr. The album, *Tug of War*, appeared a year later, in April 1982. It was an instant chart-topper around the world, selling several millions copies and being nominated for an "Album of the Year" Grammy Award in 1983. And prior to the album's release, one of the two tracks featuring Stevie Wonder, "Ebony and Ivory," was put out as a single and also made #1 across the globe.

A number of tracks from the *Tug of War* sessions were held over, and appeared on the following year's release, *Pipes of Peace*, a follow-up to the previous album which included two duets with Michael Jackson. Released in March 1983,

the album didn't do as well as *Tug of War*, but the single with Michael Jackson, "Say Say Say", topped the American charts.

Paul McCartney had always had a wide variety of interests outside music, and now, without the pressures that had surrounded The Beatles, he was able to spend more time on them. He'd been fascinated by animated cartoons since his childhood, and in 1981 started work on *Rupert and the Frog Song*, which he wrote and produced with director Geoff Dunbar. Based on a popular UK children's character, Rupert Bear, the film was released alongside McCartney's feature film *Give My Regards to Broad Street* in 1984; a song from the Rupert film's soundtrack, "We All Stand Together," made #3 in the UK charts when it was released as a single.

Above: *Paul McCartney pictured at Air Studios, London, mixing sound for his cartoon, Rupert and the Frog Song in September 1984.*

Left: *A photograph taken during the filming of a video for "So Bad", the B side of Paul McCartney's number one single, "Pipes of Peace". The picture shows, from left to right: Ringo Starr, Linda McCartney, Eric Stewart from 10cc and Paul McCartney.*

Above: *Paul McCartney on stage with George Michael (left), Bono (3rd left) and Freddie Mercury (right) during the finale of the Wembley Stadium Live Aid concert on July 13, 1985.*

The 'Broad Street movie, however, was a financial and critical disaster; with a day-in-the-life plot similar to The Beatles' *A Hard Day's Night*. It featured Paul, Linda, Ringo, and his wife Barbara Bach, all in acting roles. But the soundtrack album was more successful, topping the chart in Great Britain after its release in October 1984.

In 1985, Paul—along with most of the world's top rock and pop names—took part in the Live Aid concert, to raise money for famine relief in Africa. Broadcast live worldwide from London, he played "Let It Be" backed by an all-star group including Bob Geldof, Pete Townshend, and David Bowie.

Above: *Paul McCartney backstage with David Bowie at the Wembley Stadium Live Aid concert on July 13, 1985.*

This spread: *Paul McCartney performing during the first concert of his New World Tour in Milan on February 18, 1993.*

Along with his wife Linda, McCartney also made time to promote his own personal causes, particularly vegetarianism. Linda even produced her own line of vegetarian foods, before her untimely death from cancer in 1998. Later that year Paul released the album *A Garland For Linda,* with the proceeds donated to help survivors of the disease. Paul has continued to campaign for vegetarianism, as recently as 2010 giving his endorsement to the "Meat-Free Mondays" campaign, encouraging people to abstain from eating meat at least once a week.

Paul has also ventured into the world of classical music, most famously in 1991 when he wrote a piece to be performed by the Liverpool Philharmonic Orchestra to celebrate their 150th anniversary, *Liverpool Oratorio*. First performed in June 1991, and featuring top names from the world of classical music, an album was released in October 1991 and topped the classical charts worldwide for many weeks—and even made it to #177 in the regular US album chart.

He was later honored as a Fellow of the Royal College of Music and Honorary Member of the Royal Academy of Music, with other projects in the classical field including *Standing Stone*, premiered at London's Royal Albert Hall in 1997,

Above*: Sir Paul McCartney shows off his medal after receiving his knighthood from the Queen on March 11, 1997.*

Left*: Paul and Linda McCartney pictured with Princess Diana after a performance of Paul's Oratorio in Lille, France, on November 15, 1992.*

Right*: Paul McCartney performing during the Super Bowl XXXIX Halftime Show on February 6, 2005.*

and 1999's *Working Classica*l, in which he placed some of his already released songs in a classical setting. And in 1997 he was named in the Queen's New Year's Honours List, knighted for services to music and becoming Sir Paul McCartney.

But Paul McCartney's first love has always been popular music, going back to the sounds he grew up with in his childhood in Liverpool, and his teenage years with the early Beatles. They were days recalled by all three surviving Beatles in the early 1990s when they got together on their huge *Anthology* project, a TV series, three double CDs, and a book all celebrating the history of the group in archive footage, taped interviews and unreleased material from recording sessions.

And, now in his late 60s, Paul continues to produce albums of quality. They range from the 1991 collection of rock 'n' roll oldies originally intended just for the Russian market, *Back In The USSR* and 1999's *Run Devil Run* in the same vein, to his 2005 critically acclaimed solo album *Chaos and Creation in the Backyard*, also the 2003 live double album, *Back in the World* comprising numbers from his 2002 "Driving USA" tour of the United States. No less than 22 of the 36 tracks on *Back In The World* feature songs from his years with The Beatles. It's a testament to the enduring popularity of the music he forged in the company of John, George, and Ringo, alongside the rich and varied output of the music he's produced in the 40 years since The Beatles broke up.

Chapter 23: After The Beatles - George Harrison

Before end of The Beatles, George Harrison had already released two solo albums, the soundtrack music for the *Wonderwall* movie and *Electronic Sounds*, an experiment in synthesizer music. But when the group split up, he still had a huge backlog of material which he released in November 1970 as *All Things Must Pass*.

The triple-disc album topped the charts in the US, UK and elsewhere, although only two of the discs featured actual songs, the third being recordings of jam sessions with his friends. The album also contained two hit singles, the chart-topping "My Sweet Lord" and the Top 10 hit, "What is Life". The album, co-produced by George with Phil Spector, included Eric Clapton, Billy Preston, and Ringo Starr on various tracks.

George's biggest triumph in the early 1970s, however, wasn't a record as such. With his friend, the Indian classical sitar player Ravi Shankar, he organized the Concert for Bangladesh held on August 1, 1971. With a total of 40,000 people attending two concerts at New York's Madison Square Garden, the aim was to raise money for famine victims in Bangladesh. The supergroup line-up, featuring Bob Dylan, Eric Clapton, Ringo Starr and Billy Preston among others, was a model for all future large-scale charity concerts such as Live Aid. The live triple album of the concerts raised more funds for the charity, topping the charts in Britain and hitting #2 in the US.

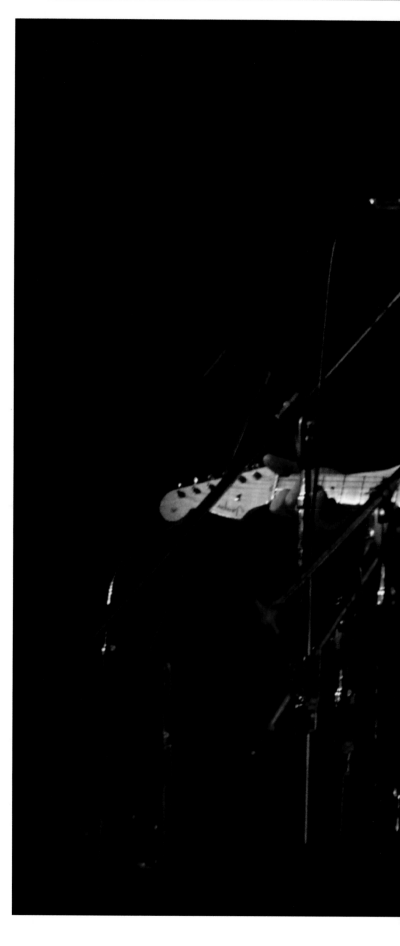

Right: *George Harrison performing at the Concert for Bangladesh at Madison Square Garden on August 1, 1970.*

George's next studio album, 1973's *Living in the Material World*, didn't do as well as *All Things Must Pass*, but still held the US #1 spot for five weeks and included the hit single, "Give Me Love (Give Me Peace on Earth)". The album's main message was George's belief in the Hindu religion, with one "non-religious" song ,"Sue Me, Sue You Blues" regretting the legal squabbles during the break-up of The Beatles.

Between 1971 and 1973 George also worked with Ringo Starr on his chart hits, "It Don't Come Easy", "Back Off Boogaloo", and "Photograph", as well as playing guitar on five tracks of John Lennon's *Imagine* album. Lennon would later say that his work on the album was the best that George had played in his life.

Above: *George Harrison and Indian musician, Ravi Shankar pictured at a press conference held in New York in July 1971 to promote the Concert for Bangladesh.*

Above Left: *(Left to right) Don Preston, George Harrison, and Eric Clapton performing together on stage at the Concert for Bangladesh at Madison Square Garden on August 1, 1970.*

Above Right: *George Harrison, backstage at 1974 concert in Salt Lake City with Jack Ford, son of President Gerald Ford.*

In 1974 George Harrison split with his wife of 8 years, Pattie Boyd. She later married his friend Eric Clapton—although the two musicians managed to remain very close, calling each other "husbands-in-law." Following the divorce he released *Dark Horse* in December 1974, recorded in the Fall while he was suffering from laryngitis. Badly received by the critics, as was a tour of North America to promote it, it still managed to hit the Top 5 in *Billboard*.

Harrison released his final album for the Apple label in 1975, *Extra Texture (Read All About It)*, before forming his own Dark Horse label, for which he recorded *Thirty Three & 1/3* through the summer of 1976. Although not achieving the chart success of his 1970 album, it received his best reviews from the critics since *All Things Must Pass*. On September 2, 1978 George married Olivia Trinidad Arias, who he had met when she was a secretary at Dark Horse. Their son Dhani had been born a month earlier.

George's final album of the 1970s was the self-titled *George Harrison*, which included the one of his best-loved post-Beatles singles, "Blow Away". Not one of his biggest sellers, the album made it to #14 on the *Billboard* chart after its release in February 1979.

As well as his own albums and working on those of others, through the 1970s George was devoting more and more of his time to other, non-musical interests. He had become a keen gardener, tending the 36-acre ground of his Friar Park mansion with the aid of a staff of 12 workers, including his two older brothers.

Above: *George Harrison and Billy Preston performing on stage during Harrison's North American tour at the Capitol Center in Landover, Maryland on December 13, 1974.*

Right: *George Harrison talking to reporters about his new album during a news conference in Los Angeles on March 8, 1979.*

Above: *George Harrison, holding 18-month-old son Dhani, with his Mexican wife, Olivia at Heathrow Airport, London, in February 1980.*

and Eric Idle in particular—and when they needed about $4 million to finish making the film *Life of Brian* in 1979, George was there to help them.

Although the company was originally formed just to back the one movie, with his partner Denis O'Brien, George went on to produce a series of ground-breaking UK films in the 1980s including *The Long Good Friday* in 1980, *Time Bandits* (with a Harrison soundtrack) in 1981, and 1986's *Withnail and I*. The company made a total of 27 movies before George eventually sold his shares in 1994.

The death of John Lennon at the end of 1980 came as a deep shock, and was obviously felt as a profound personal loss. George hadn't been in touch with John as much as Paul and Ringo through the 1970s, partly because he had never got on well with Yoko Ono. But John's murder, as well as confirming his worst fears about security from stalkers, moved George to re-write a

In fact he began to regard himself as more of a gardener than musician, and his autobiography, *Me Mine* published in 1980, was dedicated "to gardeners everywhere." The book, written with the help of ex-Beatles publicist Derek Taylor, was the only autobiography of a former member of the "Fab Four," although it concentrated more on George's post-Beatles hobbies rather than his early life and history with the band.

Harrison was also an avid fan of motor racing. He regularly attended Formula One events, had collected photographs of racing cars and drivers since childhood, and was the owner of several highly collectable vehicles.

But outside music, in the late 1970s and into the 1980s George Harrison's main business activity was concerned with his company, HandMade Films. He'd become a good friend of the team behind the *Monty Python* TV comedy series—

Above: *George Harrison pictured with Formula One driver Emerson Fittipaldi in the pits at the 1980 Canadian Grand Prix.*

Above: *George Harrison pictured with Madonna at a publicity event to promote the HandMade Films 1986 movie Shanghai Surprise in which Madonna starred.*

song he'd originally written for Ringo, as a tribute to John—"All Those Years Ago". All three ex-Beatles (and Linda McCartney) performed on the single, which reached the #2 position in the US charts when it appeared in May 1981.

Along with "Teardrops", a single released later in 1981, "All Those Years Ago" came from the album *Somewhere in England* which made it to the Top 20 albums on both sides of the Atlantic. Although it only hit the #11 spot in the US, the album sold better than George's next release, 1982's *Gone Troppo,* which only managed #108, not even making the *Billboard* Hot Hundred!

Apart from a song on the soundtrack of the high school teen movie *Porky's Revenge* in 1984 (a version of Bob Dylan's "I Don't Want To Do It"), George didn't release another record for five years after the poor performance of *Gone Troppo.* He also shunned public appearances. One rare performance was on a 1985 TV special taped in London, *Blue Suede Shoes: A Rockabilly Session* with a band billed as "Carl Perkins and Friends" including Clapton and Starr, which George apparently agreed to only because he'd been a fan of Perkins since his earliest days with The Beatles. Other one-off shows included a 1986 UK concert raising money for Birmingham Children's Hospital, playing a finale "Johnny Be Good" with Robert Plant, The Moody Blues, and Jeff Lynne's Electric Light Orchestra, and the 1987 Prince's Trust concert in London's Wembley Arena (in aid of Prince Charles' young people's charity) where he was again joined by Eric Clapton and Ringo Starr.

Left: *George Harrison pictured during a rare public appearance in 1984.*

Above: *George Harrison pictured during the shooting of a video for the Traveling Wilburys' second album.*

He joined forces with Jeff Lynne again in 1987, for his return to recording with the highly acclaimed *Cloud Nine*. Lynne co-produced the album with Harrison, which featured another all-star line-up including Lynne, Clapton, Starr, and Elton John; recorded in George's home studio at Friar Park, it made the #8 spot in *Billboard* and #10 in the UK. *Cloud Nine* also included George's last chart-topping single, "Got My Mind Set On You" and his musical tribute to the Beatlemania days of The Beatles "When We Was Fab". And in 1988 Jeff Lynne was central to George's next recording project—which more or less came about by accident—The Traveling Wilburys.

The Wilbury idea was born when Harrison, Lynne and rock 'n' roll legend Roy Orbison were having a meal together in Los Angeles in the spring of 1988. The three agreed to get together to record a B-side for George's next single release, "This Is Love", taken from *Cloud Nine*. They arranged to record at Bob Dylan's studio at his home in Malibu, and the four were joined by singer/guitarist Tom Petty, who was returning a guitar that George had left at his house. The song they recorded, "Handle With Care" was considered by the record company Warner Brothers to be too good for a B-side, and so the five musicians, who obviously enjoyed working together, decided to cut an entire album.

They decided to bill themselves as a fictitious band, consisting of Nelson Wilbury (George), Otis Wilbury (Jeff Lynne), Lefty Wilbury (Orbison), Charlie T. Wilbury (Tom Petty), and Lucky Wilbury (Dylan). The debut album, *Traveling Wilburys Vol.1* was recorded over ten days in May 1988, and released on 18 October. It was a huge success, selling over two million copies in the first six months and earning triple platinum awards in the US, where it went on to sell over three million copies.

The Wilbury's unexpected success story was marred by tragedy when Roy Orbison died of a heart attack on 6 December 1988, but the group made a follow-up album in May 1990 as a four-piece, which was released in the October as *Traveling Wilburys Vol.3*—another Wilbury joke, there was no Volume 2. Not as big a seller as their debut album, it made the Top 20 in the US, UK and other parts of the world, selling over a million copies in America alone.

Apart from The Traveling Wilburys, George's musical activity was a series of random one-offs, it didn't occupy much of his time any more—unlike his dedication to his garden. There was an appearance on Tom Petty's "I Won't Back Down" early in 1989,

and in 1996 he produced and played on "Distance Makes No Difference With Love" with his hero, Carl Perkins, as part of the rockabilly legend's final album *Go Cat Go!* And in January 1998, he played at Perkins' funeral service in Jackson, Tennessee. In 2001 he was a guest musician on *Zoom*, the album by Jeff Lynne's band The Electric Light Orchestra, and he played slide guitar on "Love Letters" for Bill Wyman's Rhythm Kings' album *Double Bill*, released the same year.

One project that was more than a one-off was his involvement alongside Paul and Ringo—with Traveling Wilbury Jeff Lynne as a co-producer—in *The Beatles Anthology* films, CDs and book. As well as the taping and editing of interviews with each former Beatle, and the assembling of all the archive film footage and sound tapes, the package also included two brand new Beatles recordings.

The series was completed after five years of planning and production, presenting a complete history of The Beatles from their own personal point of view. In America it was broadcast by the ABC network between 19 November and 23 November 1995. While promoting the series, ABC was dubbed "ABeatlesC", with some of their regular shows using Beatles songs instead of their usual opening credit themes. The *Anthology* CDs saw The Beatles in the charts yet again; on its first day of release, *Anthology 1* sold 450,000 copies, the biggest sales for an album in a single day ever.

They also released "Free As A Bird" and "Real Love" as part of *Anthology*, two songs that John had recorded in his home studio, which the other three added their voices and instruments to, making it an electronic "reunion" of all four Beatles.

The songs had been recorded by John in 1977. Paul McCartney asked Yoko Ono for any unreleased Lennon material he and the other two Beatles might be involved in, finishing the arrangement and adding extra lyrics. It was released as a single on December 4, 1995, two weeks after it appeared on the *Anthology 1* album, entering the UK charts at #2 and selling 120,000 copies in the first week. In the US it reached #6 in the *Billboard* chart, becoming The Beatles' 34th Top 10 single there.

This spread: *The Traveling Wilburys (from left to right) Bob Dylan, Tom Petty, Jeff Lynne, and George Harrison, pictured during a 1990 music video shoot.*

Above Left: *George Harrison with Ringo Starr at a party in Los Angeles, in October 1990.*

Above Right: *Ringo Starr, Paul McCartney, and George Harrison pictured together on May 30, 1995, during the production of Anthology.*

For most of the time during the late 1990s, George Harrison lived the life of a recluse, working on his garden and enjoying the company of his family. He'd always worried about being attacked by a stalker or disturbed ex-Beatles fan, especially after the murder of John Lennon, and his worst fears were confirmed on December 30, 1999, when he was attacked in his own home by an intruder.

At 3.30am Michael Adam broke into the Friar Park mansion at Henley-on-Thames through a kitchen window. Woken by the sound of broken glass, George left his bedroom to investigate, while his wife Olivia rang the police. The 33-year old intruder attacked George with a six-inch kitchen knife, inflicting seven stab wounds, puncturing a lung, and causing head injuries, before the couple overpowered him; Olivia striking him repeatedly with a fireplace poker. After the horrific attack, which lasted about fifteen minutes, George and Olivia were able to detain the intruder until the police arrived. George was treated at a local hospital, where he said to one of the staff, "He wasn't a burglar, but he certainly wasn't auditioning for the Traveling Wilburys."

The attacker, who was from Liverpool, believed he was "possessed" by Harrison, and was on "a mission from God" to kill him. He was later acquitted of attempted murder on grounds of insanity and detained for treatment in a secure hospital. George's former partners in The Beatles were informed of the attack, along with Yoko Ono. Paul McCartney told the press, "Thank God that both George and Olivia are all right. I send them all my love," while a statement from Ringo and his wife Barbara Bach at their California home said, "Both Barbara and I are deeply shocked that this has occurred. We send George and Olivia all our love and wish George a speedy recovery."

George and Olivia—who also suffered minor injuries —were said to be "deeply traumatized" by the incident, and George Harrison lived in even more seclusion for the rest of his life.

Two years before the attack in his home, George had been diagnosed with throat cancer after a lump on his neck was analyzed. He conceded that the problem stemmed from his heavy smoking in the 1960s and had the tumor successfully removed with radiotherapy. Then early in May 2001, it was announced that he had undergone a serious operation to have a cancerous growth removed from one of his lungs. In July the same year, it was reported that he was receiving radiotherapy treatment for a brain tumor at a clinic in Switzerland.

Above: *George Harrison pictured attending the 1988 San Remo Music Festival in Italy.*

This spread: *George Harrison performing with Ravi Shankar during the 1990s.*

Left: *George Harrison pictured with the Billboard Century Award award that he received at the 1992 Billboard Music Awards.*

Right: *George Harrison being met by his wife Olivia at Heathrow Airport.*

Despite his treatments and various operations, on 29 November 2001 George Harrison died in Los Angeles, with Olivia and Dhani at his side. The death certificate stated lung cancer as the cause. He was cremated at the Hollywood Forever Cemetery in LA, and as he had wished his ashes were later scattered according to Hindu tradition in the River Ganges in India.

At the news of his death, in New York fans began gathering before dawn at Strawberry Fields, the area of Central Park named after the Beatles song in the wake of John Lennon's murder in 1980. And in his hometown of Liverpool, a book of condolence was opened at the Town Hall, where official flags were flown at half-mast. The British Prime Minister of the time, Tony Blair, said, "People of my generation grew up with The Beatles, and they were the background to our lives. He wasn't just a great musician, an artist, but did a lot of work for charity as well. He'll be greatly missed around the world." A statement from Buckingham Palace said that Queen Elizabeth was "very sad to hear of the death of George Harrison," while Paul McCartney said, "He was a lovely guy and a very brave man, and had a wonderful sense of humor. He is really just my baby brother."

A year after George's death, a posthumous album, *Brainwashed*, was released. George had begun recording some of the tracks as far back as 1988, but he began to focus on getting it all together after recovering from the 1999 intruder attack, sharing his ideas for the sound of the finished tracks (and even the album's artwork) with his son Dhani. After he realized that his lung cancer (and the related brain tumor) was irreversible, he worked to get the songs finished, with Dhani and his long-time collaborator, Jeff Lynne. In fact, his final work on the album was done at a studio in Switzerland,

before his last trip to the US for what would be his final bout of cancer treatment.

When George died in November 2001, the album was not quite finished, but he had left a guide to completing it in the hands of Dhani and Jeff Lynne. After a few months the two returned to the project, working on George's unfinished songs and adding the instruments as specified in his instructions. They were even able to use the same studio timetable that George had already booked for the remaining recordings, and after sessions involving a dozen or so musicians, George Harrison's final album was completed.

Below: *Olivia Harrison holding a bouquet of flowers while standing with guitarist Eric Clapton at the start of the 2003 Tokyo premiere of the movie, "The Concert for George".*

Released on November 18, 2002, *Brainwashed* received good reviews and sold reasonably well—reaching #18 in the US, where it gained a gold disc. And in 2004, "Marwa Blues" from the album won a Grammy award for Best Pop Instrumental Performance.

On the first anniversary of George's death, November 29, 2002, The Concert for George was held at London's Royal Albert Hall. Organized by Olivia and Dhani Harrison, and under the musical direction of Jeff Lynne and Eric Clapton, proceeds from the show were to go to the Material World Charitable Foundation, an organization set up by George.

Above: *Rock greats Jeff Lynne (left) and Tom Petty (center) playing with Dhani Harrison (right), son of ex-Beatle George Harrison, at the 19th Annual Rock and Roll Hall of Fame Induction Ceremony in New York on March 15, 2004. The trio played a tribute to George Harrison.*

The all-star show included Indian music, comedy numbers from the Monty Python team, and a memorable set from "George's Band." With a line-up that included Paul McCartney, Ringo Starr, Eric Clapton, Jeff Lynne, Tom Petty, and many more, the band went through both Beatles and post-Beatles numbers associated with George, including "My Sweet Lord", "When My Guitar Gently Weeps", "Something" (which McCartney opened solo on the ukelele before the band joined in, led by Clapton), "Taxman", "Here Comes the Sun", "If I Needed Someone" and Carl Perkins', "Honey Don't".

An emotional concert closed with George's friend, Joe Brown, a star from the pre-Beatles days of English rock 'n' roll,

playing the oldie, "I'll See You in My Dreams" on the ukelele, a favorite instrument of George Harrison throughout his life. A year later, *Concert for George* was released as a live album CD, making the US Hot Hundred at #97. The DVD of the show, released alongside the album in 2003, won the 2005 Grammy award for Best Long Form Video.

In 2003 George was cited by *Rolling Stone* magazine at #21 in their list of "The 100 Greatest Guitarists of All Time". And on March 15, 2004, George Harrison, already featured there as a member of the biggest pop group of all time, The Beatles, was inducted as a solo artist into the Rock and Roll Hall of Fame.

Chapter 24: After The Beatles - Ringo Starr

Before the end of The Beatles, Ringo Starr had, like the others, begun working on solo projects. His first album under his own name, *Sentimental Journey*, was a nostalgic trip into the music he'd grown up with—not the early rock 'n' roll of his teenage years, but the songs he remembered from childhood that his family enjoyed. Numbers like "Night and Day" "Stardust", "Bye Bye Blackbird" and the title song, were regular 'standards' written by some of the great American songwriters. With George Martin producing, Ringo invited various names to write the musical arrangements for individual tracks, including Paul McCartney, Quincy Jones, and Maurice Gibb of The Bee Gees. The album sold well considering the unlikely material, and reached #7 in the UK album charts. Importantly, it established Ringo as a solo voice alongside the other three Beatles after the break-up of the band.

For his next album, *Beaucoups of Blues*, Ringo—a long-time fan of country music—flew to Nashville, Tennessee in June 1970, to record with a session band of big-name C&W players. They included pedal steel guitarist Pete Drake (who also produced the album), guitarist, Charlie Daniels, Charlie McCoy on harmonica, and Elvis Presley's original drummer, DJ Fontana. Released in September 1970, the album didn't do as well as Ringo's previous, although everyone agreed his vocal style was more suited to the country sound. Recorded during the *Sentimental Journey* sessions in March 1970, Ringo's first hit single, "It Don't Come Easy" appeared in April 1971 and made it to #4 in both the UK and US charts.

Right: *Ringo Starr in a 1989 studio portrait.*

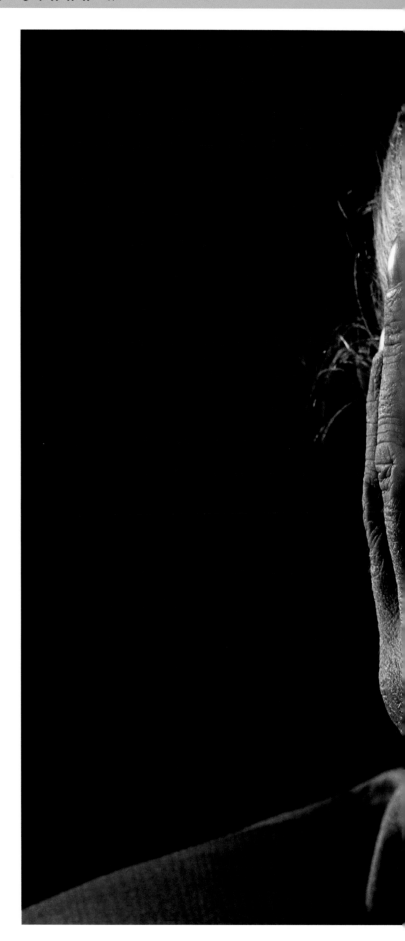

In 1972 Ringo released "Back Off Boogaloo" while he was directing the documentary *Born To Boogie* with Marc Bolan's group, T. Rex. The single, produced by George Harrison, was one of his most successful, reaching #9 in the *Billboard* chart and #2 in the UK.

But his next major recording project was in 1973, when over a six-month period from March he put together *Ringo,* involving all three of his ex-Beatle colleagues on various tracks. The opening track, "I'm The Greatest", written by John Lennon, had John, George and Ringo playing together for the first time since their group's break-up, and fueled press rumors of a Beatles reunion—which of course would never happen. Released in November 1973, *Ringo* nearly topped the *Billboard* chart at #2, and sold over a million copies, with two singles from it hitting the US #1 spot, "Photograph", which Ringo co-wrote with George Harrison, and the oldie "You're Sixteen".

Above: *Ringo Starr and his wife, Maureen pictured walking through an airport terminal en route to a holiday in Switzerland in 1971.*

Right: *Ringo Starr dressed as a spaceman to promote his 1974 album, Goodnight Vienna.*

Through 1971 Ringo was as preoccupied with filmmaking as recording music. Always a fan of Westerns (he chose his stage name because it had a "cowboy" sound to it), he couldn't turn down the chance to act in an Italian-made 'spaghetti western', *Blindman*, which was eventually released in 1973. The same year he appeared in the bizarre UK rock movie, *200 Motels*, also starring Frank Zappa and his Mothers of Invention, and The Who drummer, Keith Moon. His voice featured on the video soundtrack of an animated film by his friend, Harry Nilsson; *The Point*, first broadcast on US television in February 1971.

Ringo also started a furniture company, Ringo Or Robin, in 1971, with designer Robin Cruikshank. With coffee tables priced at over $4,000 in their London showroom, items that the drummer himself designed included a fireplace shaped like a doughnut—"With three children you think of these things," Ringo told reporters. Musical work in 1971 included an appearance at George Harrison's Concert for Bangladesh.

1973 also saw Ringo Starr in one of his most memorable film roles, in *That'll Be the Day*. Set in late-1950s Britain—a time just before the beat boom which The Beatles and others would spearhead in the early 1960s—it starred singer David Essex, as a "teenage rebel" who leaves home and a good education in pursuit of a rock 'n' roll lifestyle. Praised at the time for its gritty realism, it was a hard-hitting drama that confirmed Ringo's ability in front of the movie camera.

A far less successful movie release came the following year, when Ringo and Harry Nilsson decided to make a spoof horror film, *Son of Dracula*. With Ringo playing Merlin the Magician, the film was very badly received when released in April 1974 and was soon only showing on the drive-in and midnight movie circuit.

While *Son of Dracula* was quickly disappearing without trace, Ringo was busy in Los Angeles recording his fourth solo album, *Goodnight Vienna*. Although with a similar all-star line-up to *Ringo*, the only ex-Beatle on the album was John Lennon, who even did the voiceover for a TV commercial promoting it. With its striking cover adapted from the classic 1950s science fiction film, *The Day the Earth Stood Still*, with Ringo emerging from a flying saucer, the album reached #8 in the US chart, eventually earning a gold disc.

Two singles were taken from the album; the first, Ringo's cover version of The Platters' 1955 hit "Only You (And You Alone)" made the US Top 10 at #6 in November 1974, then "No No Song" hit #3 in February 1975.

Ringo played another outlandish film role when he appeared as the Pope in an over-the-top movie about the classical composer, Franz Liszt called *Lisztomania*. Released in October 1975, the film also starred The Who's Roger Daltrey, and was directed by Ken Russell, who had also worked with Daltry in *Tommy*, released earlier that year.

Top Right: *Ringo Starr with Harry Nilsson (center) and drummer Keith Moon (right), of The Who. The three are seen attending the West Coast premiere of the musical film, That'll Be The Day.*

Right: *Ringo Starr pictured jamming with Marc Bolan, his co-star in Born To Boogie.*

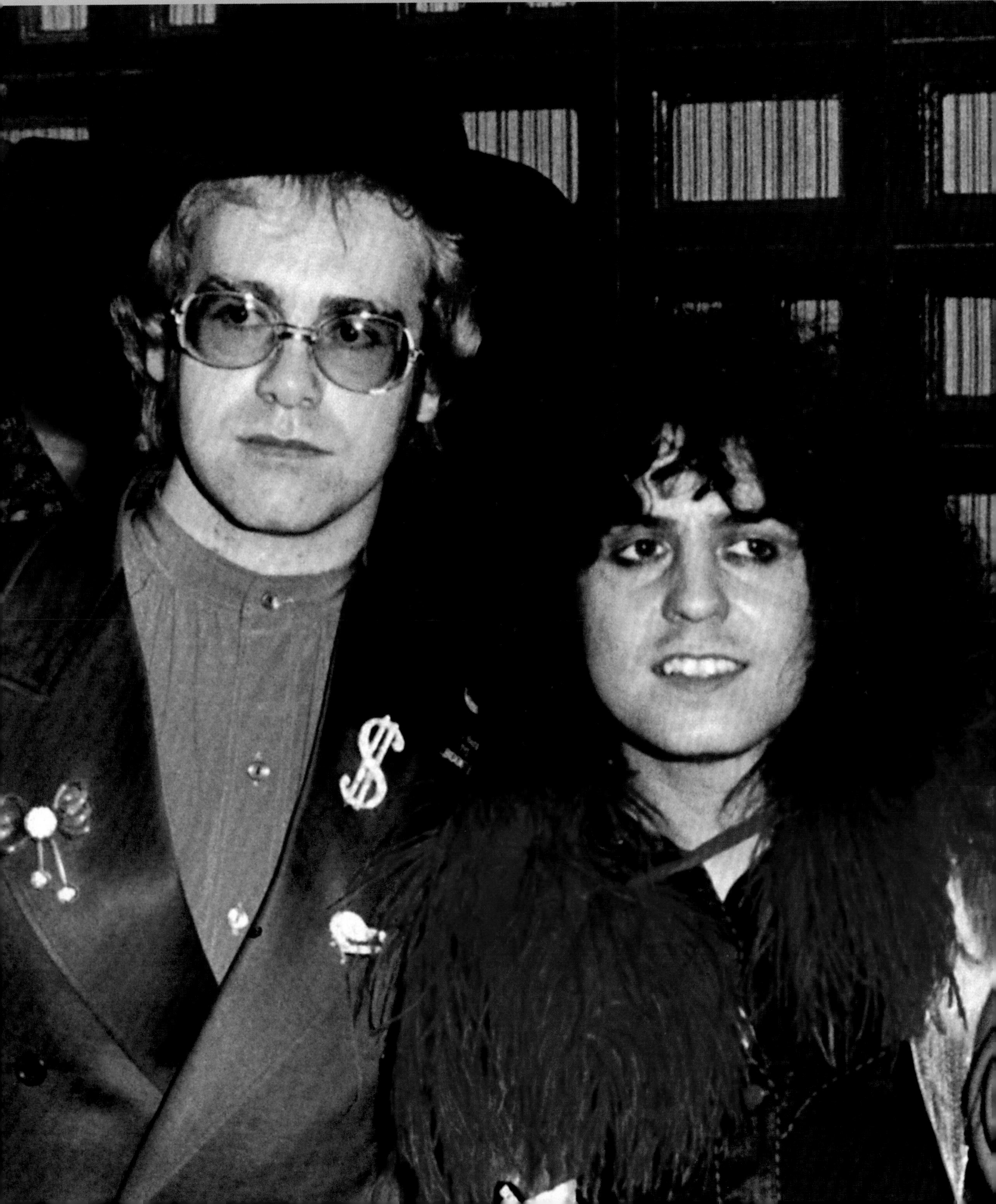

This spread: *Ringo Starr at the 1972 premiere of Born To Boogie, with fellow British musicians, Elton John (left), Marc Bolan (2nd left), and Mickey Finn (right).*

Left: *Ringo Starr wearing a black tuxedo during a guest appearance on US TV show, The Smothers Brothers Show in 1975.*

Below: *Ringo Starr pictured dressed for his role as the "Pope" in Lisztomania.*

Far Left: *Ringo Starr and Barbara Bach holding hands after their civil marriage ceremony at Marylebone Register Office in London, on April 27, 1981.*

Left: *Ringo Starr costumed for his role as Atouk in the movie Caveman, strumming a guitar during break in filming in March 1980.*

The next five years saw Ringo's recording career going through a series of changes, mostly for the worse. His contract with EMI and the Apple label had come to an end, and for 1976's *Ringo's Rotogravure* with Atlantic Records he stuck to his tried-and-tested formula of having famous rock star friends write songs and play on his albums. This time the cast included Eric Clapton, Melissa Manchester, and Dr John, plus John Lennon and Paul McCartney, but the line-up didn't help the album get any further than #28 in the US chart. It seemed the winning formula was wearing a bit thin, so he and the record company decided something new was needed.

The result, however, was even more of a disaster, both musically and commercially. The 1977 album, *Ringo the 4th* put the vocalist/drummer in a slick disco-dance setting, which certainly didn't suit his voice. So titled because, although it was Ringo's sixth album, it was his fourth rock album, the record got no higher than #162 in the US chart, and Atlantic Records dropped Ringo from their artist roster soon after. One critic claimed that *Ringo the 4th* destroyed Starr's career and that the ex-Beatle never commercially recovered from it.

In 1978, having now signed with Portrait Records, Ringo released *Bad Boy*. Although musically an improvement on the previous album, the album only reached #129 in *Billboard*, despite featuring in a prime-time TV special in America (called *Ognir Rrats*—"Ringo Starr" spelled backwards) and Portrait went on to cancel Starr's contract in 1981, while he was making his next album.

Away from the recording studio, Ringo appeared in the 1979 documentary film about The Who, *The Kids Are Alright*, interviewing the band's drummer Keith Moon. The following year, he starred in a film that would change his life, *Caveman*. Financed by George Harrison, the slapstick comedy was where Ringo met the American actress and model, Barbara Bach, previously best known as a glamorous Bond girl in the 1977 James Bond movie, *The Spy Who Loved Me*.

Ringo had divorced his wife Maureen in 1975, after ten years of marriage and three children (Zak, Jason, and Lee). After falling in love on set, Ringo and Bach were married on April 27, 1981, a few days after the film's release.

In early 1980, Ringo decided to go back to his old method of putting together an album; get some musical friends to write songs to take part in the recording. First he got Paul McCartney involved, followed by Stephen Stills, Ronnie Wood

Above: *Ringo Starr and Barbara Bach leaving the apartment block where John Lennon lived, the day after he was killed.*

of The Rolling Stones, and Harry Nilsson. He planned to have his other two Beatles bandmates on board and after making some tracks with George, he met with John in New York in November. Lennon handed him the demo tapes of two songs: "Nobody Told Me" and "Life Begins at 40". They set a date to record them, with John producing, for January 1981, but it was not to be. After John's murder, Ringo couldn't face recording the songs, which would later be released on posthumous Lennon albums.

After the shock of John's death, Ringo resumed recording the album—*Stop and Smell the Roses*—which was released in November 1981. Although not a big seller, just creeping into the *Billboard* Top 100, it was considered a return to his old form for Ringo, and a single of George's track, "Wrack My Brain" gave Starr his final US Top 40 hit, reaching #38 in December 1981.

During the early 1980s, music took a back seat for Ringo. There was one album, *Old Wave*, recorded in his new home studio, Startling Studios, in the house at Tittenhurst Park that he had bought from John Lennon in 1973. In the wake of John's murder Ringo had moved there permanently when he felt it was no longer safe to live in America.

Old Wave was produced in 1982 by Joe Walsh, whose band, The Eagles had recently broken up, but Ringo couldn't find a label that wanted to handle it. RCA Records eventually agreed to distribute the album in June 1983, but only in Canada, Australia, New Zealand, and Japan. It was later released as a CD in the US, in 1994.

Right: *Ringo Starr joking with photographers as he and his wife, Barbara Bach arrive at the Moulin Rouge in Paris on September 26, 1984 to attend a gala benefit starring Frank Sinatra.*

Below: *Ringo Starr playing the piano in the studio, accompanied by his wife Barbara Bach.*

Above*: Ringo Starr and his All-Star Band pictured during a break from rehearsals in 1995. Back row (left to right) Mark Rivera, Zak Starkey, Felix Cavaliere, Billy Preston. Front row (left to right) Randy Bachman, Ringo Starr, Mark Farner, and John Entwistle.*

Right*: Ringo Starr playing the drums during his 1989 tour.*

In 1984 and 1986, Ringo provided the voiceover narration for the UK children's TV series, *Thomas the Tank Engine & Friends*, based on the Thomas books which were hugely popular with young children in the UK. He also portrayed one of the characters, Mr Conductor, in the first season of the program's US spin-off, *Shining Time Station*, which was shown on PBS in 1989.

But a more troubling aspect of Ringo's life in the 1980s emerged in 1988, when he and Barbara Bach attended a detox clinic in Tucson, Arizona for problems with alcoholism, which the drummer had been struggling with for some time.

Above: *Ringo Starr performing on stage, August 30, 2001 at Universal Amphitheater in Los Angeles.*

At the end of December in 1994, Ringo suffered a great personal loss when his ex-wife, Maureen died of complications from treatment for leukemia. Ringo and Maureen's husband Isaac Tigrett, along with her four children and mother, were at her bedside when she died. Paul McCartney wrote the song "Little Willow," which appeared on his 1997 album *Flaming Pie*, in her memory, dedicating it to her children.

Two of Ringo's albums appeared on the Mercury label in 1998, *Vertical Man* and *VH1 Storytellers*, both with a new producer, Mark Hudson. It was the beginning of a nine-year partnership with Hudson and his band, The Roundheads, who were the core of the backing group on both records. *VH1 Storytellers* was a recording from the popular US cable TV series, in which rock stars would play in front of a small studio audience and talk about their music between numbers.

Ringo's album of his appearance on the show was released in October 1998, but the TV show, which went out in the May, was a promotion for *Vertical Man* which appeared in June. Another album featuring famous guests (including Paul McCartney and George Harrison), it peaked at #61 in the US charts, Ringo's best performance since *Ringo's Rotogravure* in 1976.

Hudson went on to produce three more albums with Ringo —the Christmas album, *I Wanna Be Santa Claus* in 1999, 2003's *Ringo Rama* (another "all star" affair), and the well-received *Choose Love,* released in 2005—before their final album together in 2008, *Liverpool 8*. Despite its title, the album (which saw Hudson replaced by Dave Stewart midway through the project) had little to do with Liverpool.

That same year, however, did see Ringo acknowledging his home city, when he opened the celebrations after it had been made European Capital of Culture. And later in 2008, he hit the headlines again when he announced he would be refusing to grant any further requests for autographs and such, causing a commotion among fans and the media.

As well as personal appearances on talk shows and charity concerts—in January 2010 he appeared on the *Hope for Haiti* global benefit show as a celebrity phone operator—Ringo continues to make music into the second decade of the 21st century. His album *Y Not*, recorded in 2009 and released in January 2010, sold over 7,000 copies in America during its first week of release. The big-name line-up would include Paul McCartney—with Ringo Starr, the only surviving members of The Beatles.

Following the six-week treatment, Ringo felt able to throw himself back into music and in July 1989, Ringo Starr & his All-Starr Band made its debut in front of 10,000 people in Dallas, Texas. The band consisted of celebrity musicians, each given their own spot accompanied by the rest. The first line-up included Joe Walsh, Dr John, and Billy Preston, and there have been 11 versions of the band where "everybody on stage is a star in their own right," up to the tour that took place in the summer of 2010.

Inspired by the success of the first All-Starr Band, in 1992 Ringo released his first album in nine years, *Time Takes Time*, with another impressive guest list including Brian Wilson of The Beach Boys and Harry Nilsson, and produced by four of the top producers of the time, Don Was, Jeff Lynne, Peter Asher and Phil Ramone. Although it got good reviews, many welcoming it as Ringo's best studio work since the early 1970s, the album failed to chart. A spin-off single, "Weight Of The World" only managed to reach #74 in the UK.

Top: *Ringo Starr arriving at a news conference in January 2008 to mark the start of Liverpool's year as the European Capital of Culture in Liverpool.*
Above: *Ringo Starr and his wife, Barbara Bach arriving at the 52nd annual Grammy Awards in Los Angeles January 31, 2010.*

The publisher would like to thank the following for permission to reproduce the following copyright material:
t = top, b = bottom, l = left, r = right, c = center

Front Cover: Michael Ochs Archives/Getty Images

Back Cover: Fiona Adams/Redferns

Front Flap: Michael Ochs Archive/Getty Images

Back Flap: David Redfern/Redferns

Corbis Images: 54/55, 74/75, 84/85, 98/99, 108/109, 120/121, 128/129, 136/137, 148/149, 156/157, 178/179, 190/191, 194/195, 230/231, 244, 245, 247 (both), 248/249, 250, 251 (tl), 252/253, 254 (t, c), 255, 257, 258 (both), 259, 260 (both), 261 (t, bl), 262 (both), 263, 264 (all), 265, 266 (both), 267 (both), 268/269, 270 (b), 271, 273, 274 (all), 277 (t), 278, 279/280, 283, 284/285, 286, 288 (both), 289, 291, 292 (both), 296 (tl, tr, br), 297, 298 (b), 299 (both), 301 (both).

Getty Images: Endpapers, 1, 4 (both), 5 (both), 7, 9, 10, 11 (t, bl, br), 12, 14 (both), 15, 16, 17, 18 (both), 19, 21, 22, 24, 25, 26, 27 (t, bl, bc, br), 28, 29 (both), 30 (l & r), 31 (both), 32 (both), 33 (both), 34, 35, 36, 37 (t), 38 (both), 39, 40 (both), 41, 42, 45, 46, 47 (both), 48, 49 (both), 50, 52, 53 (both), 57 (both), 58, 61 (both), 63, 65 (both), 66 (both), 67 (both), 69, 70, 71, 72, 73 (both), 77 (t, bl, br), 79, 81 (both), 82, 83 (tr), 87, 88, 89, 90 (b), 91 (tl, tr, bl, br), 93 (both), 94, 95, 96 (both), 97 (tl, b), 100 (l, c, r), 101, 103, 104, 105, 106 (both), 107 (bl, br), 111 (tl, tr, b), 112, 113, 114 (both), 115 (both), 117 (both), 119 (t, bl, br), 122 (both), 123, 125, 126, 130, 131 (t), 133, 134, 135 (both), 138, 139 (tl, tr, b), 141 (both), 143, 144, 145 (b), 146, 147, 150, 151 (both), 153, 154 (both), 155 (both), 158, 159, 160 (both), 161, 163 (both), 165, 166, 168, 169, 170 (t), 171, 173 (both), 175, 176 (both), 177 (both), 180 (both), 181, 182, 183, 184 (t, bl, br), 185, 187, 188 (both), 189 (both), 192, 193 (r), 196, 197 (both), 199 (both), 200, 202 (t, bl, br), 203, 204, 205, 206 (both), 207 (both), 208 (t, b), 209 (all), 210, 211 (r), 212 (tl, tr, b), 213, 215 (tl, b), 217, 218 (r), 219, 220 (both), 221, 222, 223, 224, 227 (both), 229 (tc, tr, bl, br), 233, 234, 235 (both), 236, 237 (t), 239 (both), 240 (l), 246, 251 (tr), 261 (br), 275 (t), 282 (tr), 293 (tr), 300, 303.

Time & Life Pictures/Getty Images: 2, 80 (b), 102, 145 (t), 167, 254 (b).
Science & Society Picture Library/Getty Images: 37 (b), 204 (t).
Popperfoto/Getty Images: 51, 60, 64, 68, 80, 83 (tl), 86 (t), 90 (t), 92, 97 (tr), 107 (t), 131 (b), 193 (l), 208 (c), 225, 229 (tl), 237 (b).
Bob Thomas/Getty Images: 61.
Terry O'Neill/Getty Images: 62.
WireImage/Getty Images: 170 (b), 218 (l).
FilmMagic/Getty Images: 282 (tl).

Press Association: 127, 241, 243, 270 (t), 275 (b), 276 (both), 277 (b), 286, 293 (b), 294/295, 296 (bl), 298 (t).

TopFoto: 201, 211 (l), 232 (b), 240 (r).

Every effort has been made to obtain permission to reproduce copyright material, but there may be cases where we have been unable to trace a copyright holder. The publisher will be happy to correct any omissions in future printings.